Mediterranean Politics
Volume 1

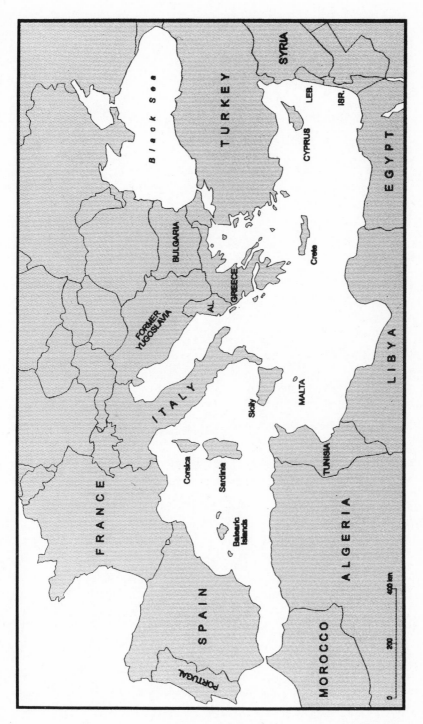

Frontispiece The Mediterranean area

Mediterranean Politics

Volume I

Edited by
Richard Gillespie

Pinter Publishers
LONDON

Fairleigh Dickinson University Press
MADISON • TEANECK

Pinter Publishers Ltd
25 Floral Street, Covent Garden
London WC2E 9DS, United Kingdom
and Associated University Presses
440 Forsgate Drive, Cranbury, NJ 08512, USA

First published in 1994

British Library Cataloguing in Publication Data
A CIP catalogue record for this book is available from the British Library

ISSN 1354-2982
ISBN 1 85567 189 1 (Pinter)
ISBN 0-8386-3609-8 (Fairleigh Dickinson)

Set in Monotype Ehrhardt by Ewan Smith,
48 Shacklewell Lane, London E8 2EY
Printed and bound in Great Britain by Biddles Ltd,
Guildford and King's Lynn

Contents

Notes on Contributors

José Amodia is head of Spanish at the University of Bradford and editor of *ACIS*, the Journal of the Association for Contemporary Iberian Studies. He writes on Spanish politics and is working on a political biography of Torcuato Fernández-Miranda.

Ewan Anderson is reader in Geopolitics at the University of Durham. His books include *Iraq and the Continuing Middle East Crisis* (Pinter, 1991), *Water Resources in the Arid Realm* (Routledge, 1992) and *An Atlas of World Political Flashpoints* (Pinter, 1993).

Ekavi Athanassopoulou is completing a doctoral thesis on 'The United States, Great Britain and Turkey's Search for Security, 1945–1952' in the History Department at the School of Oriental and African Studies, London. She is responsible for the column on Turkish foreign affairs in *Turkey Briefing*.

Stephen Calleya is a doctoral student in the Department of Politics and International Studies at the University of Warwick, where his thesis is on 'Mediterranean Security in the Post-Cold War World'.

Martha Crenshaw is professor of government at Wesleyan University, Middletown, Connecticut, where she has taught since 1974. She is an expert of political violence and the author of *Revolutionary Terrorism: The FLN in Algeria, 1954-1962*.

George Doukas is a doctoral student in the School of Languages and Area Studies at the University of Portsmouth, researching on the communist parties of southern Europe. He has published articles on the Greek Communist Party and on democratic consolidation in Greece.

Dominic Fenech is senior lecturer in Modern History and coordinator of the interdisciplinary Contemporary Mediterranean Studies programme at the University of Malta. His main research interests relate to the modern history of international relations, with special reference to the Mediterranean.

Richard Gillespie is professor of Iberian and Latin American Studies at the University of Portsmouth. He is the author of *The Spanish Socialist Party* (Oxford University Press, 1989) and co-editor of a forthcoming book on Spanish foreign policy. He is currently writing a book on Spain and the Mediterranean.

George Joffé is deputy director of the Centre for Geopolitics and International Boundaries Research at the School of Oriental and African Studies in London. He is the author of over seventy articles on the

Middle East and North African affairs and is co-author of four studies of the Iran–Iraq war.

Kyriakos Kentrotis obtained his doctorate in Germany and is currently a research fellow at the Institute for Balkan Studies, Thessaloniki. He specializes in contemporary Balkan affairs and has published several works on ethnic problems and minorities.

Georgios Kostakos received his doctorate in International Relations from the University of Kent and is now coordinator for research and training at the Hellenic Foundation for European and Foreign Policy (ELIAMEP) in Athens.

Gerd Nonneman is lecturer in International Relations at Lancaster University and a specialist on the Middle East. His publications include (with E. Ehteshami) *War and Peace in the Gulf* (Ithaca Press, 1991) and *The Middle East and Europe* (Federal Trust, 1993).

Gianfranco Pasquino is professor of Political Science at the University of Bologna and adjunct professor at the Bologna Center of the Johns Hopkins University. His most recent books include *La nuova politica* (Laterza, 1992) and *Come eleggere il governo* (Anabasi, 1992).

Philip Robins is head of the Middle East programme at the Royal Institute of International Affairs, Chatham House, London. His most recent book, *Turkey and the Middle East*, was published in 1991 and his doctoral thesis on the consolidation of Hashemite power in Jordan will appear during 1994.

Keith Salmon is senior lecturer at the University of Luton. His research interests relate to Spain's economic development (industrial restructuring, the public sector, tourism and regional development). His books include *The Modern Spanish Economy* and *Andalucía, an Emerging Regional Economy in Europe*.

İlter Turan is professor of Political Science at Koç University, Istanbul, and has held visiting appointments at several American universities. He publishes in both English and Turkish, mainly on Turkish political institutions, political culture and political behaviour.

List of Abbreviations

ALN	*Armée de Libération Nationale* (National Liberation Army, Algeria)
BCF	Balkan Communist Federation
CC	*Coalición Canaria* (Canary Islands Coalition)
CCN	*Conseil Consultatif National* (National Consultative Council, Algeria)
CCOO	*Comisiones Obreras* (Workers' Commissions, Spain)
CDS	*Centro Democrático y Social* (Democratic and Social Centre, Spain)
CDT	*Confédération Démocratique du Travail* (Democratic Confederation of Labour, Morocco)
CiU	*Convergència i Unió* (Convergence and Union, Catalonia, Spain)
CM	Council of the Mediterranean
CSCE	Conference on Security and Cooperation in Europe
CSCM	Conference on Security and Cooperation in the Mediterranean
DC	*Democrazia Cristiana* (Christian Democracy, Italy)
DPMNU	Democratic Party of Macedonian National Unity
ECO	Economic Cooperation Organization
EDB	European Development Bank
EFTA	European Free Trade Association
EIB	European Investment Bank
ERM	Exchange Rate Mechanism
ETA	*Euskadi Ta Askatasuna* (Basque Homeland and Liberty)
EU	European Union
FAN	*Forces Armées du Nord* (Armed Forces of the North)
FAT	*Forces Armées Tchadiennes* (Armed Forces of Chad)
FFS	*Front des Forces Socialistes* (Front of Socialist Forces, Algeria)
FIS	*Front Islamique du Salut* (Islamic Salvation Front, Algeria)
FLN	*Front de Libération Nationale* (National Liberation Front, Algeria)
FYROM	Former Yugoslav Republic of Macedonia
GATT	General Agreement on Tariffs and Trade
GCC	Gulf Cooperation Council
GIA	*Groupe Islamique Armée* (Armed Islamic Group, Algeria)

HB	*Herri Batasuna* (Popular Unity, Basque Country, Spain)
HCE	*Haut Comité d'État* (High State Council, Algeria)
IBRD	International Bank for Reconstruction and Development
ICO	Islamic Conference Organization
ICRC	International Committee of the Red Cross
IDF	Israeli Defence Force
IMF	International Monetary Fund
IMRO	Internal Macedonian Revolutionary Organization
IPU	International Parliamentary Union
ISGA	Interim Self-Governing Authority (Israeli authority, Palestine)
IU	*Izquierda Unida* (United Left, Spain)
JNA	Yugoslav National Army
KKE	*Kommounistikó Kómma Elládas* (Communist Party of Greece)
MDOM	*Mouvement d'Opposition Marocain* (Moroccan Opposition Movement)
METAP	Mediterranean Environmental Technical Assistance Programme
MINURSO	UN Mission for a Referendum in Western Sahara
MNLA	Macedonian National Liberation Army
MNP	*Mouvement National Populaire* (National Popular Movement, Morocco)
MP	*Mouvement Populaire* (Popular Movement, Morocco)
MSI	*Movimento Sociale Italiano* (Italian Social Movement)
NACC	North Atlantic Cooperation Council
NATO	North Atlantic Treaty Organization
ND	*Néa Dimokratía* (New Democracy, Greece)
OADP	*Organisation de l'Action Démocratique et Populaire* (Organization of Democratic and Popular Action, Morocco)
PA	*Parti de l'Action* (Party of Action, Morocco)
PASOK	*Panellínio Sosialistikó Kínima* (Panhellenic Socialist Movement, Greece)
PCI	*Partito Comunista Italiano* (Italian Communist Party)
PCS	*Parti du Centre Social* (Party of the Social Centre, Morocco)
PDI	*Parti Démocratique pour l'Indépendence* (Democratic Party for Independence, Morocco
PDS	*Partito Democratico della Sinistra* (Democratic Party of the Left, Italy)
PI	*Parti Istiqlal* (Istiqlal Party, Morocco)
PISGA	Palestinian Self-Governing Authority
PKK	*Partiya Karkaran Kurdistan* (Kurdistan Workers' Party)
PLI	*Partito Liberale Italiano* (Italian Liberal Party)
PLO	Palestine Liberation Organization

PND	*Parti National Démocrate* (National Democratic Party, Morocco)
PNV	*Partido Nacionalista Vasco* (Basque Nationalist Party)
POLAN	*Politikí 'Anixi* (Political Spring, Greece)
PP	*Partido Popular* (People's Party, Spain)
PPS	*Parti du Progrès et du Socialisme* (Party of Progress and Socialism, Morocco)
PRI	*Partito Repubblicano Italiano* (Italian Republican Party)
PSDI	*Partito Socialdemocratico Italiano* (Italian Social Democratic Party)
PSI	*Partito Socialista Italiano* (Italian Socialist Party)
PSOE	*Partido Socialista Obrero Español* (Spanish Socialist Workers' Party)
RNI	*Rassemblement Nationale des Indépendents* (National Assembly of Independents, Morocco)
RPP	People's Republican Party (Turkey)
RPR	*Rassemblement pour la République* (Rallying for the Republic, France)
SAP	*Sans Appartenance Politique* (Without Political Affinity, Morocco)
SHP	*Sosyal Democrat Halkçi Parti* (Social Democratic Populist Party, Turkey)
UC	*Union Constitutionelle* (Constitutional Union, Morocco)
UCD	*Unión del Centro Democrático* (Union of the Democratic Centre, Spain)
UDF	*Union pour la Démocratie Française* (Union for French Democracy)
UGT	*Unión General de Trabajadores* (General Workers' Union, Spain)
UGTA	*Union Générale des Travailleurs Algériens* (General Union of Algerian Workers)
UGTM	*Union Générale des Travailleurs Marocains* (General Union of Moroccan Workers)
UMA	*Union Maghreb Arabe* (Arab Maghreb Union)
UMT	*Union Marocaine du Travail* (Moroccan Labour Union)
UNDOF	UN Disengagement Observer Force (Golan Heights)
UNDP	United Nations Development Programme
UNEF I	First UN Emergency Force (Suez Canal)
UNEF II	Second UN Emergency Force
UNFICYP	UN Force in Cyprus
UNFP	*Union Nationale des Forces Populaires* (National Union of Popular Forces, Morocco)
UNHCR	UN High Commissioner for Refugees

UNIFIL   UN Interim Force in Lebanon
UNIIMOG   UN Iran–Iraq Military Observer Group
UNIKOM   UN Iraq–Kuwait Observation Mission
UNOGIL   UN Observation Group in Lebanon
UNPA   UN Protected Areas (Croatia)
UNPROFOR   UN Protection Force (former Yugoslavia)
UNTSO   UN Truce Supervision Organization (Palestine)
UNYOM   UN Yemen Observation Mission
USFP   *Union Socialiste des Forces Populaires* (Socialist Union of
            Popular Forces, Morocco)
WEU   Western European Union

Introduction
Our Focus on the Mediterranean

Richard Gillespie

In recent years the Mediterranean has forced itself more and more on to the agendas of international meetings. It has increasingly attracted the attention of both policy makers and observers of world events. For some it has been the rise of Islamic fundamentalism in North Africa that has stimulated interest. Others have been fascinated by the monumental political changes that are occurring in Italy, or by the rise of Turkey to the status of a regional power, particularly in the aftermath of the Cold War and Gulf War. Meanwhile the Bosnian tragedy and the threatened extension of the Balkan conflict have become concerns of people in virtually every country of the world.

The European Union has recently become more sensitive to Mediterranean problems, particularly due to the recent increase in regional conflicts and the growth in migration from the southern to the northern shores of the 'inner sea'. The reinforcement of EC Mediterranean policy since the late 1980s reflects a growing understanding that if Europe does not concern itself with the problems of its southern neighbours, then these problems will be exported northwards in the form of population movements and serious threats to stability and security.

Mediterranean Politics appears for the first time, reflecting this new interest but also seeking to stimulate wider interest and to contribute to a deeper understanding of contemporary trends. The volume is a response to the relative neglect of the Mediterranean in contemporary social science literature. If further justification for the birth of the yearbook is needed, it is surely that the northern European countries remain less sensitive to Mediterranean issues than their southern European partners – and yet regional problems relating to security and migration, for instance, affect Europe in general.

The yearbook aims to provide informed critical analysis of recent trends and events in the Mediterranean area. Its title reflects a prime concern with politics. This does not mean, however, that the volume will be concerned solely with elections, the fortunes of governments, the rise and fall of political forces, and regional conflicts. Over the coming years, we also intend to

focus upon the area's serious environmental problems, its destabilizing economic trends and crucial social issues, all of which inevitably give rise to
political initiatives aimed at resolving these problems.

Mediterranean specialists have traditionally differed over the geographical
scope of their notion of the Mediterranean. Rather than opt for the more
modest notion, limited to the riparian states, or for the broader notion,
which takes in all of the Black Sea and the Middle East, our volume will
adopt a flexible policy. The yearbook's central concern is with the countries
bordering the Mediterranean and with events and trends that affect this
area. Here, we shall seek to cover key recent developments on a comprehensive basis. Flexibility, meanwhile, will be employed in relation to the
periphery, which will receive attention in so far as events there affect the
politics of the riparian states.

In accordance with this policy, we shall not seek to cover all important
aspects of Middle Eastern affairs (which are served relatively well by existing
literature); we will, however, examine Middle Eastern events when they are
of relevance to the politics of the core Mediterranean states, as the Gulf
conflict was in the early 1990s. The same principle applies to the Black Sea
states, which will mainly be of interest to the yearbook when developments
there are of direct importance to Turkey. The Balkans are in such a state of
flux that a firm policy on coverage there would be premature.

Among the European states, Portugal and France may both be regarded
as peripheral. Despite their historical maritime involvement in the Mediterranean, most Portuguese feel little empathy with the people of this area;
but Portugal does act on occasion as a 'southern European' state. France
has more of a geographical claim to being considered 'Mediterranean', yet
clearly does not possess this identification to the extent that Italy, Spain
and Greece do. Our policy will be periodically to consider the Mediterranean interests and policies of Portugal and France, both members of the
'5+5' forum embracing southern Europe and the Maghreb; the yearbook
will not, however, provide comprehensive coverage of French and Portuguese
domestic developments.

Over the next few years, we shall attempt to cover Mediterranean affairs
in as balanced a manner as possible, looking to the south as well as to the
north and to both the eastern and western reaches of the Sea. We shall
focus both on the countries of the area themselves and on initiatives taken
elsewhere to address the pressing problems of the Mediterranean. Above
all, this policy will translate into regular analysis of the European Union's
developing Mediterranean policy and of other international proposals, such
as the attempt to convoke a Conference on Security and Cooperation in the
Mediterranean (CSCM) modelled on the Conference on Security and Cooperation in Europe (CSCE).

Chapters in the volume will be arranged in three principal clusters. The first section will focus broadly on developments affecting the whole of the Mediterranean, or a large part thereof. The second will be concerned with the external relations of Mediterranean states, irrespective of whether these point inward or point towards the Mediterranean periphery and beyond. The third section will address major events, recent trends and issues in the domestic politics of the area. It will not be possible to include chapters on every Mediterranean state in every volume of the yearbook, but we intend to provide comprehensive coverage of all the major developments. The growth in political violence in Egypt and the strain on the Qadhafi regime in Libya are among our priorities for future coverage.

We also hope in future to include occasional research notes (although not conference reports). Finally, regular features of the yearbook from the outset will be a chronology of Mediterranean events and a statistical appendix providing indicative economic data.

In this volume, we begin with an analysis of the ways in which thinking on the security of the Mediterranean has changed in recent years. Ewan Anderson and Dominic Fenech show that, while the end of the Cold War has brought new opportunities for global cooperation, it has also increased the incidence of smaller scale conflicts. The causes and symptoms of instability are diverse: boundary disputes, water shortages, economic disparities, arms proliferation, Islamic fundamentalism, demographic trends, and terrorism. It is argued that traditional military-based concepts of security are outmoded and that a new security architecture is needed for the Mediterranean.

While these authors see the CSCM proposal as still relevant, George Joffé regards it as too complex to be operationalized; he sees better prospects for cooperation between the European Union and the Maghreb, as a means of tackling regional problems. Certainly, many of the causes of instability can be related to the growing imbalance between economies to the north and south of the Mediterranean; and European governments have recently shown a readiness to strengthen the EU's economic relationship with Morocco and perhaps Tunisia. Yet the EU's Mediterranean policy remains very modest in relation to the huge size of the problems, and as Joffé points out, European and North African viewpoints on the purpose of cooperation differ quite significantly. Concern is also expressed that increased economic relations could strengthen the political status quo in the Maghreb, and thus shore up political features that remain an obstacle to North African development.

Following these framework chapters, Gerd Nonneman and Georgios Kostakos examine the problems arising from the pursuit of peace in the area. Notwithstanding the vagueness of the Israeli-PLO peace declaration of September 1993 and the subsequent set-backs, Nonneman underlines the potential of this breakthrough and argues that there will be more progress, albeit halting, during 1994. Kostakos meanwhile offers a survey of UN peace missions in the Mediterranean, focusing chiefly on Cyprus and former Yugoslavia. A disproportionate share of UN operations have been in the Mediterranean and all too often the peacekeepers are confronted with situations in which there is no peace to keep. Kostakos sees the Cyprus case as showing how peace-keeping missions can have negative consequences, in that they can freeze the political problem; he suggests that in future the UN should place greater emphasis on conflict prevention.

The Balkans inevitably also provide the subject of some of our chapters on the external relations of Mediterranean states. Kyriakos Kentrotis and Philip Robins respectively analyse Greek and Turkish reactions to the Balkan conflict. Greece's security concerns have met with little sympathy in the European Union, partly one suspects due to the country's persisting good relations with Serbia and also because of lingering perceptions of Greece as the Union's *enfant terrible*. Greece pursued a maverick foreign policy under the Panhellenic Socialist Movement (PASOK) in the 1980s and the re-election of Papandreou's party in 1993 provoked nervousness in Europe, despite PASOK's recent pragmatism. The chapter by Kentrotis explains Greece's fears concerning the Macedonian question, and argues that, while Athens may have little option but to compromise on the issue, this would not resolve the historical issue, which would resurface sooner or later.

Turkey's concerns relate more to the fate of the Bosnian Muslims and the threat of the conflict spreading closer to home. Philip Robins shows how skilfully the Turkish authorities have managed the Bosnian issue through taking the line that only through the mobilization of the major powers and international institutions can effective external action be taken. Internal leadership changes (analysed later in the volume by İlter Turan) distracted public attention from the Bosnian question for a while, but before the end of the year Turkey involved itself again as a mediator in the fighting between Bosnian Muslims and Croats.

Ekavi Athanassopoulou meanwhile examines Turkey's Black Sea regional policy, aimed at alleviating political differences and achieving regional stability via economic cooperation. She shows how this cooperation project has become more limited over the last three years due to the persistence of regional rivalries and Turkey's own domestic distractions (economic problems, the Kurdish uprising, the advance of Islam and leadership changes).

Malta's external outlook is attracting more interest due to its involvement in the '5+5' forum and its application to join the European Union. Stephen Calleya shows that even a small state can contribute to the debate about Mediterranean security needs, especially when the more grandiose proposals have run into deadlock. Malta has proposed the creation of a Council of the Mediterranean (CM) to at least regularize dialogue among member states. One is struck by the degree of imitation of European institutions in the debate so far: the CSCM proposal is inspired by the CSCE, the CM idea by the Council of Europe. No doubt this is partly a function of the need to involve non-Mediterraneans in the construction of any viable new security framework, but one can surely question whether any project inspired by a European experience, even if 'adapted' to local realities, can really satisfy the requirements of the Mediterranean.

Domestic developments form the subject of our final section. Of particular importance in 1993 was Italy's radical process of political restructuring, authoritatively discussed by Gianfranco Pasquino. His chapter shows how events and reforms in Italy prepared the way for a far more uncertain political future, devoid of Christian Democrat domination.

Less dramatic changes have occurred in Spain, yet the Socialists' loss of their absolute parliamentary majority after a decade in office quickly affected the character of political life. José Amodia reflects on the first decade of Socialist rule and shows how in the election of June 1993 the PSOE, weakened by corruption scandals, factional strife and the economic recession, relied more heavily on Felipe González than ever before. The loss of Socialist hegemony brings with it the prospect of an enhanced role for Parliament, but has also complicated Spanish political life by strengthening the bargaining position of the Catalan and Basque nationalists.

Morocco also held elections in 1993, although to a parliament that to date has played much less of a role than the Spanish Cortes. Besides analysing the election results, George Joffé discusses the nature of the Moroccan political system and explains why the Islamic fundamentalists remain relatively weak. The religious status and political dexterity of King Hassan are central to his argument, and the role of the king is also seen as crucial in determining whether democratic participation will be expanded in the coming years.

Algeria, Morocco's traditional rival in North Africa, has meanwhile been retreating from the reform process initiated in the late 1980s. Martha Crenshaw focuses on the background to the political violence and its increase in 1993, a year that saw Europeans becoming (as in Egypt) a favourite target for terrorists. Crenshaw's argument is that the terrorist problem in Algeria will not be solved by repressive means since the insurgents are far too decentralized and the military authorities lack political legitimacy.

While Algeria sank more deeply into crisis, the eastern Mediterranean experienced significant political changes during 1993. PASOK returned to office in Greece, just as the country was preparing itself for the EU presidency, amidst northern European misgivings. George Doukas shows how Andreas Papandreou's party owed its electoral victory largely to the fall in public support for the New Democracy government, a product of its austerity measures and foreign policy setbacks.

By contrast, Turkey saw new political leaders emerging as a result of the death or retirement of incumbents. İlter Turan discusses the tradition of a strong centralized state and other factors deemed responsible for the remarkably long periods of office hitherto enjoyed by Turkish political leaders. This pattern is now under challenge, however, in part due to generational change. Turan suggests that the arrival on the scene of a new set of party leaders may herald a future in which political careers become less secure as public interest in political participation grows. This would represent quite a democratic advance for Turkey, although ironically one that could be traced back to distinctly non-democratic origins: the army's disruption of political life in the early 1980s, when the motives behind military intervention were anything but democratic.

PART ONE
THE REGIONAL SCENE

1

New Dimensions in Mediterranean Security

Ewan Anderson and Dominic Fenech

Between the fall of the Berlin Wall (1989) and the disintegration of the Soviet Union (1991), the long confrontation between NATO and the Warsaw Pact, the dominant factor in post-war global security, evaporated. In many parts of the world, particularly Central Europe, the effects were cataclysmic. In the Mediterranean, a prominent theatre of East–West confrontation, changes were not immediately obvious. For a number of reasons, among them the peripheral status of the Mediterranean in relation to Europe, the great diversity of the component parts of the region, and the deep historical roots of the region's many problems, the end of the Cold War could not possibly herald peace in the Mediterranean. Naturally, however, the abrupt withering of the single most important feature of post-war international relations was bound to have far-reaching effects on the region. The confrontation between the two superpowers had indelibly defined the international system (Evert, 1991) and effectively overshadowed all other local and regional contradictions.

Its removal has both left a clear-cut legacy and altered security assumptions. On the military front, there is only one superpower and therefore an analysis of Mediterranean security must take into account the views of the United States. The correlation of forces has been completely altered, but the beneficiaries, the countries of the Western alliance, are still largely in disarray over security policy. The vulnerabilities of the former southern flank of NATO were in the main apparent and were the subject of much military planning. Now, the strategic significance of the Mediterranean itself is a question for debate.

A further key geopolitical aspect is the accepted existence of a global North–South fracture zone, which is perhaps most clearly demarcated as a boundary down the centre of the Mediterranean. As Rathbone (1992) observed: 'The Mediterranean is both a cross-roads and frontier. The Mediterranean is the point of contact between two dissimilar worlds.' In the Mediterranean basin the differences – political, economic, social and

9

strategic – on either side of the line are most obviously accentuated, the more so now that the role of the chief actors of East and West is no longer so overbearing. Such differences have an obvious bearing upon the current, more broadly defined concept of security. Indeed, the implications of North–South differences for the region's security are more serious because they are real, engrained differences, unlike the East–West division, which was externally induced. If the East–West division can be removed by decisions and circumstances quite external to the Mediterranean, the North–South division can only be narrowed by the wishes of the indigenous actors themselves. Thus, the old balances have been upset, but new ones have yet to emerge (Evert, 1991).

Although, therefore, the end of the East–West conflict has provided new opportunities for international cooperation and has significantly reduced the possibility of global conflict, one other result has been an increase in the probability of regional, smaller-scale crises, particularly in certain regions. One such region, in which a combination of negative factors is concentrated in a particularly explosive fashion, is the Mediterranean basin. While the immediate effects of the breaching of the Berlin Wall were less obvious in the Mediterranean than in several other regions, the aftermath, particularly exemplified in the cases of Yugoslavia and the Middle East, has been seismic. The range and complexity of potential problems rival those in any other region of comparable size. Thus, even for the Mediterranean, 1989 will undoubtedly be recorded in European history as a turning point, ranking alongside 1789, 1848, 1919 and 1945 in significance (Williams and Williams, 1993).

BACKGROUND

The Mediterranean has been described as 'a region of great cultural and religious diversity, of sometimes difficult encounters of Catholics, Muslims and Orthodox, where empires have clashed and collapsed, causing large movements of population and leaving a trail of unsolved nationalistic and ethnic tensions' (de Vasconcelos, 1991). Such has been the long historical consequence of the region's geography as an intercontinental junction. Modern history, then, that is to say the mainly Eurocentric history of the past four centuries, not only is synonymous with the marginalization of the Mediterranean region in relation to the continent of Europe, but also with the region's surrender to foreign influence and conquest from the North.

The decline after the sixteenth century of the old Mediterranean power bases of East and West – the Catholic Habsburgs and the Muslim Ottomans – belonged to the same process that saw the rise of France, Britain and eventually Prussia and Russia to great power status. This shifting of the centre of gravity in international relations from the Mediterranean to the north of Europe and the attendant weakness of the Mediterranean states, made the region doubly susceptible to external influence and domination. On the one hand, by virtue of its skirting the European continent, the sea and the region as a whole came to possess an important function *vis-à-vis* the security of Europe; what in recent decades has been termed the 'southern flank'. On the other hand, Mediterranean territory became potentially colonial or paracolonial territory, either for its own sake or as a step towards more global imperial designs. Thus, the geopolitical properties of the Mediterranean combined with its inherent political weakness to attract the attention of every power concerned with European and world affairs.

This dual utility that the region acquired in the eyes of the big European powers has meant that the big powers of modern and contemporary history have regarded the Mediterranean as a vital extension, but not necessarily an intrinsic part, of Europe. This has abetted to no small degree the relative underdevelopment of the region, both politically and economically. Indigenous developments on the European side of the Mediterranean, notably nationalist struggles in the Balkan peninsula, inevitably became entangled with big power interests, often producing thwarted outcomes which bore the seed of future conflict. On the other hand, the non-European sooner or later came under the direct control, in one form or another, of the European powers. The Second World War signalled the end of the Europeans' 'big power' and imperial status, the coming into being of the superpowers and the proliferation of newly independent, but undeveloped states, and the resultant East–West and North–South divisions of the world. In the Mediterranean, with its long legacy of big power rivalry and imperialism, the East–West and North–South divisions and Western and Soviet perceptions of their 'vital interests' in the region, and persisting disparity between especially the European and non-European banks of the littoral introduced new terms for essentially old, interconnected problems.

The Mediterranean is littered with regional problems whose roots are earthed deep in history. Although the overshadowing East–West confrontation, no less than, say, nineteenth-century big power rivalries, often became an extremely important variable in such conflicts, its termination did not automatically open the way to their resolution. The Arab–Israeli conflict, the Cyprus question, the Yugoslav problem, the external policies of radical states, terrorism, militant fundamentalism, or South–North emigration – such problems do not owe their existence to the Cold War. However, what the Cold War did was either to render them more intractable through foreign intervention and patronage, or else to contain them and their effects, or indeed simply distract attention away from them. Superpower competition being at once a complicating and a stabilizing factor in these regional issues, its abrupt termination necessarily had an impact, variously destabilizing, conciliatory or provocative of new problems. The cases of Yugoslavia and the Middle East, both dense with a history of native rivalries compounded by great power competition and intervention, illustrate the staggering effects of the Cold War's end on regional conflicts. In both cases, it is difficult and certainly too early to conclude whether the impact has been salutary or dangerous to security.

In the case of Yugoslavia, the many and complex problems connected with south Slav nationalism were not, of course, created by the Cold War. However, the fears generated by the Cold War did constitute an external cement for an otherwise disparate union, such that the removal of those fears released (as opposed to created) the powerful centrifugal movement that ended definitively the Yugoslav national experiment. Seen through more optimistic eyes, the break-up of Yugoslavia represents not the failure of a singular nationalist experiment, but the fulfilment of several nationalisms. What is sure, both where Yugoslavia and the rest of the Balkans are concerned, is that the Cold War imposed stability on a region well known for its potential threat to international, no less than national, peace. Historical experience suggests that nationalist triumph in Balkanized regions can create more problems than it solves.

In the Middle East, the seeds of conflict are eminently historical. Western imperialism had been grafted upon existing conflict long before the Cold War. The Cold War then turned the entire region into a major area of superpower competition, resulting in arms proliferation that promoted successive wars, sometimes regarded as superpower proxy wars. In the longer run, however, the scale of US and Soviet patronage produced a simplified form of regional cold war, resting on mutual deterrence, with Syria counterpoised to Israel. In the Israeli–Syrian contest over Lebanon it was possible for the two to wage a completely localized war without declaring one. Concurrently, war broke out in the other most delicate part of the Middle East, the Gulf, between Iraq and Iran, a war in which superpower patronage was present, but far less defined than it was on the Mediterranean bank of the Middle East. The end of the Cold War led to a rapid succession of events: superpower collaboration to negotiate a ceasefire in the Gulf; Soviet abandonment of Syria and the consequent erosion of the erstwhile balance of power with Israel; Iraq's bid for mastery of the Middle East once the Soviets retreated and Syria ceased to represent a credible counterpoise to Israel; full-scale war on Iraq concerted by the remaining superpower; linkage between the Second Gulf War and the Arab–Israeli conflict; and superpower, but mainly American, sponsorship of the Arab–Israeli peace process. Thus, in the case of the Middle East, the end of the Cold War resulted in destabilization, warfare and peacemaking, in that order. It is not to be assumed, of course, that the process stands in its concluding phase.

The multitude of Mediterranean problems is therefore a legacy of native problems with deep historical roots compounded over time with great power competition, interference, conquest or patronage. The historical interaction of native movements, especially nationalist movements in their many variations, with external interests has produced complicated problems which cannot be unscrambled by the mere disappearance of a single factor – the Cold War – however dominant it was.

NEW CONCEPTS OF SECURITY

In the past, security has been defined largely in a military context, a viewpoint reinforced by the bipolar nature of the global geopolitical scene. It is already obvious in the first year or two of the post-Cold War era that the reduction in the potential for global conflict has resulted in a wide variety of other threats to security. Beyond the narrow confines of traditional military thinking, it is clear that there are economic, social and environmental threats to security. The collapse of the economies, the denial of human rights, the persecution of minorities, discrepancies in living standards and the degradation of the environment can all affect the maintenance of security. Such vulnerabilities are felt even by the one remaining superpower. Grover (1993) considers that US post-Cold War strategy is determined by three geo-challenges:

1. the geo-economic challenge, caused by the tri-polar division of the world along trading bloc lines, together with the growth of instant global communications and other technologies, the development of transnational corporations and the emergence of a well educated global labour force;
2. the geopolitical challenge, resulting from America's relative economic decline, economic competition from its traditional military allies and regional tensions threatening its global interests; and
3. the challenge to military geography of effectively projecting power over distance, given the constraints of greatly reduced budgets and the loss of overseas bases.

In the Mediterranean basin, the marked discrepancies between the North and the South have already been indicated. Indeed, the economic and social development of the European Union will only exacerbate the differences which already exist. However, even within and between member states of the Community, there already exist serious economic, social and environmental problems. Thus, a holistic approach to security is required, but in adopting this, the old dimensions must not be neglected.

OLD DIMENSIONS OF SECURITY

Many geostrategic aspects of the Mediterranean remain as relevant today as they were two thousand years ago (Train, 1988). The sea has always provided a vital line of communication, whether for trade, migration or military campaigns. In more modern times, this role was enhanced by the opening of the Suez Canal in 1869, and the Mediterranean provides the vital oil lifeline to Western Europe and North America. The sea is divided into two major basins with interconnecting choke points, which have long been of military interest. Gibraltar, Sicily, Malta, Carthage and Crete have each, at various times over the centuries, been the focus of military campaigns. The Turkish straits, the Sicilian straits and the Straits of Gibraltar were all considered of major significance during the Cold War period and, although diminished in importance, their military potential has by no means been eliminated (Brogan, 1989). The importance of the Suez Canal as a key global flashpoint (Anderson, 1993) was again emphasized during the Gulf conflict, when its closure could have had serious consequences for the deployment of the US-led forces. A particular focus of NATO planning was the Turkish straits, since these limited the access of the Soviet Black Sea fleet from its ice-free bases to the Atlantic or the Indian Oceans. Given the volatility of many of the former Soviet republics, together with the fact that Russia remains a global naval power, the strategic importance of the Turkish straits must still be considered. Thus, even in terms of traditional military thinking, the Mediterranean basin exhibits a wide variety of problems.

NEW DIMENSIONS OF SECURITY

New sources of threat to the peace and stability of the Mediterranean basin can be seen to arise not only from a more broadly defined concept of security, but also from the rapidly changing pattern of conflict in neighbouring areas (Anderson, 1993). The arc of crisis runs through the Mediterranean into Central Europe, the Balkans and South Central Asia, via the Persian/Arabian Gulf. Despite the recent accords and the continuation of peace talks, the Arab–Israeli dispute continues to be the major Middle Eastern strategic concern. However, the disintegration of the Soviet Union increases the potential for conflict within the Gulf region as the former republics realign with either Turkey or Iran. Events in the former Yugoslavia are, of course, directly related to the Mediterranean, but to the north, potential for conflict must be clearly recognized in Macedonia and Moldova, to mention only the more obvious possibilities. On the southern side of the Mediterranean, conflict continues in Western Sahara and Sudan, with potential flashpoints in Algeria and along the Egypt–Sudan border.

These issues in neighbouring areas of Europe, Asia and Africa pose security problems on a potentially global rather than regional scale and therefore the involvement of the United Nations and, more obviously, the United States, must be examined. Recently, the UN has encountered severe problems in both Bosnia and Somalia. Peacekeeping must be preceded by peacemaking and in both cases the UN forces entered zones of conflict. In the absence of peace, impartiality can be impugned and the presence of UN forces may actually exacerbate the tension. The Mediterranean basin and its immediate surroundings have been the scene of continuous UN activity since 1948 (see Kostakos, this volume).

The interests of the United States follow from the concept of the New World Order, developed in his 1990 *National Security Strategy of the United States* by the then president, George Bush, and, for the Mediterranean, have been analysed by Dismukes and Hayes (1991). The Mediterranean is seen as particularly significant in the larger national security context in that it abuts on to two of the four areas defined as being critical to the growth of the world economy: North America, Western Europe, Northeast Asia and the Persian/Arabian Gulf. To the north, NATO remains the linchpin of US engagement in Europe and the Mediterranean offers a natural location for this continued involvement. Indeed, as Dismukes and Hayes point out, even before Operation Desert Storm , the focus of NATO was beginning to shift to the south and east, towards the Mediterranean. Other related concerns include the territory of the former Soviet Union, the chief reason for the continuous US involvement in Europe. The danger of conflict arising from the Soviet disintegration is considered to be focused immediately to the east of the Mediterranean. Apart from the religious, linguistic and ethnic tensions in the Balkans, which have already produced limited warfare, there are the obvious effects of environmental disasters from the nuclear and chemical industries within the region. To the south and east, the arc of crisis continues to present threats to US interests, particularly in that access to the Persian/Arabian Gulf may be at risk.

Therefore, it is concluded that the Mediterranean, a region in which the causes of instability are intensifying rather than attenuating, remains an area in which the US has vital interests. Furthermore, it forms a geopolitical unit with the Persian/Arabian Gulf, where US interests are similarly vital (Dismukes and Hayes, 1991).

REGIONAL SOURCES OF INSECURITY

Within the broader definition, there is a vast array of potential security problems: disputed boundaries, water shortage, nuclear and chemical weapons proliferation, terrorism, nationalist and separatist grievances, militant fundamentalism and demographic imbalance. In most cases, such concerns spill over national borders and assume regional importance.

The problem of international boundaries as a threat to security can be particularly well illustrated within the Mediterranean basin, where boundary disputes rest on mixtures of security considerations and resource appropriation. Among the most intractable boundary disputes are those between Israel and its neighbours: Lebanon, Syria and Jordan. If the present peace agreement holds and the political will survives, there must be some possibility of a settlement, but there are fundamental issues at stake for all four countries. The Chad–Libya dispute over the Azou Strip has already resulted in warfare, but the case was placed before the International Court of Justice in 1990. The boundary that divides Cyprus is also a source of continuing tension and forms part of a longer-running confrontation between Turkey and Greece. The other most obvious set of boundary problems involves the former Yugoslavia. Indeed, the religious, linguistic and ethnic variations within Bosnia-Herzegovina seem so complex as to virtually defy allocation, let alone demarcation. These are only the more obvious cases of dispute or potential dispute onshore, but offshore a further range of problems arises.

Here again, the complex topography of the Mediterranean lends itself to disputes. Although both states belong to NATO, Greece and Turkey have been locked in dispute on the question of sovereignty over the Aegean Sea for over twenty years and the dispute, compounded with the Cyprus problem, has brought them close to armed conflict on three occasions: in 1974, 1976 and 1986/87 (Blake, 1992). According to the 1992 UN Convention, signed by Greece, but not by Turkey, every coastal state can claim a territorial sea of twelve nautical miles in width. The full entitlement of Greece, therefore, would extend sovereignty over 71 per cent of the Aegean. Given the likely presence of oil in the northern Aegean and the necessity to protect its shipping, Turkey claims that the Aegean presents 'special circumstances' and should be divided according to a median line boundary. The position is further exacerbated by an airspace dispute, which has not yet been fully resolved. Elsewhere in the Mediterranean there are still many boundaries to be finally settled, including much of the median line between the northern and southern states and the sea around Cyprus.

A further key problem with economic, political and social implications is water. With limited areas of drainage basin and dry summers, the Mediterranean is, in general, an area of water shortage. Notable exceptions are France and Turkey, but more than balancing them are Israel, Jordan, Egypt, Libya and Malta, which rank among the countries with the lowest per capita consumption of water in the world. There is a long history of water shortage, and basin irrigation was introduced into the Nile valley in about 3300 BC. Egypt claims to have the world's oldest dam irrigation, constructed some five thousand years ago (Anderson, 1992). The greatest of the ancient aqueducts, the Aqueduct of Carthage, was built in the second century AD, stretched for some 141 km and had a capacity of 31.8 million litres per day. However, owing to the rapid rates of population increase and therefore the requirements for agriculture and industry, particularly in the countries of the eastern and southern Mediterranean, the problems of water supply maintenance are now far more acute and complex. As the situation has deteriorated, there have already been conflicts over transboundary water flows. In fact, Dr Boutros Ghali, Secretary-General of the United Nations, has stated that: 'The next war in the Middle East will be over water, not politics' (*The Independent on Sunday*, 6 May 1990).

At present, concern has centred on three catchments: those of the Jordan, the Tigris–Euphrates and the Nile, and assessments have been made of the potential for conflict, resulting from resource geopolitics (Agnew and Anderson, 1992).

In an area with so much potential for conflict and instability, the dangers of arms proliferation are obvious. For a number of reasons – among them the atmosphere of crisis that has hung over many parts of the Mediterranean, superpower clientism, the instability of certain regimes, the role of the armed forces in government, or simply national prestige – many states, despite their often scarce resources, have consistently allocated big budgets during the past forty or fifty years to maintain large defence establishments. Additionally, several countries in and around the Mediterranean possess weapons of mass destruction. France and Israel are nuclear powers, while parts of the former Soviet Union, within range of the Mediterranean, have nuclear weapons stockpiles The proliferation of such weapons in the region is an ever present threat, particularly in the case of Libya, Iran and Iraq. A related danger, in that they may be seen as a substitute for nuclear weapons, is posed by chemical weapons. Within reach of the Mediterranean is the greatest concentration of chemical weapons holders in the world: Russia, republics of the former Soviet Union, France, Syria, Iraq, Iran, Israel, Egypt, Libya are all known to possess chemical weapons stockpiles. A contrast can be drawn with the rest of non-Mediterranean Africa and Latin America in which, in each case, there is only one country in possession of chemical weapons.

Terrorism is another security threat that haunts the Mediterranean, precisely because so many flashpoints and grievances are concentrated in the region. In October 1985, the Italian cruiseship *Achille Lauro* was hijacked in the Mediterranean (Clutterbuck, 1990) and this act has remained a symbol of terrorism at sea. Virtually every Mediterranean riparian country has witnessed acts of terrorism, whether in Southern Europe, the Balkans, the Middle East or North Africa. While the major concentration of active terrorist organizations is undoubtedly in the Levant, terrorist activities are currently of major significance in Turkey, Egypt and Algeria. Even the islands of Corsica and Sardinia, not normally in the front line of terrorist atrocities, have not been immune (*The Economist*, 22 August, 1992). The gamut of Mediterranean terrorists ranges from frustrated nationalists to regional separatists, political visionaries, religious fanatics or simply brigands.

This sheer variety of grievances, organizations and manifestations of terrorism indicates the extent of the problem.

Moreover, although terrorism usually stems from local or regional grievances, it often knows no boundaries. Terrorism is exported from Iran, Syria, Israel and, probably, Libya and, in many cases, is effectively state-sponsored. Furthermore, by its very nature, terrorism is linked to international crime, including the illegal transfer of arms and drugs smuggling. In turn, punitive action against terrorism can and does often entail violations of international sovereignty or human rights. Terrorism, being the expression of frustrated individuals, groups or even states unable to attain their aims or rectify their grievances by lawful or conventional means, constitutes a defiance of the established order, at the national or international level, by those who perceive themselves ill-served by it. Thus, under certain aspects, the high incidence and variety of terrorism in the Mediterranean illustrates not just the concentration of problems in one region, but the very rejection by its perpetrators of the international order and/or the modern state, both seen as creations of the West.

Another, more popular, expression of such rejection, whether voiced by violence or not, is the spread of Islamic fundamentalism, which has been gaining momentum in recent years. Especially since the Islamic revolution in Iran, fundamentalism has been the spectre of every Muslim state from Turkey to Morocco. More recently, fundamentalism, both Shi'ite and Sunni, has emerged more convincingly as a threat to the established order, most notably in Egypt and Algeria, but also in the incipient state of Palestine. The hostility between the state and fundamentalists in most countries has resulted in more recourse to violence by the latter and increasingly repressive measures by the former, threatening further the stability of the state. From an overall Mediterranean point of view, on account of its rejectionist tendency, it underlines further the division between the European and non-European shores of the Mediterranean.

Such a division, already deeply marked in terms of the different levels of development, is further highlighted by the equally rejectionist attitude on the European side against immigration from the South. One of the most deep-seated causes of insecurity lies in the marked difference between the demographic structures of the European and the non-European Mediterranean. The population of North Africa, from Egypt to Mauritania, 90 million in 1980, will rise to 153 million by the end of this century and to 241 million by 2025 (de Vasconcelos, 1991). Furthermore, with over 50 per cent of the population under the age of 15, the region is set to be afflicted by the 'youth bulge' when competition for education, jobs and other opportunities increases severely. Already, unemployment is rampant and the escape route of emigration to Western Europe has been virtually closed. With rising unemployment in Western Europe and increasing numbers of immigrants expected from Eastern Europe, the situation is likely to worsen. 'The Mediterranean is to Europe what the Río Grande is to the United States' (*The Times*, 5 February 1992).

Millions of Muslim immigrants have already entered France, Italy and Spain and this continued immigration from the South is an open challenge to the development of the European Union. Movements of labour across the Mediterranean, for long a feature of the economies of the region, have always involved the potential for social problems, but when the migrants are refugees, the situation can be greatly exacerbated (McColl, 1993).

Thus, an examination of the new dimensions of security reveals that, on the regional scale, there are many potential threats. Most involve a complex interrelationship of political, economic, social and environmental factors. Added to these difficulties, of course, each Mediterranean state has its own security problems and concerns.

A NEW SECURITY ARCHITECTURE?

…the world today needs more than the nation-state to organize global peace, to promote global welfare, to diffuse globally the fruits of science and technology, and to cope with global environmental problems. All of these things can be done more effectively and rationally if nation-states are encouraged to co-operate in the setting of a larger community that reflects what unites them and submerges what has traditionally divided them (Brzezinski, 1993).

In terms of purely military security, the Mediterranean region poses many actual and potential problems. If a more broadly based definition of security is used, the Mediterranean emerges with more possible geopolitical flash-points than any other region of comparable size. The vital question that must then be posed concerns what kind of structure can best be employed to address the issues and reduce the possibility of conflict. This debate is at present in its early stages, if only because until now little headway has been achieved in addressing the Mediterranean basin as a single region, with riparian states acknowledging a common security interest.

Around the Mediterranean, but not across it, there is no shortage of organizations experienced in dealing with security issues. The European Mediterranean is represented by at least some member states in five bodies originally constructed within the framework of the Cold War: NATO, the European Union (EU), the Western European Union (WEU), the Conference on Security and Cooperation in Europe (CSCE) and the North Atlantic Cooperation Council (NACC). NATO has been described as 'the most successful alliance in history' (Kinkel, 1992), but it has yet to redefine its role following the demise of the Warsaw Pact. The main advantages advanced for the retention of NATO as the guardian of Europe include its long and successful record, its tested structure, crucial for post-Cold War disarmament verification and monitoring, and the fact that it ensures the continuing concern of the United States with Europe. Against this it has been argued, particularly in France, that the economic strength and global importance of the EU demand that Europeans, alone, should be responsible for the security of the continent. The CSCE and the NACC include a far wider range of interests, but, again, membership is restricted to the countries of Europe, together with the republics of the former Soviet Union.

By contrast, on the non-European side of the Mediterranean, comparable security organizations are conspicuously absent. Two subregional groupings for economic integration involving Mediterranean Arab states were established in 1989. One, the Arab Co-operation Council, was brought to a *de facto* end by the Gulf Crisis soon after. The Arab Maghreb Union remains, but appears stalled. The only organization with potential would seem to be the Arab League, a body that has grown in stature since the resumption of the Middle East peace talks. However, like the European organizations, it has responsibilities far wider than the Mediterranean and within the region is restricted geographically.

It would appear that, for it to be viable, any regional security structure would have to involve as many of the region's states as possible, especially when the region in question already contains deep divisions within it, divisions that existing security structures around the Mediterranean have not healed. Any attempt to impose stability on the region or to take care of the security of one side by erecting defences against the other, say, by recasting NATO into an organization for the defence of Europe from its non-European neighbours, or by formulating a European common defence policy, directed at the non-European Mediterranean, is not likely to bridge the divisions that exist within the region and that constitute the most important overall threat to its security.

Accordingly, the most suitable idea, because it recognizes the inseparability and complementarity between security and cooperation in a region that is otherwise divided, is that of involving the Mediterranean in a system of security and cooperation along the lines of the CSCE process (Ghebali, 1992). The concept was launched by Italy and Spain in 1990, at the CSCE conference on the protection of the Mediterranean's ecological system, held in Palma de Mallorca. The Conference on Security and Cooperation in the Mediterranean (CSCM) was welcomed as a possibility, but, as yet, many basic problems, including that of membership, remain and the idea has still to be pursued effectively, diplomatically. None the less, since the CSCM would provide a unifying forum for the region as a whole and would be concerned with security, however broadly defined, it remains at present potentially the most effective suggestion.

REFERENCES

Agnew, C.T. and Anderson, E.W. (1992), *Water Resources in the Arid Realm*, London: Routledge.

Anderson, E.W. (1993), *An Atlas of World Political Flashpoints*, London: Pinter.

Anderson, E.W. (1992), 'The Political and Strategic Significance of Water', *Outlook on Agriculture* 21, 4:247-53.

Blake, G.H. (1992), 'International Boundaries and Territorial Stability in the Middle East: an Assessment', *GeoJournal* 28, 3: 365-73.

Brzezinski, Z. (1993), *Out of Control*, New York: Maxwell Macmillan International.

Brogan, P. (1989), *World Conflicts*, London: Bloomsbury.

Clutterbuck, R. (1990), *Terrorism, Drugs and Crime in Europe after 1992*, London: Routledge.

de Vasconcelos, A. (1991), 'The New Europe and the Western Mediterranean', *NATO Review*, October: 27-31.

Dismukes, B. and Hayes, B.C. (1991), 'The Mediterranean Remains Vital', *Proceedings of the USNI*, October: 45-9.

Evert, M. (1991), 'Emerging Power Balances in the Mediterranean', *Mediterranean Quarterly*, Summer : 9-14.

Ghebali, V.-Y. (1992), 'CSCM - a Chance for Peace in the Middle East?', *International Defense Review* 2: 111.

Grover, B. (1993), 'The "Geo" of the United States National Strategy', *GeoJournal* 31, 2: 141-8.

HMSO (1992), Statement on the Defence Estimates, London: HMSO.

Kinkel, K. (1992), 'NATO's Enduring Role in Europe', *NATO Review* 40, 5: 3-7.

McColl, R.W. (1993), 'The Creation and Consequences of International Refugees: Politics, Military Action and Geography', *GeoJournal* 31, 2: 169-77.

Rathbone, T. (1992), 'WEU and Security in the Mediterranean', *Letter from the Assembly*, July: 17-20.

Train, H. (1988), 'Maritime Strategy in the Mediterranean', *Adelphi Papers 229, Prospects for Security in the Mediterranean Part One*: 49-60.

Williams, C.H. and Williams, S.W. (1993), 'Issues of Peace and Security in Contemporary Europe', in Williams, C.H. (ed.), *The Political Geography of the New World Order*, London: Belhaven, 100-131.

2

The European Union and the Maghreb

George Joffé

Since the end of the war against Iraq in 1991, Europe, particularly the European Union, has become the dominant concern of the foreign policies of the Maghreb states – Libya, Tunisia, Algeria, Morocco and Mauritania: the five states which, since February 1989, have made up the Union Maghreb Arabe (UMA). Events in the Middle East, particularly the defeat of Iraq and the impending end of the Arab-Israeli conflict, have significantly reduced North African interests there (Joffé 1993: 6-7). Africa remains isolated from North African affairs by the geographic barrier of the Sahara – there is still no proper communications link across the desert.

More importantly, the imperatives of trade and regional security have refocused North African minds on the Mediterranean and the European Union. It is Europe, after all, that provided 53.5 per cent of their imports and absorbed 31.8 per cent of their exports in 1990 (see Table 2.4). It is Europe, too, that absorbed up to 2.3 million migrant workers from North Africa at the end of the 1980s (Escallier 1991: 96). And, finally, despite the continuing tensions over regional issues such as the Western Sahara, it is Europe that now dominates the North African security agenda, as NATO begins to consider the implications of its 'southern flank'.

THE SECURITY ISSUE

Up to 1990, two basic factors governed the strategic significance of North Africa. The first was the Cold War and the second was the issue of regional security and hegemony.

The Cold War and the superpowers

The Cold War lent a particular importance to the North African coastline. The reason was that it dominated the western Mediterranean and the all-important naval trade route from the Black Sea and the Gulf through the

Straits of Gibraltar to the Atlantic. This was of primary importance to Europe because of its dependence on Middle Eastern and North African oil and gas. North African states – Libya and Algeria and, to a much lesser extent, Tunisia – were also major energy suppliers to Europe.

In 1989, for example, Algeria satisfied 8.8 per cent of European natural gas consumption through the Trans-Med line to Italy (11.2 billion cubic metres out of a total consumption of 126.1 billion cubic metres) and 91.1 per cent of European demand for liquefied natural gas (LNG) (15.4 billion cubic metres out of a total demand of 16.9 billion cubic metres) – overall, 11.6 per cent of Western Europe's gas needs. These exports of LNG went to Belgium, France and Spain, while Libya supplied a further 1.5 billion cubic metres (8.9 per cent of the European total) to Italy and Spain. North Africa, in short, satisfied 20.5 per cent of Western Europe's gas consumption, while 35.0 per cent of the supplies came from the Soviet Union, 20 per cent from Norway and 23.7 per cent from the Netherlands' North Sea fields. In the same year, the Middle East supplied 31.5 per cent of European oil demand and North Africa provided a further 15.4 per cent of the 12.51 million barrels per day consumed throughout Europe (BP, 1990: 24).

In reality, however, European security concerns over these flows were absorbed into the wider issue of Western security in the face of the perceived Soviet threat. The major security burden fell, therefore, on the USA, particularly in naval terms, although European powers, particularly along the north Mediterranean coastline, provided additional naval support. Interestingly enough, however, defence provision as far as North Africa was concerned was not specifically coordinated through NATO, as the region was considered to be 'out-of-area' to the Western alliance. Instead, only naval provision and accompanying air support fell within the NATO ambit and then only in so far as it formed part of the general defence arrangements for the whole of the Mediterranean region – NATO's 'southern flank'. North Africa itself was not seen as a major strategic concern, except for the fact that it could offer military facilities to one or other of the superpowers or their allies. The major concern for the USA, Europe and NATO, therefore, was to prevent the Soviet Union from obtaining a permanent presence in the region.

Although the US Sixth Fleet did have permanent bases in the central Mediterranean region, the Soviet naval equivalent, the Black Sea Fleet, did not. The American presence depended on facilities in Italy and Greece. During the 1980s, when Spain joined the NATO alliance, Spanish ports also offered facilities and France, though not formally in NATO's integrated military structure, increasingly coordinated with the alliance. Indeed, much superpower activity in the North African region was devoted to either acquiring access to permanent base facilities – as was the case with the Soviet Union – or to denying them to potential opponents – the objective of the USA and Western Europe.

This became particularly important after 1972, when the Soviet Union lost access to Alexandria as a result of the decision of Egyptian President Anwar Sadat's decision to break Cairo's links with Moscow. Thereafter, Soviet naval power was never able to restore its presence in the central or the western Mediterranean. Although it obtained berthing facilities at Benghazi and Tripoli in Libya and at Mers el-Kebir in Algeria, as well as bunkering facilities off Malta, it never enjoyed permanent port facilities in the region again. The Soviet naval presence in the Mediterranean declined in consequence.

This Soviet naval decline was mirrored by the Soviet Union's relative weakness in military terms generally throughout North Africa. Soviet military equipment was, it is true, sold in significant quantities to Libya (around $15 billion-worth during the 1970s and 1980s) and to Algeria (where the armed forces were substantially dependent on Soviet equipment until President Chadli Benjedid's visit to Washington, the first by an Algerian leader, in 1985). There were even similar sales to Morocco shortly after independence. Algeria and Libya, as a consequence of their arms purchases, also harboured large numbers of Soviet military technical personnel – 600 to 700 in the case of Libya and up to 2,000 in Algeria – and depended on Soviet strategic and tactical principles for their military planning.

This was never, however, transformed into dependence on Soviet protection, even in Libya, despite a treaty of fraternity between Tripoli and Moscow in 1973. Soviet ground forces and air forces never enjoyed strategic access to North Africa, any more than did Soviet naval forces. Nor does North Africa seem to have figured particularly highly in Soviet strategic planning. This was, no doubt, in part due to the fact that Soviet arms supplies were a matter of hard-headed commercial interest as much as one of strategic purpose. The arms had to be paid for, even if long-term credit arrangements were negotiated with Libya – where the collapse of the Soviet Union in 1991 left both Russia and the Ukraine holding Libyan military debts of $2 billion each! It also reflected, however, an acute sensitivity about communism within the two states most directly concerned – Libya and Algeria. The official ideologies of both were not sympathetic to Soviet communism and diplomatic friendship was never allowed to develop into formal alliance patterns which would have given Moscow a strategic toehold, at least, in North Africa.

This arms-length relationship between Libya and Algeria, on the one hand, and the Soviet Union on the other, was similar to the relationship enjoyed by the USA with North Africa's two moderate, pro-Western states – Morocco and Tunisia. Morocco, it is true, did participate annually in the US 'Bright Star' military exercises from the mid-1980s onwards, and both countries provided facilities for the Rapid Deployment Force of Central Command, set up by President Carter in the aftermath of the Iranian revolution in 1979 as a means of guaranteeing the defence of Arab oil states in the Gulf. Ironically enough, when there was a real threat to these states – after Iraq's invasion of Kuwait in August 1990 – the USA made virtually no use of these facilities! Both Morocco and Tunisia also enjoyed regular military aid from the United States. Neither, however, entered into close military cooperation with Washington. Indeed, in 1984 Morocco shocked the Reagan administration by signing a regional unity agreement, the 'Arab–African Union', with Libya, a state already regarded with considerable hostility by the USA.

As far as Europe was concerned, North Africa's military significance was limited and was, above all, a French concern. By the end of the 1980s, there were still residual anxieties about the fact that, in naval terms, North African states could potentially control the strategic line of communication that ran through the Mediterranean from the Suez Canal to the Straits of Gibraltar along which flowed oil from the Gulf. But the major European anxiety was over the nature of security inside North Africa itself. Algeria, after all, once independence had been achieved in 1962, appeared to be the dominant power there and European states, particularly France, were by no means certain that this situation accorded with their own strategic concerns in the region. France therefore provided military support to Morocco and Tunisia, supplying most of their military equipment as well as training. Spain, too, became a major military supplier to Morocco during the 1980s. By the 1990s, there were some French strategists who even argued that the acquisition of missile technology by Algeria could be a threat to France itself, particularly if Algeria were to become an Islamic state.

Regional security

The touchstones of European concerns about the security situation in North Africa came to focus around the issues of potential conflict between Algeria and Morocco over the Western Sahara, which Morocco had unilaterally annexed after Spain's withdrawal in February 1976, and the actual conflict between Libya and Chad which was symbolized by the Aozou Strip dispute. The Western Sahara conflict not only involved European anxieties over Algerian and Moroccan ambitions to establish an hegemony over the region but also caused considerable anxieties in the early years over the stability of government in Morocco, particularly if its annexation of the Western Sahara could not be sustained. However, by the mid-1980s, it had become evident that Morocco would not relinquish its hold over the Western Sahara and that it increasingly regarded the Sahrawi referendum on self-determination demanded by both the United Nations and the Organization of African Unity as a convenient means of legitimizing *de jure* Rabat's *de facto* integration of the former Spanish colony into metropolitan Morocco.

This left European powers with an embarrassing diplomatic conundrum. No European state accepted Morocco's justification for the annexation of the Western Sahara in November 1975, not least because the International Court of Justice's advisory opinion, handed down the previous month, had rejected Moroccan claims to sovereignty over the region, although it did admit that there were links between it and Morocco in the pre-colonial period (ICJ 1975: 60). At the same time, the European Commission had the responsibility for the regular negotiation of a fishing treaty with Morocco and this raised the embarrassing question of whether or not Western Saharan waters were included. Although the wording of these treaties (they were usually renegotiated every three years) was deliberately ambiguous on this point, European, particularly Spanish, fishing practice granted Morocco effective recognition of the legality of its presence in the Western Sahara.

Indeed, there has been a growing tendency in European capitals and within the Union to try to ignore the Western Sahara issue. Responsibility for its solution now lies with the United Nations, which is trying to organize the all-important referendum despite continuing tensions between Morocco and the Polisario Front. One reason why Europe can afford to ignore the Western Sahara issue for the moment is that the Sahrawis' most important patron, Algeria, is profoundly weakened by its internal crisis over the future form of government there and over its looming confrontation with the powerful, even if banned, Islamist movements. This has meant that the vital diplomatic and military–logistical support necessary for a more active Polisario response to Morocco's unwillingness to cooperate over the referendum except on its own terms has been lacking ever since 1988.

Algerian passivity over the Western Sahara issue mirrors its weakness in regional strategic terms as well. Its armed forces are significantly smaller in size than those of Morocco (125,000 in the regular Algerian armed forces, together with 23,000 paramilitary personnel and a defence budget of $560 million, compared with 195,000 in the regular Moroccan armed forces, along with 40,000 paramilitary personnel and a defence budget of $1.264 billion in 1991). In any case, since the country-wide riots in October 1988 and particularly since the army-backed coup in January 1992, which brought the democratic experiment in Algeria to an abrupt end, military and governmental concerns have been dominated by domestic factors.

Quite apart from these issues, Algeria has also engaged in diplomatic démarches which have limited its ability to wholeheartedly support the Polisario Front and the Sahrawis. In February 1989, Algiers joined Rabat, Tunis, Tripoli and Nouakchott in creating the UMA (Union Maghreb Arabe), a regional confederation designed to both defuse diplomatic tensions and to create a regional common market. Article 27 of the founding treaty bound the members together in mutual defence, for an attack on any one of them would be construed to be an attack on all. Clearly, Algeria now could only support diplomatic initiatives to bring the Western Sahara issue to a successful conclusion without threatening Morocco!

In essence, therefore, Algeria's domestic crisis and economic weakness in the wake of the 1986 collapse in oil prices have forced it to abandon the pretensions to regional hegemony that it harboured in the 1970s and early 1980s. Morocco has not been able to enforce its own regional power instead, but it has at least been able to confront Algeria on equal terms. Nor has the UMA arrangement acted, as Algeria hoped, as a means of forcing a solution to the Western Sahara conflict. Instead Morocco has been able to insist on its own interpretation of rights of sovereign control there, with very little opposition from its UMA partners. Indeed, Tunisia, Libya and Mauritania appear to have virtually accepted the Moroccan thesis by default. The problem for Europe, then, has been considerably eased by the acquiescence of regional states in Morocco's *de facto* annexation of the territory. European states can, in effect, simply ignore the issue – except at the level of international law – by pointing to North African indifference towards it.

The decline of Algerian regional power and influence has had other effects as well, particularly upon the situation of Libya. Algeria had traditionally been seen as the strategic hinterland for Libya. Indeed, in July 1977, when border incidents escalated into full-scale war between Libya and Egypt, it was the Boumedienne government in Algiers that persuaded the Sadat regime to end the fighting because of its threat to intervene in support of Libya if the conflict continued. At the same time, Algeria had also been the guarantor of Tunisian independence against the Libyan threat, as was implicit in the Treaty of Concord and Fraternity which the two countries signed in March 1983. With the collapse of Algeria's diplomatic role in regional terms after 1988 and the creation of the UMA as a vehicle for defusing regional tensions, Libya has become a region-wide responsibility and problem.

Thus, the UMA states reluctantly acquiesced in the imposition of sanctions against Libya as a result of British and American claims about its responsibility for the destruction of an American airliner over the Scottish town of Lockerbie in December 1988 and of French claims of Libyan involvement in the destruction of a UTA aircraft over Chad in September 1989. However, together with Egypt, they tried to mitigate the harshness of the sanctions and, led by Morocco, worked behind the scenes to persuade Western states to moderate their attitudes. Some years earlier, Morocco and Algeria had played significant roles in defusing tensions in the aftermath of Libya's defeat in Chad in March 1987 and in persuading the Qadhafi regime to take its claim to the Aozou Strip in northern Chad to the International Court of Justice at The Hague.

Indeed, Libya's relations with Chad have been the other major touchstone of European concern over the security situation in North Africa. In the wake of the Libyan intervention in Chad in mid-1980 on behalf of the then president, Goukouni Oueddeye, and Libya's unilateral decision to retreat two years later, as Hissan Habré successfully forced the incumbent out of the presidency, France, in particular, became very worried about the situation in Chad. When, in mid-1983, Libya once again supported Goukouni Oueddeye in an attack on the Habré regime, France sent military aid to N'Djamena in the form of 3,000 men who manned a ceasefire line along the sixteenth parallel right across central Chad.

Further French military aid was provided in February 1986 when Libyan forces aided Goukouni Oueddeye's rebel army to move southwards in an attempt, in its turn, to recover control of Chad. Over the next year, France and the United States vied with each other for a dominating role in N'Djamena as each provided military aid to the Habré regime to bolster it against the Libyan-backed onslaught of Oueddeye's FAN (Forces Armées du Nord) forces. Eventually, in March 1987, Habré's FAT (Forces Armées Tchadiennes) units, freshly equipped by France and the USA, hit back at the FAN and at Libyan army units in northern Chad.[1] In a lightning campaign, Libyan units were destroyed or forced back into Libya.

It was at this juncture that Libya's North African neighbours played a significant role. Both Morocco and Algeria eventually persuaded the Qadhafi regime that, in the wake of its defeat in northern Chad, it would do best to abandon ambitions inside Chad itself. Instead, Libya would place its claims to the Aozou Strip – the ostensible cause of its interest in Chadian affairs – before the International Court of Justice at The Hague. Libya had, after all, had satisfactory experiences before the Court in the past, in resolving its boundary disputes with Tunisia and Malta. It was, therefore, prepared to submit to the same process again in determining where its international boundary with Chad was really located. Morocco ensured that the Habré regime agreed to submit to the same procedure. In any case, Libya achieved its final revenge over Hissan Habré in December 1990 when it supported a rival, Idriss Deby, in a successful bid to wrest control of Chad from the Habré regime.

Current security concerns

The security concerns of European states in the western Mediterranean today reflect North African anxieties over the possibilities and implications of Western interventionism, as a result of the West's antagonism towards Libya because of its alleged role as a terrorist state. However, Europe also has wider concerns based on anxieties about instability amongst the UMA countries, largely as a result of developmental failures and the demographic explosion there (Joffé, 1992: 61). The archetypal example is, of course, Algeria, although there have long been similar concerns over the future course of government in Tunisia and Morocco. This has resulted in a series of proposals, particularly from southern Europe and from the Maghreb's traditional protector, France, for new security arrangements.

Perhaps the best-known is the 'CSCM proposal' for a Conference on Security and Cooperation in the Mediterranean, put forward by Spain and Italy in September 1990 (Ministero degli Affari Esteri 1990). This builds on security cooperation agreements that already exist between, for example, Morocco and Spain over air defence, and it is patterned on the CSCE system. The CSCM proposals were designed to deal with all the problems of the Mediterranean, including those of the Levant, and they even anticipated covering the Gulf region as well. The primary purpose was to create a stable system of regional cooperation based on three 'baskets' dealing with security, economic cooperation and human rights. The CSCM project required that participant states would (1) respect the territorial integrity and border inviolability of member-states, (2) aid regional economic development, (3) reject the use of force and abandon armament programmes, and (4) practise tolerance and begin a dialogue over political, cultural and religious matters. The proposal was to involve the EU; all Mediterranean littoral states; the GCC, Yemen, Iran and Iraq; and the USA and Canada.

The proposal was, of course, far too complex to be acted upon in the short term and in any case it ran counter to an alternative proposal put forward by France. This was the 'five plus four' proposal, later modified to include Malta and now known as the 'five plus five' proposal. It basically brings together the four EU states of France, Italy, Spain and Portugal, together with Malta, as the states most directly affected by Mediterranean security issues, and the five North African states that form the UMA – Libya, Tunisia, Algeria, Morocco and Mauritania. Its primary purpose is to provide a framework for regional security issues outside both the Western European Union and NATO. It is also designed to be a forum for the discussion of common issues, particularly those of migration and economic development.

Migration from North Africa is seen as one of the biggest threats to security in Southern Europe in the medium term. North African states are experiencing annual population growth rates of between 2.5 and 3 per cent and their combined populations are expected to rise from the current level of 67 million to between 100 and 140 million by the year 2025. The problem is that growth in employment opportunities satisfies only about half the demand at 200,000 places annually. Only Libya is a labour-deficit economy, and labour demand there is largely satisfied by Egypt (Nonneman 1992: 202-3). In the wake of the Second Gulf War, the potential opportunities for migrants from the Arab-speaking world have largely disappeared, as the Gulf states themselves seek migrant labour from Asia.

Europe is thus the obvious and preferred destination for North African migrants. There are, however, over 2.3 million North African migrant workers already present in Europe – between 8 and 10 per cent of the European labour force – and European states are determined that this figure should not rise, in view of the growth in xenophobia and racism there. There is a certain irony in this, since French demographers have shown that, by 2025, there is likely to be a 30 per cent shortfall in indigenous European labour supply in precisely those areas in which North Africans traditionally work. There are some claims that the shortfall will be made up from labour from eastern Europe and the former Soviet Union, but this is unlikely for domestic political reasons. From a North African point of view, however, the demographic crisis which the region faces requires concerted action involving Europe, and the 'five plus five' proposal provides a forum for this, as does, in economic terms, the EU Commission in Brussels.

There is, of course, a further anxiety expressed by North African states for which the 'five plus five' proposal offers some means of relief. This is the anxiety about possible direct military intervention, particularly in Libya. The other states in the UMA are both embarrassed and disadvantaged by Western attitudes towards Libya because they are tied to Libya's defence by article 27 of the UMA's founding treaty. It is not clear whether the obligation of mutual defence contained in this clause would apply in circumstances where the attack was engendered as a result of terrorist activities on the part of the target state. However, public opinion inside the Maghreb would not differentiate and would thus deny to the governments concerned the freedom of action to make such a distinction themselves. That is, after all, what happened in the case of the war against Iraq in 1991.

As far as Libya is concerned, there is evidence that similar constraints apply already. As mentioned above, all four states were very reluctant to support the sanctions imposed on Libya in April 1992 and December 1993 because of its refusal to surrender the people accused of the Lockerbie and UTA bombings to Britain, France or the USA. Extended sanctions or an actual attack on Libya would cause serious problems in their relations with the West, not least because of domestic popular reaction inside North Africa itself. The 'five plus five' proposal, if it were fully operative, would provide a far more equitable forum – and one seen in North Africa to be equitable – for the resolution of this kind of issue. It remains to be seen, however, to what extent such a forum can be transformed into a practical reality.

Political Islam

Europe also has, as have North African governments, an acute concern over the implications of Islamic fundamentalism in the region. Here, once again, the touchstone is Algeria, where European states have been in a quandary as to what to do. The quandary arises because of Europe's mixed objectives in regard to the region. On the one hand, there is a normative desire to support progress towards the institution of democratic regimes in North Africa and towards full observance of human rights there. On the other hand, there is considerable anxiety in Brussels and in national capitals over the threat to regional stability represented by Islamic fundamentalism. This anxiety also extends towards Europe's own Muslim migrant populations, particularly in countries where a majority or a significant minority of migrants come from North Africa – France, Spain and the Benelux countries.

In Algeria these two concerns seem to be operating in direct contradiction and European states have, therefore, had ambivalent attitudes towards the situation there. In January 1992, France began by arguing that the democratic process should not be interrupted. However, just over a year later, after parliamentary elections in France which brought a conservative government to power, official opinion changed markedly and open support was offered to attempts to re-establish public order. Towards the end of 1993, the French government also encouraged Algerian government leaders to contemplate dialogue with 'responsible' Muslim leaders – after having demonstrated its own hostility towards Islamic fundamentalism in France by a series of arrests and expulsions. This ambivalence in France has been mirrored, with somewhat more restraint, by other concerned governments, particularly those of Italy and Spain, and by the European Union Commission in Brussels.

Behind this ambivalence lies an unresolved contradiction between preferences for legitimate, responsible and democratic government – 'good governance' – or political stability as a basis for economic development. Indeed, European anxieties over Islamic fundamentalism in North Africa, like those of the United States within the wider context of the Middle East, are basically related to these two apparently contradictory objectives. They are apparently contradictory because, in the last analysis, 'good governance' is the only way to ensure real political stability. However, in the process of achieving it, there can be plenty of potential for instability, particularly with regimes – such as that in Algeria in 1991-92 – which have lost fundamental popular trust.

The problem is that, whilst recognizing the need for radical political change, most European governments do not see Islamic fundamentalism as an appropriate means by which change and subsequent political stability can be achieved. They are well aware that popular support for such movements is powerfully fed by popular discontent over economic reform as much as because of popular anger with existing government. They also realize that few Islamic fundamentalist movements are genuinely prepared to tolerate democratic dissent or opposition. Indeed, in Algeria this refusal to tolerate the democratic option, on the grounds that it is non-Islamic (*jahiliyya*), was expressed quite explicitly by Islamist spokesmen. Thus, to have permitted the democratic process to have continued there in January

1992 would have led to profoundly undemocratic consequences. It certainly would not have led to political stability.

Stability in the short term is seen as a desirable objective because of the implications for foreign investment. Western governments have not forgotten their experiences in Iran in 1979 as a result of the Islamic revolution there. However, Islamic fundamentalist movements today are generally not opposed to foreign investment or to the operations of the free market, provided basic requirements of social justice are met. This has been certainly true of the FIS (Front Islamic du Salut), whose representatives went out of their way in December 1991 and January 1992 to reassure foreign investors in Algeria. Western investors are still not convinced, however, and Morocco and Tunisia are considered as far safer havens for foreign investment.

Moroccan and Tunisian attitudes towards Islamic fundamentalism have been quite different from those of Algeria (see Joffé 1991). The Tunisian authorities have long been exercised over the dangers of such movements since they developed in the early 1970s. However, it was in the early 1980s that a crisis developed over Islamist activities there, starting with the abortive rebellion in the southern town of Gafsa in 1980. By 1987 the then president, Habib Bourguiba, was demanding that the leadership of the major Islamist movement, the Harakat al-Ittijah al-Islami (Islamic Tendency Movement) should be executed, a demand that led to his replacement (Boulby 1988: 614). His successor, Zine al-Abidine ben Ali, despite an early attempt to placate and integrate the movement, now renamed the Nahda (Renaissance) party in an attempt to be accepted as a legitimate political party, has opted for confrontation instead. Tunisia considers that Islamist movements in North Africa are part of a much wider Islamist conspiracy derived from Iran and, latterly, Sudan. They must therefore be opposed, and Tunisia has joined with Egypt, Algeria and, to a lesser extent, Morocco in adopting a hostile attitude towards them. In this the Tunisian government enjoys full European support, despite growing disquiet over human rights abuses there.

In Morocco, the Islamist movement has always been far weaker than in any of the other North African countries. The major reason for this is the religious legitimization possessed by the Moroccan sultanate through its status as Amir al-muminin (Commander of the Faithful). As a result, it has proved very difficult for the Islamist movement to characterize the political system as inherently illegitimate. It is also true that the Moroccan security services have been very efficient at controlling the growth of such opposition, although it did play a part in the country-wide disturbances in January 1984. The Moroccan government also believes that external influences support Islamic fundamentalism inside the country, and it thus supports other countries in North Africa in their opposition to such influences. For Europe, however, the success of the Moroccan authorities in holding Islamic fundamentalism at bay has been a source of relief.

Whatever the situation may be currently, however, Europe is still left with the conundrum as to what to do over the phenomenon of Islamic fundamentalism. Even though the problem may have been contained for the moment, except perhaps in Algeria, it is quite clear that Islamic fundamentalism will continue to be, in one form or another, a significant element within regional political systems. There will also be a similar development within Europe itself amongst the North African migrant populations there. Perhaps the most important question is whether or not Islamist movements in the future will be prepared to accept political pluralism. If they are, then they will not a priori represent a threat to regional stability. If they are not, then the North African political scene is likely to be turbulent and North African governments will continue with their repressive policies despite Western complaints over human rights abuses, on the grounds that Islamist intransigence can only be countered by force.

THE ECONOMIC DIMENSION

Although issues of security may seem to top the European agenda, this is not the case as far as North African states are concerned – except, perhaps, for Algeria. Since the end of the Cold War, North African diplomacy has concentrated on regional relations, particularly with Europe. The Non-Aligned Movement has disappeared; North African interests in Middle Eastern affairs have been curtailed as a result of the disintegration of the Arab world in the wake of the war against Iraq in 1990-91 and the initiation of the Middle East peace process; and the process of economic reform during the 1980s has forced North African governments to review their relationships with their major trading partners. In short, it is now the European Union that dominates North African diplomatic and commercial horizons.

The demographic dimension

North African states are in the grip of a demographic explosion (see Table 2.1). Within thirty years, their populations will have more than doubled and even today more than 50 per cent of their populations are under thirty years old. The average regional growth rate is of the order of 2.3 per cent and it is conventionally assumed that GDP growth rates must at least match this if there is not to be an absolute decline in living standards. In fact, because of the additional demand on services made by rapidly growing populations, GDP growth rates must be significantly higher if this objective is to be achieved.

George Joffé

Table 2.1 Demographic growth in the Maghreb, 1960–2025 (million persons)

	1960	1990	2000	2025	1960–90 (%)	1990–2000 (%)
Algeria	10.8	25.0	32.9	52.0	2.8	2.8
Libya	1.3	4.5	6.5	14.0	4.1	3.6
Mauritania	1.0	2.0	2.7	5.0	2.4	2.9
Morocco	11.6	25.1	31.6	47.0	2.6	2.3
Tunisia	4.2	8.2	9.9	14.0	2.2	2.0
Total	28.9	64.8	83.6	132.0	2.4	2.3

Source: United Nations Development Programme, 1992; World Bank, 1992; Maghreb Quarterly Report 7 (Aug/Sept 1992).

In fact, it is most unlikely that this will be achieved easily and the demographic problems are already creating massive social problems. In Algeria, for instance, 30 per cent of the population under the age of twenty-five and 17 per cent of those under the age of thirty (who make up 70 per cent of the Algerian population) are unemployed.

Table 2.2 Active population in the Maghreb, 1987 (population – millions/rates – %)

Population	Morocco	Algeria	Tunisia	Total
Total population	23.4	22.6	7.5	53.5
Active population	8.7	5.3	1.9	15.9
Occupation rate	37.1	23.6	25.2	29.7
Number unemployed	1.6*	1.1	0.3	3.0
Unemployment rate	18.4	21.4	14.4	18.9

* Including 851,000 under-employed rural workers
Source: Lacoste, 1991: 486.

Nor will this situation ease, for the Algerian government creates less than half (100,000) the 256,000 jobs needed annually. In Morocco, where 268,000 new jobs are needed every year but where the state sector does not even meet half that figure, unemployment is officially admitted to be 17 per cent of the workforce and is reliably estimated to be rising beyond 25 per cent. When under-employment in rural areas is included, the true figure rises towards 50 per cent. The same situation applies in Tunisia, where 75,000 new jobs are required annually but only 45,000 are created by the state (Lacoste 1991: 421). Only in Libya is there a shortage of labour, which is made up by migrants – 180,000 Egyptians, 40,000 Tunisians and 15,000 Moroccans (Nonneman, 1992: 202-3).

Migration, however, does not offer a real alternative by which this excess labour force can be absorbed. Europe, with its 2.3 million Maghrebi migrants, has made it clear that it will not accept significantly greater numbers, even though French demographers have calculated that, by the year 2025, Europe will suffer from a labour shortage, running at 30 per cent of the total labour force, precisely in those areas in which Maghrebi migrants usually work. In any case, it is expected that such shortfalls will be made up by migrants from eastern Europe, if indeed more migrants are tolerated at all. The Middle East and particularly the Gulf, which had been alternatives up to 1990, are now also closed to Maghrebi migrants. This is in part due to the reduced funds available in the Gulf region as a result of its contributions towards the costs of Operation Desert Storm and in part because of a regional preference for labour from non-Arab sources, particularly Asia.

Table 2.3 Development Assistance to North Africa

	Algeria	Libya	Mauritania	Morocco	Tunisia
1980					
aid ($ mn)	176	17	176	894	232
aid/GDP (%)	0.5	0.1	25.8	4.8	2.8
aid/exports (%)	1.2	–	65.2	27.3	65.2
1985					
aid ($ mn)	173	5	209	785	163
aid/GDP (%)	0.3	–	29.5	5.8	1.9
aid/exports (%)	1.3	0.1	58.1	27.3	6.0
1989					
aid ($ mn)	171	6	184	482	316
aid/GDP (%)	0.3	–	19.7	2.1	3.0
aid/exports (%)	2.1	0.1	25.8	4.8	2.8

Source: Lacoste, 1991: 441–56.

The only solution to this crisis will be radical improvements in regional economies. Given Europe's dominance in Maghrebi trade patterns (Tables 2.4 and 2.5), this must inevitably mean that economic change will be largely conditioned by the way in which the relationship of North African states with the European Union develops.

Table 2.4 UMA trade with the EU 1990 (ECU million)

	1990			1989/90 (% change)	
	Imports	Exports	Balance	Imports	Exports
Algeria	6,940	4,966	-1,974	19	5
Libya	7,888	2,655	-5,233	25	-9
Mauritania	239	221	-17	-5	-8
Morocco	3,042	3,559	516	14	10
Tunisia	2,250	2,971	721	14	17
TOTAL	20,359	14,372	-5,987		
% EU	4.4	3.0			
% UMA	53.5	38.1			

Source: Eurostat; World Bank.

Table 2.5 The role of the EU in UMA country trade, 1990 (% of total trade)

	Imports	Exports
Algeria	55.6	37.0
Libya	83.2	22.3
Mauritania	35.4	44.6
Morocco	33.7	57.1
Tunisia	34.8	56.6
TOTAL	53.5	31.8

Source: World Bank.

The EU, in turn, both for security reasons and because of its desire to minimise migration flows into Europe, has an acute interest in fostering such economic change. Given the fact that official development assistance has become far less generous in recent years and that, in any case, official aid has been relatively insignificant except in the case of Morocco and, more particularly, Mauritania, this cannot be the means by which modernization will occur. Equally, the debt problems (Table 2.6) of North African states mean that neither official nor commercial loans offer a viable route to capital access for development. Instead, all North African states except Libya have been obliged to follow IMF and World Bank stabilization and restructuring programmes during the 1980s (see Horton 1990 for Morocco). Nor have innovative ideas, such as Tunisia's proposal for a debt recycling development bank, found much favour.

Table 2.6 Foreign debt, 1991 ($bn)

Country	Total debt	Long-term debt
Algeria	28.6	27.6
Libya	–	–
Mauritania	2.3	2.0
Morocco	21.2	20.9
Tunisia	8.3	7.6

Source: World Bank, *Debt Tables 1992*, Washington.

In any case, current attitudes towards economic development emphasize the role to be played by export earnings and direct private foreign investment within a free market economy (World Bank 1991: 109–27). Direct private foreign investment is uncertain, however, as Table 2.7 makes clear.

Table 2.7 Private investment in the Maghreb, 1980 and 1991 ($ million)

Country	1980	1991
Algeria	349	0
Libya	–	–
Mauritania	27	0
Morocco	89	320
Tunisia	235	150

Source: World Bank, 1993: 282–83.

Indeed, more recent figures underline this, for Morocco has seen private foreign investment rise to around $500 million in 1993 – largely from European sources – while Algeria claims to have captured promises of up to $5 billion-worth of investment in the oil sector over the next five years. None the less, whatever the future role of direct private foreign investment, it is clear that, as North African economies become integrated into the global economy, it is Europe that will continue to dominate, both as a trading partner and as an investment source.

The European dimension

The Maghreb states have long enjoyed a close relationship with the European Union, partly as a result of the latter's 'South Mediterranean Policy' which has been designed to foster close cooperation between Mediterranean countries and Europe, and partly because of the colonial legacy which left

North Africa with economies designed to satisfy the European market, particularly in France and Spain. The relationship has been expressed since 1976 through a series of cooperation agreements which replaced the earlier association agreements signed in 1969 with Tunisia, Algeria and Morocco. Libya has never had any preferential trading arrangements with Europe or the Community.

The Cooperation Agreements were designed to regularise export arrangements between the Union and the Maghreb states, particularly in the field of agriculture, in return for Community development aid as provided through the European Development Bank in a series of bilateral financial protocols. The emphasis on agriculture existed because industrial exports from the Maghreb states were governed by the Treaty of Rome, which provided for unrestricted entry into the Community. In reality, however, such exports, mainly from Tunisia and Morocco, consisted primarily of textiles and thus fell outside the GATT-inspired Staflex agreements which limited entry of other developing countries' textile products into Europe in order to protect European textile producers. As a result, a series of so-called 'voluntary restraint agreements' were negotiated between the Community and Maghreb textile producers which created what were, in effect, quota limits on textile exports. Libya and Algeria, as hydrocarbon exporters to Europe, experienced no restrictions on the export of oil and gas. Morocco, similarly, suffered from no barriers to its phosphate exports (Morocco is the world's third largest phosphate producer and its largest exporter).

The cooperation agreements did, however, affect agricultural exports to Europe - mainly of citrus (Morocco), early vegetables (Morocco and Tunisia) and wine (Algeria and Morocco) or olive oil (Tunisia). In some cases, such as wine and olive oil, a quota system was used to limit exports. More generally, however, European producers were protected by the 'reference price system'. This provided a special tariff for exports outside specific periods (when export to Europe was unrestricted because identical European products were not available) so that Maghrebi wholesale prices *inside* Europe were the same as the recommended Common Agricultural Policy price. This was the reference price and clearly discriminated against North African agricultural produce in favour of the European producer.

The Spanish–Portuguese transitional regime

The system caused considerable resentment in North Africa, particularly when local industry, such as the tomato paste industry in Morocco in the 1970s and 1980s, was adversely affected. However, it did provide Maghreb states with privileged access to the Community market at a time when other markets were difficult to develop as viable alternatives to the old colonial export patterns. In 1986, however, an event took place that was to upset this comfortable arrangement. This was the accession of Spain and Portugal to the European Community with a transition period of ten years.

It soon became clear to Morocco and Tunisia that, with Portugal and Spain as integral parts of the European Community, now the European Union, Europe would be more than self-sufficient in *all* agricultural produce, particularly in those commodities in which the two countries had specialized. Even their advantage over Europe in regard to earlier harvesting seasons would be eroded. A special transition regime was quickly negotiated for Maghrebi states as well. This provided for reductions in customs duties and an eventual end to the reference price system in 1996, the year in which Spain and Portugal would be fully integrated into the Community. Instead a quota system was to be introduced so that exports above the quota limit would be subjected to a 'countervailing charge' – in effect, a reference price under another name. What was worse, from the North African point of view, was the fact that the annual quotas were to be set at the average annual level of the 1980–84 period – which had been a period of drought and thus of low production and exports in North Africa. Despite massive protests from Rabat and Tunis, all the Community would offer were some cosmetic improvements and the promise of additional financial aid, to help overcome the stresses of economic reconstruction (both countries were engaged in the rigours of IMF-style economic reconstruction at the time).

It must be remembered that these developments only briefly predated the end of the Cold War and the subsequent fragmentation of the Arab world as a result of the war against Iraq in 1990–91 (Joffé 1993). Thus, as North Africa became progressively divorced from Middle Eastern affairs politically, European economic control became ever more significant on its diplomatic horizon. Maghrebi states, in short, became increasingly concerned about the Mediterranean dimension of their foreign policies and this inevitably meant that they became increasingly concerned over European intentions as far as the European Community was concerned.

The Single European Market

It was at this point that the second major event which has shaped their current relationships with Europe began to evolve. This was the creation of the Single European Market which came into operation on 1 January 1993, just three years before the Spanish and Portuguese transitional regime was due to come to an end. In theory, this should not have affected the Maghreb–Community relationship at all. After all, no mention was made of future additional restrictions on agricultural imports into Europe nor were the Treaty of Rome's industrial import provisions affected.

In reality, however, certain of the Single Market provisions had a profound significance for North Africa. This was because the Single European

Market raised a series of non-tariff barriers against non-Community exporters. Chief amongst these was the requirement that imports into the Community in future would have to meet European industrial standards – something which no North African manufacturer could do without incurring massive investment costs. Tunisia and Morocco, in particular, raised a barrage of complaints over what they saw as unfair discrimination against them, both in terms of the end of the Spanish and Portuguese transitional regime and as a result of the introduction of the Single European Market.

The GATT Uruguay Round

A further problem, although not one of the European Community's making, concerns the GATT Uruguay Round. One of the most public disputes during the negotiations for this latest process of liberalization of world trade has been over the question of agricultural export subsidies. This has involved the USA, the European Community and the Cairns Group. The latter group of states wanted to see all agricultural export subsidies removed; Europe and the USA only differed over the speed with which such subsidies should be reduced.

There is, however, a major concern that directly affects North Africa. This is that all North African states are cereal importers. In the 1984–86 period, for example, Morocco produced on average 5 million tonnes and had to import a further 2.2 million tonnes; domestic production only satisfied 69 per cent of domestic needs. In Algeria, where 2.9 million tonnes were produced and 3.9 million tonnes were imported, domestic production only covered 43 per cent of demand. The situation in Tunisia, with a domestic cereal production of 1.2 million tonnes on average and imports of the same amount, was a little better, with production covering 50 per cent of demand (Lacoste and Lacoste 1991: 463).

One of the reasons for these imports is that domestic production in North African countries experiences costs that are substantially above world price levels for cereals. There is therefore, in effect, domestic cereal price support, in that imported cereals and world price levels are prevented from competing directly with domestic production. This procedure is designed to ensure that urban drift off the land is minimized. Now, however, the Uruguay Round terms require that there should be free competition in domestic markets and this will ensure that North African domestic production will become completely uneconomic. As a result, unless North African governments take special measures, the destruction of the agricultural sector will proceed apace, with the inevitable social consequences of increased urban drift and unemployment. One of the main beneficiaries will be the European Union, which is a major cereals supplier to North Africa, in competition with the USA.

The North African response

Apart from protesting at these new discriminatory developments, North African governments, led by Tunisia and Morocco, have attempted to create viable alternatives to total dependence on Europe in economic terms. One of the most significant has been the attempt to create regional economic and political integration. This is exemplified by the creation of the Union Maghreb Arabe in Marrakesh in early February 1989 (see Sutton 1972: 191–202 and Aghrout and Sutton 1990: 115–39). The UMA was designed to be a confederation of North African states that would defuse their regional diplomatic problems and create the basis for economic integration. It represented the culmination of political aspirations that harked back to the struggle for national liberation in the 1950s and 1960s.

Table 2.8 Intra-UMA trade, 1989 ($ million)

| Destination | Exporting country | | | | |
	Algeria	Libya	Morocco	Mauritania	Tunisia
Algeria	–	–	2.8	10.9	63.3
Libya	–	–	90.3	–	112.7
Morocco	–	46.0	–	–	15.8
Mauritania	24.0	–	2.6	–	1.8
Tunisia	77.0	14.0	33.7	22.3	–
Total	101.0	60.0	129.4	33.2	193.6

| Origin | Importing country | | | | |
	Algeria	Libya	Morocco	Mauritania	Tunisia
Algeria	–	–	0.2	52.5	84.9
Libya	–	–	51.1	0.1	15.8
Morocco	3.0	99.0	–	2.8	49.4
Mauritania	11.0	–	–	–	24.5
Tunisia	70.0	124.0	33.4	1.9	–
Total	84.0	223.0	84.7	57.3	174.6

Source: IMF, *Direction of Trade Yearbook 1990*.

Table 2.9 Intra-Maghreb trade, 1989 (% of total trade)

Destination	Exporting country Algeria	Libya	Mauritania	Morocco	Tunisia
Algeria	–	–	2.8	0.1	2.2
Libya	–	–	–	2.7	3.9
Mauritania	0.3	–	–	0.1	0.1
Morocco	–	0.6	–	–	0.5
Tunisia	0.9	0.2	5.5	1.0	–
TOTAL	1.2	0.8	8.3	3.9	6.7

Origin	Importing country Algeria	Libya	Mauritania	Morocco	Tunisia
Algeria	–	–	13.1	0.0	1.9
Libya	–	–	0.0	0.9	0.4
Mauritania	0.1	–	–	–	0.6
Morocco	0.0	2.3	0.7	–	1.1
Tunisia	0.8	2.8	0.5	0.6	–
TOTAL	0.9	5.1	14.3	1.5	4.0

Source: IMF, *Direction of Trade Yearbook 1990*; World Bank.

It also represented the realization of United Nations proposals for regional economic integration that had developed in the late 1960s. Finally it resolved the tensions created during the 1980s, as first Algeria and then Morocco sought to create their own structures for regional integration (Nonneman 1992: 193–203).

Unhappily, two factors have militated against the UMA's success since its foundation. The first is that, although there is no doubt that the region would benefit from the complementarity offered by the four major economies involved – with Libya and Algeria as hydrocarbon producers, Algeria as a nascent industrial economy alongside Tunisia and Morocco, and Morocco and Tunisia as agricultural exporters – and from the economies of scale that the regional market would permit – through the integration of industry on a region-wide, rather than a national basis, trade patterns do not encourage this. As Tables 2.8 and 2.9 demonstrate, inter-regional trade is minimal and there is thus little incentive for regional economic integration. Indeed, the integration that has taken place has mainly been political in nature, as the joint ventures along the Algerian–Tunisian border regions or the integration of power networks or joint oilfield exploitations proposed between Tunisia and Libya indicate.

The second factor is linked to this lack of regional commercial integration. It is the fact, already noted above, that Europe is by far the dominant trade partner of all the states concerned. Associated with this is the long-standing determination of at least two North African states – Morocco and Tunisia – to strengthen these links, with Morocco in 1987 even applying for European Community membership. More recently, Libya also has sought to persuade European states of its essentially Mediterranean outlook, with the suggestion in 1993 that Arab nationalism should be abandoned in favour of Libya becoming the 'Kuwait of the Mediterranean'. In Algeria, the argument is couched in slightly different terms but the outcome is the same; essentially the choice is now seen to be between 'modernism' in the European sense (even though Europe is now obsessed with postmodernism – Gellner, 1993) and the Islamic or Algerian nationalist alternative.

THE FUTURE

In practical terms, these conflicts mean that North African states have essentially opted for closer association with Europe, rather than an alternative either based on their traditional links with the Middle East or on the potential of regional integration. Middle Eastern affairs have concentrated on the peace process between Israel and the Arab world in which North Africa plays a marginal role, despite Morocco's close association with attempts at *rapprochement* over recent years. The Non-Aligned Movement, in which Algeria played such a pivotal role during the 1970s and 1980s, has disappeared amongst the detritus of the post-Cold War period. The UMA, although now denuded of much of its content, will continue to serve as a regional forum. However, the hopes of an economic alternative based on regional integration now seem irrelevant to what is actually happening on the ground.

At the same time, the European Union has also realized that its proposals for minor rectification of the 'South Mediterranean Policy' proposed in 1990 by Commissioner Juan Abel Matutes were quite inadequate. During 1992, proposals cautiously emerged from Brussels for the creation of a free trade zone in parts of North Africa, similar to what has been proposed for the EFTA countries and for the Visegrad Group in former Eastern Europe. The proposal was first extended to Morocco, with Tunisia expected to follow. Algeria was to be excluded until the political and economic situation there had clarified, and there was no question of extending the proposal to include Libya while the quarrel over the Lockerbie bombing continued to poison EU–Libyan relations. By the end of 1993, Morocco and the European Union Commission were locked in detailed negotiations over the transitional arrangements to be instituted for the creation of such a free trade zone. Similar detailed negotiations were expected with Tunisia during 1994.

Although the formal negotiations over the free trade area with Morocco were confined to purely economic issues, there is a significant political and diplomatic dimension as well. After all, if Europe is prepared to tie itself to Morocco in economic terms, there is an implied acceptance of the political dispensation there as well. The regime of King Hassan thereby acquires a significant degree of European Union-sanctioned respectability and support as a result of these commercial and economic agreements. Europe, on the other hand, acquires a Mediterranean dimension to its policy imperatives that, up to 1990, was almost completely lacking. In short, the relationship between North Africa and Europe for the first time shows the potential for political and economic symbiosis, which has been rejected by Europe since the end of the colonial period. The wheel has truly come full circle and the European Union seems to have finally recognized that it is a Mediterranean as well as a continental power.

NOTE

1. In 1987 alone France supplied FFr 1.67 billion-worth of aid, of which military aid comprised FFr 516 million. The USA provided $94 million in military aid between 1983 and 1988, together with a further $128 million in economic and emergency aid (Anon 1989: B193–B194).

REFERENCES

Aghrout, A. and Sutton, K. (1990), 'Regional economic union in the Maghreb', *Journal of Modern African Studies*, 28, 1.
Anon. (1989), 'Chad: peace seems on the horizon', *African Contemporary Record 1987–88*, 20, New York: Holmes and Meier.
Boulby, M. (1988), 'The Islamic challenge: Tunisia since independence', *Third World Quarterly*, 10, 2 (April): 590–615.
BP (British Petroleum) (1990), *BP Statistical review of world energy*, (June), London.
Commission of the European Communities, *Eurostat*, Brussels.
Escallier, R. (1991), 'Une région bouleversée par les flux migratoires', in Lacoste, C. and Y. (eds), *L'Etat du Maghreb*, Casablanca: Editions le Fennec.
Gellner, E. (1993), *Postmodernism, reason and religion*, London: Routledge.
Horton, B. (1990), *Morocco: analysis and reform of economic policy*, Washington: World Bank.
International Court of Justice (1975), *Western Sahara: Advisory Opinion*, The Hague: ICJ–Peace Palace.
International Monetary Fund (IMF), *Direction of Trade Yearbook*, Washington: IMF.
Joffé, E.G.H. (1993), 'The implications of the new world order for the Middle East and North Africa', in Chapman, S., *The Middle East and North Africa 1993*, London: Europa Publications.
Joffé, E.G.H. (1992), 'European Security and the new arc of crisis', in IISS, *New dimensions in international security*, Adelphi Paper 265 (Winter 1991/92), London: IISS/Brassey's.

Joffé, E.G.H. (1991), 'Iran, the southern Mediterranean and Europe: terrorism and hostages', in Ehteshami, A. and Varasteh, M. (eds), *Iran and the international community*, London: Routledge.

Lacoste, C. and Lacoste, Y. (1991), *L'état du Maghreb*, Casablanca: Editions le Fennec.

Maghreb Quarterly Report, London.

Ministero degli Affari Esteri (1990), *Italian–Spanish Non-Paper on CSCM*, Rome, 17 September.

Nonneman, G. (ed.) (1992), *The Middle East and Europe: an integrated communities approach*, London: Federal Trust for Education and Research.

Sutton, K. (1972), 'Political association and Maghreb economic development', *Journal of Modern African Studies*, 10, 2.

United Nations Development Programme (1992), *World Development Report*, New York.

International Bank for Reconstruction and Development (1992), *World Tables*, Washington: World Bank.

World Bank (1991), *World development report 1991: the challenge of development*, Oxford: Oxford University Press.

World Bank (1992), *World development report 1992: development and the environment*, Oxford: Oxford University Press.

World Bank (1993), *World development report 1993: investing in health*, Oxford: Oxford University Press.

3

The Middle East Peace Process

Gerd Nonneman

Unexpected change came to the Arab–Israeli theatre in the course of the peace process initiated in Madrid in 1991 – although for any hopes raised, as many have been dashed. Even after the start of the process, prior to the change from Likud to Labour in Israel, both Arabs and Israelis appeared to be as far removed as ever from an accommodation of their differences. The uprising in the occupied territories (the *Intifada*) raged on, and the Israeli Prime Minister, Yitzhak Shamir, reassured his right-wing constituents that participation in the peace conference by no means implied any readiness for territorial concessions; indeed, the retention of the occupied territories became one of his election campaign's priorities. Mutual fears, suspicions and bitterness retained their potency, being reinforced by, and in turn reinforcing, existing perceptions and myths. On the Arab side, popular perceptions continued to see Israel as a foreign and illegitimate implant that had usurped the local population's rights and land with the help of the West. For many Israelis, the Arabs – and in particular the PLO and Syria – remained bent on Israel's destruction, depriving the Jewish people of the chance to live in peace and security in their historic homeland. It was true, of course, that the *de facto* expansion of Israel and the creation of the refugee problem had not been imaginary – nor were the stated policies of some smaller religious parties which were advocating the transfer of all Palestinian Arabs out of the occupied territories; these fed Palestinian and Arab fears and perceptions. At the same time, it was also true that Israel had had to face a number of military threats from its neighbours, along with Palestinian violence, and a continuing stream of statements from a variety of radical groups vowing to free all of Palestine from Israeli control.

The end of the Cold War, the evaporation of the Soviet Union's superpower status, and the implications that this had for regional balances and policies of both regional and international powers, appeared to help drive the Middle East in the direction of a more 'orderly' system. This trend was demonstrated by the PLO's historic recognition of Israel and its acceptance of a two-state solution in 1988, and the readiness of the radical Arab states (such as Libya and Syria) to mend fences with Egypt despite its peace treaty with Israel. Equally striking was the Arab–Israeli peace process that was initiated in Madrid in the wake of the Gulf war of 1990–91. The war, and the way in which it unfolded, was yet another illustration of the new global environment and dynamics. The conflict also highlighted the need to address the Palestine question, in part because of the nefarious effect that its continued festering was likely to have on Middle Eastern attitudes towards the West and towards pro-Western governments in the region. It was against this background that the US – mainly in the person of the then Secretary of State James Baker – was able to engineer the start of the Madrid process.

THE MADRID PEACE PROCESS

The peace process, which had been launched in Madrid on 30 October 1991, received a boost from the election victory of the Labour Party in Israel in June 1992 and the formation of a new government under Yitzhak Rabin the following month. The new prime minister had run his election campaign on the basis of a pledge to get the peace process moving forward. The previous five rounds of the bilateral Arab–Israeli negotiations in Washington had resulted in deadlock, essentially over Israel's unwillingness to discuss territorial compromise. The Israeli proposals for an Interim Self-Governing Authority (ISGA) tabled at the fourth round were far removed from the Palestinian aspirations contained in their own 'Palestinian Interim Self-Government Authority' (PISGA) proposals: there was to be no withdrawal or even redeployment of troops, no freeze on settlements (which were creating geographic and demographic facts in the occupied territories), and no authority for the ISGA beyond functional/administrative responsibility. In this context US President Bush on 24 February 1992 laid down his official condition for the granting of $10 billion in loan guarantees for Israel (needed towards the cost of absorbing new Soviet Jews): all new settlement in the occupied territories had to be stopped. (See *Middle East International*, 24 January 1992, 7 February 1992 and 6 March 1992).

Officially, the Palestinian–Israeli negotiations were conducted in the framework of the bilateral Jordanian–Israeli talks. Jordan's own separate negotiations with Israel were less problematic than those of the others, as a *de facto modus vivendi* had already been in place for some considerable time. Provided that Jordan could feel assured that it would not become the dumping ground for Palestinians under the so-called 'Jordanian option', and that significant progress was made on the sub-track with the Palestinians, an understanding between Israeli and Jordanian negotiators was unlikely to be too elusive. In the Israeli–Syrian negotiations it was always clear that nothing could be achieved unless some compromise could be reached over the Golan Heights – annexed by Israel. A breakthrough in these negotiations was a precondition for any serious progress on the Israeli–Lebanese track;

the key issues in the latter are Israel's occupation of parts of southern Lebanon, and the activities of Hizbollah.

Meanwhile the multilateral talks agreed upon in Madrid had also started; at the first meeting in Moscow in January 1992, working groups were established to deal with regional economic development (to be chaired by the EC), arms control, environment, water, and refugees. The EC's role in the development group was justified by its experience in regional integration; Commissioner Matutes had put forward a draft plan in late 1991, aimed at improving regional integration in the region between Israel, Egypt, Jordan and the West Bank, later to be widened to Saudi Arabia, Syria and Lebanon. The first round of this working group took place in Brussels in May 1992. EC peace envoy Leonardo Mathias, who chaired the talks, agreed with the Palestinian position that there could be no real progress in the multilaterals without 'tangible results' – then absent – in the Arab–Israeli bilateral talks. The multilaterals themselves also remained hamstrung, however, as illustrated by the Israeli boycott of the Brussels meeting, as well as the working group on refugees in Ottawa, also in May: while all the other delegations welcomed representatives of the Palestinian diaspora, Israel refused to accept their right to be represented. Total failure obtained in the working group on water, with the Palestinians blaming Israel for refusing to recognize Palestinian national rights over water resources (*Middle East Economic Survey*, 18 May 1992: C1; *Middle East International*, 7 February 1992, 29 May 1992; *Le Monde*, 11 September 1993).

In July 1992 Prime Minister Rabin offered to halt all the housing projects in the occupied territories that had been started after 1 January that year, and to stop subsidising settlers – but he excluded what he called 'security settlements'. To this was added his statement in August that 'not every inch of the Golan is sacred' (*Middle East International*, 24 July 1992, 11 September 1993). On 10 September 1992, Rabin for the first time explicitly referred to the possibility of giving up some of this territory in return for total peace. The Syrian response was that any conclusion of a peace agreement could only be on condition of total Israeli withdrawal from the Heights. While this Syrian contemplation of the possibility of peace was in itself significant, no tangible further progress appeared to have been made by the end of 1993. Nevertheless, the summer of 1992 saw the general atmosphere and tone of Arab–Israeli negotiations becoming more positive. Crucially for Israel, the US Administration released the $10 billion loan guarantees. Yet again hopes faded; the seventh and eighth rounds in October and December proved virtually sterile, deadlock prevailing over the issues of Jerusalem (Israel claiming it – against international law – as its own indivisible capital) and the level of eventual Palestinian independent authority. In the second round of multilateral talks on refugees (Ottawa, November 1992), the issue of Palestinian representation was skirted but the Israeli delegation rejected the working group's competence to discuss family re-union policy – the context within which unofficial Israeli proposals to allow perhaps up to 50,000 Palestinians to return had been made (see *Middle East International*, 29 May 1992, 6 November 1992, 20 November 1992). (The proposal itself could be seen against the background of repeated international reaffirmation of UN Security Council Resolution 194 of 1948, which gave Palestinian refugees – then numbering some 750,000, by 1993 some 3.5 million – the right to return or receive compensation.) Talks edged forward again in this working group's third session on 11–13 May in Oslo, when Israel for the first time agreed to discuss the family reunion issue (*Le Monde*, 11 September 1993).

In response to increased agitation and a number of killings, the Israeli government on 18 December 1992 deported 413 Palestinians – alleged activists of the Hamas movement – to southern Lebanon. The negotiations immediately ground to a halt, and in the unanimously agreed UN Security Council Resolution 799, the deportations were condemned, a reversal was requested, and the applicability of the Fourth Geneva Convention to the occupied territories, including East Jerusalem, was reaffirmed. Under US pressure, on 1 February 1993 Israel offered to let 100 deportees return. This brought an immediate positive response from the US, UN Secretary-General Boutros-Ghali, and the EC. Even though the European Parliament on 11 February passed a resolution calling for increased EC pressure on Israel to return all deportees, using the lever of the mooted cooperation pact, the Commission and Ministers refused to contemplate freezing negotiations over the pact due to start in March. A deal was reached at the UN (following US pressure to veto any sanctions against Israel over the full application of Resolution 799) whereby Israel promised to speed up the return of the remaining deportees and stated that deportation was not an integral part of its policy. On 15 March, Rabin in a meeting with US President Clinton announced that Israel accepted Resolutions 242 and 338 as being applicable to the achievement of peace. Nevertheless, the Palestinian negotiators refused to receive the subsequent US invitation to the ninth round of the bilateral talks in Washington, on the grounds that there was still no Israeli commitment to end the deportations. At the same time, the situation in the occupied territories worsened to the extent that the Israeli government sealed off the territories from the rest of Israel (*Middle East International*, 8 January 1993, 5 February 1993, 19 February 1993, 19 March 1993, 16 April 1993).

Restarting the peace process required a further move in April, whereby the US and Israel both reaffirmed Resolutions 242 and 338, and Israel accepted Faisal Husseini – an East Jerusalem resident – as a member (effectively the leader) of the Palestinian delegation. Israel also promised to allow back a number of the Palestinians deported since 1967, and to speed up the return of the others; and stated that it had 'no plans for future deportations'. Round nine convened in Washington on 27 April. Three weeks of talks, however, did not lead to any progress. Both in the occupied territories and within the Palestinian negotiating team, doubts about the talks were increasingly expressed (reflected in increased violent opposition against the peace process); only on 15 June 1993 did it prove possible to convene the next round, after a virtual order from PLO chairman Arafat to the Palestinian negotiators to accept the invitation. However, round ten proved fruitless as well. A US paper with 'ideas' for continuing the negotiations, presented at the end of the round, was rejected by the Palestinians, for being almost identical to Israeli positions. Indeed, the paper no longer appeared to consider the occupied territories 'occupied', but subject to sovereignty claims by both sides; and Jerusalem was excluded from the scope of negotiations for the interim period. This was interpreted by many observers, along with the Palestinian team and the PLO, as a substantial turn-around in US policy, and a premiss that ignored both previous UN resolutions and the apparent achievements of the peace process thus far. As of mid-1993, opposition to the talks as futile – expressed even by Dr Haidar Abdul-Shafi, one of the team's most prominent members – was spreading fast in Palestinian circles (see *Middle East International*, 30 April 1993, 11 June 1993, 9 July 1993).

The context that helped make the initiation of the process possible, however, had not altogether dissipated. Indeed, the resolution of the Arab–Israeli conflict remained more feasible than at any time before the summer of 1991. Yet, as Efraim Karsh has pointed out (in Nonneman, 1992: 112), it was clear that 'in order to surmount such an acrimonious legacy, any peace settlement between Arabs and Jews would have to be innovative, rejecting the obsolete formulas and relying on unorthodox diplomatic means and novel conceptual frameworks. A number of basic conditions [had to] be fulfilled'. First, such a settlement would have to be comprehensive, addressing peace between Israel and all its neighbours including the Palestinians. Second, it would have to

> be based on mutual recognition of each other's legitimate rights and interests, namely, the Arabs' right to regain the territories lost in 1967 and the Palestinian right for self determination, on the one hand, and Israel's right for regional acceptance and secure existence, on the other. In practical terms, this means an Israeli withdrawal to the pre-June 1967 borders with minimal territorial adjustments in strategic areas and the establishment of an independent Palestinian state on the West Bank and the Gaza Strip (preferably confederated with Jordan) in return for a genuine peace which includes unequivocal *de jure* recognition, full diplomatic relations, unrestricted freedom of movement and fully-fledged economic ties.

And finally, major external involvement would need to be both available and accepted, both for the purpose of offering guarantees and for the necessary infusion of resources to make a deal stick (ibid.). The difficulty in arriving at any such solution was exacerbated by the persistent atmosphere of distrust referred to at the outset of this chapter, and the respective domestic political contexts of Palestinians and Israelis. It is this hurdle that the Norwegian-sponsored secret Israeli–PLO talks from January to August 1993 helped to clear.

THE OSLO AGREEMENTS

An eight-month series of secret and mostly informal meetings sponsored by Norway's foreign minister, and involving a very small group of Israeli and PLO representatives, unbeknown either to their own domestic constituencies, or to foreign powers such as the US, achieved a sufficient level of trust and understanding to compose a draft declaration of principles, aiming at mutual recognition and a framework for peace. On the Israeli side, the key players were Foreign Minister Peres (indirectly) and his deputy, Yossi Beilin. Prime Minister Rabin gave his fiat once it appeared that serious progress could indeed be made. On the Palestinian side, the negotiating team involved in the Madrid peace process was left in the dark, while only Yasir Arafat (indirectly) and a small group of confidantes were involved, particularly Mahmoud Abbas – considered by many the architect of the accord – and Abu Alaa, the PLO's main economic strategist. On the sidelines, Nabil Shaath, a close Arafat adviser long active in the search for compromise, was also involved.[1]

From both the Israeli and PLO sides, this effort was spurred by the realization that the deadlock in the occupied territories was becoming increasingly politically untenable, with the radical Hamas and other militant forces chipping away at support for the more pragmatic PLO. For the PLO leadership, and for Arafat in particular, success in this initiative would enable a triumphant re-engagement in the region as well as internationally. For Rabin, a peace settlement would be the crowning of his career in politics; specifically, it would be a way to achieve two key interrelated elements on the prime minister's agenda: disengagement from the Arab-majority occupied territories, and securing the Jewish and democratic nature of the Israeli state. It is in this context that the Knesset on 19 January had finally lifted the ban on contacts with the PLO.

On 26 August, Foreign Minister Peres announced that Israel intended to withdraw from 'Gaza and Jericho first', and the PLO Executive Council began a debate on the draft declaration reached in Oslo. On 30 August, the draft declaration of principles was approved by the Israeli cabinet, and was made public by both sides. The following day, the eleventh round of the

Washington negotiations began, but delegates there could do little but await events. On 1 September, Peres for the first time publicly stated that Israel could recognize the PLO if it renounced violence and deleted the references in its charter to the elimination of the Israeli state. Reactions from the international community were generally effusive – even though there was some initial annoyance in the US at not having been involved. Moves to re-establish American contacts with the PLO began soon after. Among the Arab states, the Gulf Co-operation Council (GCC) states and Egypt offered full support. Of the other key players, King Hussein of Jordan came out in favour on 4 September, and President Asad of Syria, while not supporting the initiative, did not reject it. Iraq and Iran both issued strong condemnations.

Two statements with major significance for the Palestinians were made on 6 September by Itamar Rabinovitch – the chief negotiator on the Israeli–Syrian track – and Deputy Foreign Minister Beilin. The former said that the matter of a Palestinian state was an 'open question', while Beilin stated that the Arab section of Jerusalem could some day become an autonomous quarter (*Le Monde*, 11 September 1993). Earlier official statements had always rejected both ideas out of hand. While it remained unclear who the two officials could in fact speak for in the Israeli establishment, their words helped to reassure some sections of Palestinian opinion.

On 9 September, further negotiations in Paris resulted in an agreement on mutual recognition between Israel and the PLO. Yasir Arafat promised to call for, and enforce, an end to Palestinian violence. This opened the way for the grand 13 September signing ceremony in Washington, where the final Declaration was signed by Shimon Peres and Mahmoud Abbas. Against expectations, and Prime Minister Rabin's original preference, it proved possible to bring both leaders together on the White House lawn. After conciliatory speeches from both, the now famous Arafat–Rabin handshake took on historic symbolic significance.

In addition to making official mutual recognition, the agreement aims at a permanent settlement based on UN Security Council resolutions nos. 242 and 338, after a five-year transitional period during which a degree of autonomy will be established for Palestinians in Gaza and the West Bank, under a 'Palestinian Interim Self-Government Authority' (PISGA). Israel committed itself to an eventual withdrawal from occupied territory; in a first stage, such withdrawal would begin in Gaza and Jericho. A timetable was agreed as follows:

13 October 1993:
— the agreement enters into force;
— start of the establishment of a Palestinian police force;
— transfer of power in certain functional spheres;
— negotiations for interim period arrangements begin.

13 December 1993:
— (deadline for) agreement on withdrawal of Israeli military forces from the Gaza Strip and Jericho.

13 April 1994:
— the Israeli withdrawal from the Gaza Strip and Jericho should be complete;
— the 5-year transitional period begins;

13 July 1994:
— the redeployment of the IDF in the West Bank must be under way;
— elections for PISGA are held;
— once PISGA is inaugurated:
    (1) the Israeli Civil Administration in the occupied territories is dissolved;
    (2) the military government is withdrawn from the occupied territories.

13 April 1996:
— negotiations on permanent status commence.

13 April 1999:
— the final status should be agreed.

The declaration leaves much that is only vaguely defined and relegates some of the more difficult issues to the future. For many Palestinian opponents of the agreement, this was sufficient reason for their stance: in their view, the PLO had squandered its last card – recognition of Israel and the ending of the uprising – in return for no more than some minor transfer of managerial authority, and without any prospect of the establishment of a Palestinian state. The latter possibility, nevertheless, was precisely one of the main fears of Israeli opponents of the peace deal, and was voiced by the leadership of the Likud party. Nevertheless, between 60 and 70 per cent of both Palestinians in the occupied territories and Israelis appeared to be in favour of the peace plan, according to opinion polls held in the aftermath of the signing. With the exception of Iraq and Iran, most of the international community expressed strong support for the agreement. On 14 September, Jordan and Israel, also in Washington, signed their own agreed 'agenda' for peace. Initial hopes that a breakthrough with Syria was in the offing were fuelled when President Asad instructed his ambassador to attend the 13 September signing ceremony. But although not actively opposing the agreement, both the Syrian and, inevitably, the Lebanese, leaderships let it be known that they frowned on a separate deal of this kind. By the end of 1993, as noted earlier, a Syrian–Israeli accommodation appeared no closer. Immediate difficulties in implementation and interpretation of the Israel–

PLO declaration emerged. These focused essentially on questions over (1) the size of the 'Jericho' referred to in the declaration; (2) what exactly would be understood by 'withdrawal' (of what, and where to?); (3) who would control the border (crossings) where the autonomous areas border on Jordan and Egypt; and (4) the PLO's ability to organize a sufficiently well-trained and -manned police force in time to maintain security within the areas evacuated by Israel – particularly in the face of militant organized and violent opposition by Palestinian groups. Medium- and long-term differences and difficulties remain largest over (1) the question of Jerusalem; (2) the number of refugees (post-1967) for whom return would be considered; (3) the future of settlements in the autonomous areas, and who would have control over which – if any – aspects of their, and their inhabitants', activities; and (4) the ultimate level of self-government envisaged. In addition, there is the underlying and ineluctable importance of the water issue: to a large extent Israel is dependent upon water sources in the West Bank and the Golan Heights. Failing a secure arrangement for Israeli access to the water it needs, any concessions over territorial control in the relevant areas seem unlikely.

Questions over the level of autonomy which will be achieved figure highly on the agenda of those Palestinians suspicious of the agreement. Even supporters concede that the agreement does not guarantee that the ultimate effect may not be legitimation of Israeli control, rather than real self-government. Indeed, whereas at present Israel is considered to be in breach of international law and conventions (because of (a) the occupation itself; and (b) the abolition of the local civilian administration in 1948 and the establishment of its own civilian administration in 1980), *de facto* Israeli involvement in the territories would be legitimized following the agreement's implementation. If such involvement amounted to effective control (and at least for the settlements it would certainly be that), Palestinians would have gained little beyond a measure of administrative responsibility, while having lost the recourse to international law. In their current form, Israel's proposals – based on the negotiations in the framework of the Madrid process – envisage PISGA's authority (and possibly that of any subsequent authority) to be:

1. not applicable to the settlements;
2. not applicable to external relations, external security and sovereignty;
3. not applicable to decisions on which categories of people have the right to reside;
4. exercised jointly with Israel for land and resources;
5. exercised jointly with Israel for infrastructure;
6. partial in internal security (e.g. limited with regard to jurisdiction over settlers and linking roads);

7. applicable to (a) courts and police; (b) economic sectors such as trade and taxation; (c) municipal services; and (d) other functional spheres such as health and education. Here, however, 'joint liaison committees' are envisaged to supervise decisions and implementation. There is also room for doubt over whether PISGA legislation would be primary, or secondary only, dependent on primary legislation by Israel.

On the other hand, supporters could claim that, even if a positive outcome was not guaranteed, moves towards it had now at least become possible. A log-jam had been broken. Specifically, they could also point to the fact that the Jerusalem issue had been put on the agenda; that Palestinian residents of East Jerusalem could take part in the elections; that Israel had recognized Resolutions 242 and 338 as the basis for a settlement – therefore committing itself to land-for-peace; that there was now an irrevocable recognition of a Palestinian people, along with the relevance of their political rights and the legitimacy of their political representation; that the issue of the refugees (albeit only those of 1967) had been put on the agenda; and that there was now a prospect of international political and economic support for the Territories, with all the benefits that this would bring.[2]

With respect to the latter, the international community did indeed show itself fairly generous. Economic development in the West Bank and Gaza was generally recognized as of crucial importance if long-term stability was to be achieved and if the improvements in people's daily lives were to be brought about which would maintain support for the peace process. A Palestinian study group had worked out a development plan requiring some $11.2 billion over six years. The World Bank, in an amended version of its own study on the subject, estimated that $4.7 billion would be needed over five years. A major appeal for assistance, launched by US President Clinton, succeeded in attracting pledges of $2 billion within the first few weeks following the 13 September signing. The EC, with the most extensive experience in economic assistance to the Palestinians, took the lead with a commitment of $620 million. The US offered $500 million, Japan $200 million, and the GCC states are believed to have offered some $200 million – although the modalities in this case are not clear. As of late 1993, doubts remained, however, over which priorities would be chosen, who should administer the aid and the development programme (indeed, how much control would reside with the PLO's political leaders, rather than Palestinian and other economic experts), and how (if at all) donor coordination would proceed.

Initial cautious optimism, however, soon became mingled with increasing Palestinian disappointment over the lack of visible changes in Israeli security policy on the ground, and lack of progress in the negotiations that began in Cairo and Taba on 13 October. The killing of several Palestinian leaders in

the occupied territories, probably by Palestinian opponents, further heightened concern, and instances of violent incidents between Israeli settlers on
the one hand and militant Palestinians on the other, by late 1993 appeared
to be giving rise to a vicious circle of increasing bitterness and mutual
suspicion and a shrinking level of support for the peace process. A number
of Israeli Defence Force security operations in the West Bank and Gaza,
leaving several dead and injured and a number of houses destroyed, was
one element in the equation of increasingly violent confrontation. The
radical Islamic Hamas movement and other Palestinian opponents of the
agreement and of the PLO gathered strength and support, as results appeared to remain elusive. In particular, Israel refused to release more than
a few hundred of the 12,000 or so Palestinian prisoners who were being
held in many instances without proper trial, and insisted on treating the
issue as a point of negotiation rather than as a question of human rights
and due legal process. An early release of the more than 8,000 who were
acknowledged not to have been involved in criminal violence would doubtless
have brought major returns in the form of support for the peace process, at
little or no cost to Israel, and was for this reason strenuously sought by the
PLO negotiators.

The delegations in technical committee meetings in Taba to work out
the details of security and logistics for the planned Israeli withdrawal by 13
April 1994 were led by, respectively, Nabil Shaath and General Shahak (the
Deputy Chief-of-Staff of the IDF). While the two men appeared to have
established a good working relationship, this proved insufficient to reach
agreement on security arrangements and on the size of the Jericho area.
Arafat established a 3,000-strong secret security organization, led by Salim
al-Zera'i (the first prisoner to be released), and the first members of the
new police force began to arrive from Jordan. Yet by itself this was not
enough to reassure the Israelis with respect to their security concerns. A
summit between Arafat and Rabin in Cairo in December failed to break the
stalemate on either issue. Thus the Declaration's first deadline – that of 13
December for the start of the withdrawal from Jericho and the Gaza Strip
– passed without effect.

This in turn helped undermine further the already diminishing faith in
the peace process among both Palestinians and Israelis. Within Israel, Rabin's
popularity was waning along with that of the agreement. At year's end, both
he and Arafat – having in effect staked their careers on the success of the
peace process – clearly needed a major breakthrough to show their respective
constituencies that the concessions made were not in vain. Failing this, the
cycle of falling support, increasing violence, and dwindling control of the
pragmatist factions (in particular Arafat's PLO) over popular emotions and
actions, appeared inevitable. Perversely, this very cycle conceivably also
increased the pressure on the Israeli Prime Minister, in particular, not to be

seen making further concessions. Arafat's own position within the PLO, meanwhile, was also becoming more difficult, as he was coming under increasing pressure both from opponents of the agreement and those in the supportive camp who were becoming disenchanted with the autocratic way in which the PLO leader was handling the process. While both leaders, therefore, found themselves facing difficult choices, the balance of probability remained that 1994 would see further, if halting, progress on implementation of the Declaration of Principles.

NOTES

1. The Norwegian foreign minister's role was in fact rather more limited than much media reporting indicated at the time the Oslo channel was unveiled. The main credit for the initiation, and subsequent facilitation, of the talks must go to a young Norwegian husband-and-wife team: the academic Terje Larsen and the Middle East specialist and diplomat Mona Juul. With Beilin's unofficial encouragement, Larsen met with Israeli academic Yair Hirschfield, whom he subsequently brought together with Abu Alaa in December 1992. Official Norwegian involvement had started on 10 September when Jan Egeland, a senior Foreign Ministry official (who would remain actively engaged) joined the second Larsen–Hirschfield meeting. On 20 January 1993 (a day after the Knesset lifted the ban on contacts with the PLO), Norwegian Foreign Minister Johan Joergern Holst joined in for the first time, in a secret meeting in Norway. Key Israeli interlocutors brought in were the Director-General of the Foreign Ministry, Uri Savir, and Foreign Ministry lawyer Yossi Sarid. For a detailed and lively account of the Oslo channel negotiations, see the excellent book by Jane Corbin (1994).

2. The author is grateful to Dr Shai Feldman and Dr Anat Kurtz of the Jaffee Institute for Strategic Studies (Tel Aviv) and Dr Yezid Sayigh of Oxford University, for sharing their insights on the issues and perceptions referred to in this and the previous two paragraphs.

REFERENCE

Corbin, J. (1994), *Gaza First*, London: Bloomsbury.
Nonneman, G. (ed.) (1992), *The Middle East and Europe*, London: Federal Trust.

4

UN Peace-keeping Missions in the Mediterranean Region

Georgios Kostakos

If one attempts a survey of United Nations peace-keeping, it is around the Mediterranean – this closed sea with remnants of ancient civilizations scattered around its shores – that one finds the greatest concentration of such operations. Together with more recent ones, some of the earliest missions are still going on. The world body has often been asked to interpose its 'blue helmets' between conflicting interests and traditions, between ethnic and/or religious and/or political and/or economic (the latter usually disguised) aspirations confronting each other in this part of the globe.

Table 4.1 shows all the peace-keeping operations undertaken by the United Nations in the Mediterranean region, both completed and still under way.[1] Not included in the list are UNYOM (UN Yemen Observation Mission, in operation 1963–64), UNIIMOG (UN Iran–Iraq Military Observer Group, in operation 1988–91), UNIKOM (UN Iraq–Kuwait Observation Mission, in operation since 1991) and MINURSO (UN Mission for the Referendum in Western Sahara, also in operation since 1991), although one could legitimately argue that these operations also belong to the broader 'Mediterranean region', the first three through its Middle East component and the fourth through its North African component.[2] Even excluding these four missions (not least for practical purposes – in order to make this survey manageable), the 'Mediterranean' UN peace-keeping operations amount to a significant portion of the UN peace-keeping total. In fact, before the end of the Cold War, Mediterranean peace-keeping took up more than half of all the relevant UN activities, involving seven out of thirteen peace-keeping operations. Of those thirteen operations, five continue today, four of them in the Mediterranean region (Goulding, 1993: 452–3 and Boutros-Ghali, 1993a: 67).

Following the end of the Cold War, large UN operations such as the ones in Namibia and Cambodia became possible, but at the same time several smaller operations, dealing with election-monitoring and assisting democratization / peace-building were established. In fact, some fifteen

58

Table 4.1 UN peace-keeping missions in the Mediterranean region

Name of mission	Headquarters	Duration
UNTSO (UN Truce Supervision Organization)	Jerusalem	1948 to date
UNEF I (First UN Emergency Force)	Gaza	1956–67
UNOGIL (UN Observation Group in Lebanon)	Beirut	1958
UNFICYP (UN Peace-keeping Force in Cyprus)	Nicosia	1964 to date
UNEF II (Second UN Emergency Force)	Ismailia (Egypt)	1973–79
UNDOF (UN Disengagement Observer Force)	Damascus	1974 to date
UNIFIL (UN Interim Force in Lebanon)	Naqoura (S. Lebanon)	1978 to date
UNPROFOR (UN Protection Force)	Zagreb	1992 to date

new operations were set up between 1988 and 1993, as opposed to thirteen before that in the years since the inception of the United Nations (UNDPI, 1993c: 8). Interest shifted from the Mediterranean to other areas too. However, the crisis in former Yugoslavia to a great extent 'made up' for that, directing once again the attention of the world organization and of world public opinion to the Old Sea region.

In what follows, a survey is attempted of the various aspects of UN peace-keeping operations in the Mediterranean region, past and present, with special emphasis placed on the latter. In the final section, some conclusions and some broader generalizations are drawn.

THE HISTORY OF UN PEACE-KEEPING IN THE MEDITERRANEAN

Peace-keeping missions in the Mediterranean region can be differentiated according to the nature of the particular conflict that each one was meant to address. Thus we have cases of inter-state conflict, mainly as a result of the Arab–Israeli confrontation, and cases of intra-state conflict, in divided societies such as Lebanon, Cyprus and former Yugoslavia.

Peace-keeping related to the Arab–Israeli conflict

The peace-keeping operations examined below all relate to the long-lasting conflict between Israel and its Arab neighbours. Since its creation in May 1948 the state of Israel has been in continuous confrontation with the neighbouring Arab states and the Palestinian–Arab population inhabiting or originating from the territories under Israeli rule (Heraclides, 1991). The various operations were created at certain points in time in order to deal with some acute deterioration of the situation. They were discontinued after the crisis was over or lingered on, and some even continue up to date, with a mandate that has often had to be adjusted to changing circumstances.

United Nations Truce Supervision Organization (UNTSO) UNTSO is officially considered by the United Nations as its first peace-keeping operation (Goulding, 1993: 452). It was established by the UN Security Council (resolution 50 of 29 May 1948) in order to supervise the truce called for in Palestine during the Arab–Israeli war of 1948 and the subsequent Armistice Agreements between Israel and its Arab neighbours. UNTSO's activities spread over the territory of five states, namely Egypt, Israel, Jordan, Lebanon and Syria. Its unarmed observers continued to play the role of go-betweens between Israel and its neighbours, although their functions underwent changes after major events such as the wars of 1956, 1967 and 1973. UNTSO personnel were used as a pool from which experienced personnel were drawn to form the basis of other peace-keeping missions later deployed in the area (see below) and beyond (such as the UN Operation in the Congo, the UN Iran–Iraq Military Observer Group, etc.). Now observers are deployed on the Golan Heights, between Israel and Syria (assigned to UNDOF – see below), in Lebanon (assisting UNIFIL – see below) and between Egypt and Israel, in Ismailia and the Sinai (UNDPI, 1993a: 3–4 and UNDPI, 1990: 15–42).

By July 1993 UNTSO's strength was expected to decrease to 224 military observers (UNDPI, 1993a: 3). The organization's maximum strength has been 572 military observers (in 1948) (UNDPI, 1990: 419). Observers come from the following countries: Argentina, Australia, Austria, Belgium, Canada, Chile, China, Denmark, Finland, France, Ireland, Italy, the Netherlands, New Zealand, Norway, the Russian Federation, Sweden, Switzerland and the United States. There have been twenty-eight fatalities (UNDPI, 1993a: 3–4).

Since its establishment UNTSO has been financed from the regular UN budget. The annual cost of the operation is US\$ 31 million approximately (UNDPI, 1993a: 4).

First United Nations Emergency Force (UNEF I) This is the first actual peace-keeping force mounted by the United Nations. Consisting of troops bearing arms, it was created under the leadership of the then Secretary-General Dag Hammarskjold and Lester Pearson, then Secretary for External Affairs of Canada. The UN General Assembly, replacing the Security Council which was incapacitated by permanent member vetoes, under the provisions of the 'Uniting for Peace' resolution of November 1950 (General Assembly resolution 377(V)), convened for an emergency special session in November 1956, in response to Israel's attack on Egypt and the UK and French military intervention in the Suez Canal. It adopted resolution 998 (ES-I) with which it asked the Secretary-General to present a plan for 'the setting up, with the consent of the nations concerned, of an emergency international United Nations Force to secure and supervise the cessation of hostilities'.[3] Subsequent resolutions determined more specifically the mandate, organization and operating rules of the force.

UNEF I took over control of the Suez Canal and its presence guaranteed the ceasefire agreed by the parties through the good offices of the Secretary-General. It also led to the complete withdrawal of the Anglo-French forces and to the gradual withdrawal of Israeli forces until complete withdrawal occurred on 6 March 1957. The territory left was put under UNEF's control (UNDPI, 1990: 59–75).

UNEF's presence was terminated in May 1967, while tension was rising between Israel and its Arab neighbours. The termination came about despite the Secretary-General's efforts to the contrary, after Egypt's refusal to accept the presence of the force on its soil any longer and Israel's refusal to let the force station on its side of the border. Soon afterwards, on 5 June 1967, full-fledged war broke out between Israel and Egypt, which was soon joined by Syria and Jordan. The 'Six Day War' resulted in a major victory for Israel (UNDPI, 1990: 75–8).

The maximum strength of UNEF I was 6,073 troops (February 1957). In the execution of its mission, it had a total of ninety fatalities. The force was financed by UN member assessments deposited in a special account and its total cost reached US$ 214,249,000. Personnel-contributing countries included Brazil, Canada, Colombia, Denmark, Finland, India, Indonesia, Norway, Sweden and Yugoslavia (UNDPI, 1990: 421).

Second United Nations Emergency Force (UNEF II) UNEF II was created by resolution 340 adopted by the Security Council on 25 October 1973 in order to monitor a ceasefire between Israel and Egypt in the Suez Canal area. The status quo there had been upset, initially by a surprise move by Egypt, whose forces had crossed the canal on 6 October, in a coordinated move with Syria which at the same time attacked Israeli positions on the Golan Heights. Israel responded to the challenge and by 21 October an Israeli armoured column had crossed the canal threatening to cut off the Egyptian Third Army, which was on the canal's east bank (UNDPI, 1990: 79–80).

The maximum strength of UNEF II was 6,973 troops (in February 1974). Troop-contributing countries included: Australia, Austria, Canada, Finland, Ghana, Indonesia, Ireland, Nepal, Panama, Peru, Poland, Senegal and Sweden. Fatalities reached fifty-two in total. The force was financed through UN member assessments deposited in a special account and total expenditure reached US$ 446,487,000 (UNDPI, 1990: 423).

The US-brokered peace treaty of March 1979 between Egypt and Israel (the Camp David Agreements), which entered into force on 25 April 1979, led to the Israeli withdrawal from the Sinai. UNEF II's presence thus became obsolete and the force's mandate was not renewed beyond July 1979 (UNDPI, 1990: 86–7).

United Nations Disengagement Observer Force (UNDOF)   While UNEF II was established in order to monitor the ceasefire on the Egyptian–Israeli front of the 1973 war, UNDOF was established in order to deal with the other front of the same war, the Israeli–Syrian one. Tension on this front remained high until an Agreement on Disengagement between Israeli and Syrian forces was signed on 31 May 1974, following a US diplomatic initiative. On that same day, the Security Council created UNDOF through its resolution 350 (1974) with the mandate to maintain the ceasefire between Israel and Syria and to supervise the disengagement of Israeli and Syrian forces on the Golan Heights (UNDPI, 1990: 99–101). Since then, the mandate of the force has been renewed periodically for six-month periods; 'that force is still there – unpublicised because it does its job so well' (Goulding, 1993: 453).

UNDOF's current strength is 1,120, assisted by the military observers of UNTSO's Observer Group Golan. By late 1993 there had been thirty-one fatalities. Contingents come from Austria, Canada, Finland and Poland, while in the past there were Peruvian and Iranian troop contributions. The annual cost to the UN of this operation is about US$ 36 million. The money comes from a special account initially established for the financing of UNEF II. Outstanding contributions reached approximately US$ 26 million by 30 April 1993 (UNDPI, 1993a: 5–6 and UNDPI, 1993c: 18).

United Nations Interim Force in Lebanon (UNIFIL)   UNIFIL was established by Security Council resolutions 425 and 426 of 19 March 1978 with the mandate to supervise the withdrawal of Israeli forces from southern Lebanon. Israel had occupied that part of the Lebanese territory in retaliation for a commando raid in Israel for which the Palestine Liberation Organisation (PLO), the dominant force in southern Lebanon at the time, claimed responsibility (UNDPI, 1990: 111–14).

UNIFIL has been unable to implement its mandate fully, because the PLO and the Israeli government never fully accepted its role. Militias supported and supplied by Israel control the zone above Israel's border with Lebanon, preventing UNIFIL's full deployment there. However, UNIFIL tries to provide the local civilian population with humanitarian assistance, important utilities and some limited protection. UNIFIL's mandate has been extended repeatedly for six-month periods (UNDPI, 1993a: 7–8). The force has thus become 'a quasi-permanent fixture. It illustrates how much easier it is to get into a peace-keeping operation than to get out of it – and the need therefore for the Security Council to satisfy itself that conditions exist for successful peace-keeping before taking the decision to set up a new operation' (Goulding, 1993: 453) – a statement quite valid with regard to other operations too.

UNIFIL now has a strength of about 5,280 soldiers, assisted by fifty-seven military observers from UNTSO and about 520 international and local civilian staff. Troops come from Fiji, Finland, France, Ghana, Ireland, Italy, Nepal, Norway, Poland and Sweden. By late 1993, 190 fatalities had been registered. UNIFIL's budget amounts to about US\$ 146 million annually. This cost is met by assessed contributions paid by the UN membership. Approximately US\$259 million was owed by member states to the UNIFIL special account for the period from the establishment of the force to 30 April 1993 (UNDPI, 1993c: 19).

Peace-keeping in cases of internal strife/divided societies

The peace-keeping operations examined under this heading do not deal with conflicts between two or more adversarial states. They refer rather to attempts made to bring about peace when a bloody dispute has occurred within the borders of a single internationally recognised state. History shows that conflicting factions within the borders of a state, belonging to different ethnic and/or religious and/or political groups, can confront each other in at least as destructive a way as in the case of conflicts between states. These are cases of internal strife within divided societies, what could be called 'civil war', although some of the protagonists, often in young and heterogeneous – and therefore precarious – states, might not consider it (or the societies themselves) that 'civil'. The United Nations has had to intervene in such cases too, in spite of its fundamental principle of non-intervention in the internal affairs of states (Article 2, para. 7 of the UN Charter). The UN operations demonstrate international concern with regard to an internal crisis which could, however, easily degenerate into an international one, by means of spill-over of the conflict into the broader neighbourhood, imminent or actual intervention by external actors, and so on.

United Nations Observation Group in Lebanon (UNOGIL)   The group was created by Security Council resolution 128 of 11 June 1958 in an attempt to ensure that there would be no illegal support in arms and/or personnel supplied to elements within Lebanon which had revolted against the (Maronite Christian) president of the country, Camille Chamoun. The resolution was supported by both the government of Lebanon and the United Arab Republic, which was accused by the former of encouraging and supporting the rebellion. About a hundred observers were finally drawn from twenty-one countries, excluding, of course, in accordance with Cold War norms, nationals of the five permanent members of the Security Council and of 'special interest' countries (UNDPI, 1990: 175–6).

Due to broader political considerations in the region (i.e. the overthrow of the Kingdom of Iraq and its replacement by a republican regime), in July 1958 a US contingent was dispatched to Lebanon, at the request of the Lebanese government. The US government publicly acknowledged that this was not the optimal response, but it had to be followed until the United Nations had the capacity to guarantee stability in the region. In the same month British forces were dispatched to Jordan in order to protect the regime there (UNDPI, 1990: 178–80).

The Secretary-General proposed successive increases in the size of UNOGIL, the strength of which reached 591 in mid-November 1958. Tension evaporated after the election of General Fuad Chehab as president of Lebanon, for he was acceptable to the Muslim leaders in the country. At the same time, the new Iraqi revolutionary government had accepted the rules of the United Nations and had been recognized by the United Kingdom and the United States. US and UK forces soon withdrew from the area, relations between Lebanon and the United Arab Republic were fully restored and UNOGIL began its withdrawal on 26 November 1958 (UNDPI, 1990: 183–5).

The total cost of the operation was US$ 3,697,742 and it was financed by appropriations through the UN regular budget. Observers were contributed by Afghanistan, Argentina, Burma (now Myanmar), Canada, Ceylon (now Sri Lanka), Chile, Denmark, Ecuador, Finland, India, Indonesia, Ireland, Italy, Nepal, the Netherlands, New Zealand, Norway, Peru, Portugal and Thailand (UNDPI, 1990: 176).

United Nations Peace-Keeping Force in Cyprus (UNFICYP)   Soon after Cyprus attained its independence, on 16 August 1960, violence broke out between the two ethnic communities of the island, the Greek Cypriots and the Turkish Cypriots, comprising about 80 per cent and 18 per cent of the population respectively. The UN was asked to intervene by Cyprus and the United Kingdom; the latter was, along with Greece and Turkey, a guarantor of the basic provisions of the Constitution of Cyprus and of the territorial integrity and sovereignty of the new state – while the former claimed that Turkey was responsible for intervention in its internal affairs and for aggression. These accusations were denied by Turkey, which in turn complained about the treatment of the Turkish Cypriots. The Security Council unanimously adopted resolution 186 on 4 March 1964, by which it established UNFICYP in order to prevent violence and contribute to the restoration of law and stability (UNDPI, 1993a: 11).

In July and August 1974 hostilities resumed, this time with the direct intervention of the Turkish army. Intercommunal strife was thus turned clearly into an international problem. After a *de facto* ceasefire, which came into effect on 16 August 1974, UNFICYP was deployed along a 180 kilometre-long buffer zone of varying width which separated the two sections of the island, the northern one occupied by the Turkish and Turkish Cypriot forces (about 36.5 per cent of the total area of the island) and the southern, Greek Cypriot one, which had received a great number of refugees who had fled from the north (UNDPI, 1990: 301–9 and Souter, 1984).

The mandate of UNFICYP has been renewed regularly by the Security Council, since 1964, usually for six-month periods. UNFICYP has been the only UN peace-keeping force financed through voluntary contributions. However, such contributions have not always been forthcoming. As a result, the force's special account presented a deficit of more than US$ 200 million, from the force's inception to September 1993.[4]

Military and civilian police personnel are contributed to UNFICYP by Australia, Austria, Canada, Denmark, Finland, Ireland, Sweden and the UK (UNDPI, 1993a: 12). The deficit has long been shouldered by the troop-contributing countries, which have had to cover the regular pay and material expenses of their respective troops, while the world organization has taken care of the operational costs of administrative and logistic support.[5] This has caused resentment among the troop-contributing countries and in 1992–93 resulted in the withdrawal of the Danish battalion (323 personnel) and in the reduction in the size of the forces of the UK (by 198 personnel), Austria (by 63) and Canada (by 61), while further withdrawals or reductions were announced.[6] It has even been proposed that 'military observers be deployed in Cyprus instead of infantry units in order to reduce the cost of the operation'.[7] This was not favoured by the Secretary-General and his representatives, who considered that 'the current political and military situation in Cyprus and in the region does not yet justify UNFICYP being converted to an observer mission'; they preferred a restructuring and reduction of the force 'to the minimum number of infantry battalions required to maintain effective control of the buffer zone'.[8]

A recent attempt to finance UNFICYP as an expense of the UN, through assessed/mandatory contributions, was not successful. A Security Council draft resolution to that effect was approved by all the Council members except Russia, which vetoed it,[9] purportedly on purely practical/economic grounds.[10] The resolution finally passed (resolution 831 (1993), adopted on 27 May 1993 with fourteen votes in favour and one abstention (Pakistan)), provided that 'with effect from the next extension of UNFICYP's mandate on or before 15 June 1993, those costs of the Force which are not covered by voluntary contributions should be treated as expenses of the Organisation under Article 17(2) of the Charter of the United Nations'. It also provided that 'UNFICYP should be restructured as a first step on the basis of the proposal ... of the Secretary-General ... with the addition of a limited number of observers for reconnaissance'. A comprehensive reassessment of UNFICYP was scheduled to take place in December 1993, when the mandate of the force was to be considered in view of developments towards a conflict settlement.[11]

This extension of UNFICYP's mandate to 15 December 1993 was estimated to cost about US$ 21.5 million, $12.5 million of which was expected to come from voluntary contributions. Significant voluntary contributions were pledged by the governments of Cyprus and Greece.[12] At its plenary meeting on 14 September 1993 the General Assembly appropriated about $8.5 million for UNFICYP's operation for the period 16 June – 15 December 1993, to be apportioned among its members.[13]

The force's currently authorized strength is 1,323, well below the maximum of 6,411 which it reached in June 1964. Some 1,050 members are infantry personnel, 223 support personnel, 38 civilian police, and 12 military observers. The observers are provided by Austria, Ireland and Hungary.[14] There have been 159 fatalities among the UN troops since the creation of the force (UNDPI, 1993a: 11).

On the 'peacemaking' front, UN-sponsored negotiations between the two communities of Cyprus continue – a long, tortuous process which seems to be leading nowhere. In the latest phase of the intercommunal talks, the Secretary-General and his representatives formulated a set of ideas that they put forward to the parties as the basis for a negotiated settlement. These ideas had emerged from previous talks between the representatives of the two communities under UN auspices and they provided, among other things, that:

— Cyprus would be a federal state with a single international personality, sovereignty and citizenship, based on the political equality of the two communities;
— constitutionally the reunited state of Cyprus should be bi-communal, with a bicameral legislative, consisting of a lower house where Greek Cypriots and Turkish Cypriots would be represented in a 70:30 ratio respectively, and of an upper house where representation would be 50:50;

— territorially, the state of Cyprus would be bi-zonal, that is 'each federated state would be administered by one community which would be guaranteed a clear majority of the population and of land ownership in the area';
— the federal constitution would guarantee the fundamental rights of all citizens, including their political, economic, social and cultural rights, as well as freedom of movement and settlement, and the right to property;
— the 1960 Treaties of Guarantee and of Alliance, appropriately supplemented, would guarantee the security of both communities, and all non-Cypriot forces not foreseen in the Treaty of Alliance would be withdrawn;
— the question of membership of the European Community should be decided by both communities in separate referenda; and
— measures that would promote good will and closer relations between the two communities would be implemented immediately following approval of the overall framework agreement by the two communities in separate referenda.[15]

This set of ideas was endorsed by the Security Council (resolutions 750 of 10 April 1992 and 774 of 26 August 1992) as 'an appropriate basis for reaching an overall framework agreement'. However, the deadlock continued. Efforts by the Secretary-General and his representatives for an agreement to be reached on confidence-building measures did not bring about any concrete result because of the Turkish Cypriot leadership's stalling tactics. This was allegedly due to deep political divisions existing within the Turkish Cypriot community, which were expected to be resolved through elections.[16]

In a letter dated 20 September 1993 from the President of the Security Council to the Secretary-General, the members of the Council endorsed the report of the Secretary-General on his mission of good offices in Cyprus dated 14 September 1993 (UN Doc. S/26438) and conveyed their continuing support to the efforts of the Secretary-General and his representatives. The members of the Council once again called on both parties to cooperate with the Secretary-General in order for an overall framework agreement to be reached promptly. In the first instance, agreement should be reached on the confidence-building proposals related to Varosha and Nicosia International Airport. The members of the Council noted with concern 'that the Turkish Cypriot side has not yet shown the necessary goodwill and cooperation required to achieve an agreement' and 'recognise[d] the important role that Turkey could play in this effort'. The Secretary-General's efforts could not continue indefinitely and, following a thorough review of the situation on the basis of a forthcoming report of the Secretary-General, the members of the Council would 'if necessary, consider alternative ways to promote the implementation of the resolutions on Cyprus'.[17]

United Nations Protection Force (UNPROFOR)   The end of the Cold War
brought about, among other things, the dissolution of Yugoslavia, Marshal
Tito's federal construction of a maverick socialist state. Fighting soon broke
out between constituent republics of former Yugoslavia, which declared
their independence, and the weakened federal centre, actually controlled by
Serbia.

In view of the unsuccessful efforts by the European Community to stop
hostilities in mid-1991 and to bring about a conflict settlement in the
framework of its Conference on Yugoslavia, the Security Council initially
intervened by imposing an arms embargo on the whole of the territory of
former Yugoslavia, through its unanimous resolution 713 (1991) of 25 September 1991. On 8 October 1991 Cyrus Vance, former US Secretary of
State, was appointed by the Secretary-General as his personal envoy for
Yugoslavia. With a view to finding a solution to the crisis, the Secretary-
General and his envoy maintained constant contact with the conflicting
parties as well as with representatives of other interested actors, such as the
EC Presidency, the CSCE Chairman-in-Office, Lord Carrington – then
Chairman of the EC Conference on Yugoslavia – and others (UNDPI,
1993b: 1–2).

Through its resolution 724 (1991) of 15 December 1991, the Security
Council approved the Secretary-General's report, which contained a plan
for a possible peace-keeping operation in the territory of former Yugoslavia.
The United Nations Protection Force (UNPROFOR) was finally established
by Security Council resolution 743 (1992) of 21 February 1992 for an initial
period of twelve months, despite the objections expressed by some political
groups involved in the conflict. The force was envisaged as an interim
arrangement which would help create the conditions for peace and security,
which in turn would lead through negotiation to an overall settlement of
the Yugoslav crisis, within the framework of the EC's Conference on Yugoslavia. Full deployment of the force was finally authorised on 7 April 1992
through Security Council resolution 749 (1992) (UNDPI, 1993b: 1–2 and
UNDPI, 1993a: 37–8).

UNPROFOR was initially deployed in three 'United Nations Protected
Areas' (UNPAs) in Croatia, namely Eastern Slavonia, Western Slavonia and
Krajina. Its goal was to monitor the federal army's withdrawal from the
whole of Croatia, as well as UNPA demilitarization – predominantly Serbian
areas – and local government, until an overall political solution to the
Yugoslav crisis was reached. UNPROFOR would also facilitate the safe
return to their homes in the UNPAs of civilian displaced persons, in support
of the work of the UN humanitarian agencies. UNPROFOR's headquarters
were initially established in Sarajevo, the capital of Bosnia-Herzegovina, to
be moved later to Zagreb, the capital of Croatia (see below) (UNDPI, 1993a:
38).

Following the deterioration of the situation in Bosnia-Herzegovina in April 1992, sanctions were imposed on rump Yugoslavia (by then consisting only of Serbia and Montenegro), through resolution 757 (1992) of 30 May 1992. An embargo was instituted on Yugoslav (Serbian and Montenegrin) products, financial and economic exchanges, sports contacts, scientific, cultural and technical exchanges, air transportation, and so on. UNPROFOR's mandate was enlarged to include the establishment of a security zone encompassing Sarajevo and its airport which would be used for a humanitarian airlift and the protection of humanitarian relief efforts (resolution 758 (1992) of 8 June 1992). UNPROFOR's presence in Sarajevo was gradually strengthened (see resolutions 761 (1992) of 29 June 1992 and 764 (1992) of 13 July 1992).

UNPROFOR's mandate and strength were enlarged by Security Council resolution 776 (1992) of 14 September 1992, in order to support efforts by the United Nations High Commissioner for Refugees (UNHCR), the International Committee of the Red Cross (ICRC) and other agencies to provide humanitarian assistance throughout Bosnia-Herzegovina.[18] Following Security Council resolution 781 (1992) of 9 October 1992, the UNPROFOR mandate was further enlarged to include the monitoring of compliance with a military flight ban in the airspace of Bosnia-Herzegovina imposed by the Security Council (UNDPI, 1993b: 8–9).

In view of alleged aerial bombardment of villages near Srebrenica by unidentified aircraft on 13 March 1993, the Security Council on 31 March 1993 adopted resolution 816 (1993) by which it extended the ban on military flights to cover various types of aircraft. Acting under Chapter VII of the UN Charter, the Security Council authorized member states, acting nationally or through regional arrangements, to ensure, by 'all necessary means', compliance with the ban on flights, in coordination with the Secretary-General and UNPROFOR. Soon afterwards, the Secretary-General of NATO, Dr Manfred Woerner, informed the United Nations that the North Atlantic Council had made the necessary arrangements to ensure compliance with the military flight ban; to that end, aircraft had been offered by France, the Netherlands, Turkey, the UK and USA and liaison cells were established at UNPROFOR headquarters in Zagreb and in Bosnia-Herzegovina (Kiseljak). The operation started on 12 April 1993 at 12.00 GMT.[19] Already since July 1992 another regional organization, the Western European Union (WEU), had undertaken to conduct embargo monitoring and, later, embargo enforcement, according to UN Security Council resolutions, by ships and aircraft offered by its member states, in the area of the Adriatic sea. Combined WEU/NATO operations were later undertaken in the Adriatic in order to enforce the tightening of the embargo on the Federal Republic of Yugoslavia (Serbia and Montenegro) under Security Council resolution 820 (1993) of 17 April 1993. WEU member states were also assisting Bulgaria, Hungary and Romania in enforcing the sanctions and the embargo on the Danube.[20]

On the perimeter of the crisis, an UNPROFOR presence was also established in the former Yugoslav Republic of Macedonia (FYROM), following a report by the Secretary-General to that effect and its endorsement through resolution 795 (1992) by the Security Council on 11 December 1992. This was done at the invitation of the government of this country and at the recommendation of Cyrus Vance and David Owen, co-chairmen of the Steering Committee of the International Conference on the Former Yugoslavia (see below), in order to avoid a possible spreading of the conflict any further into the south of former Yugoslavia. UNPROFOR would be stationed near the borders with Albania and the new Federal Republic of Yugoslavia (Serbia and Montenegro).[21] This was the first clear case of 'preventive deployment', an idea put forward by the UN Secretary-General in his report *An Agenda for Peace* (Boutros-Ghali, 1993b: 324 and Boutros-Ghali, 1992: paras. 28–32). To the 760 troops initially deployed, some 300 were added later, offered by the USA and unanimously accepted by the Security Council (resolution 842 (1993) of 18 June 1993).[22]

By May 1993, UNPROFOR consisted of about 24,000 personnel altogether, military, police and civilian. Of those about 14,000 were stationed in Croatia and the UNPAs, 9,200 in Bosnia-Herzegovina and about 760 in the Former Yugoslav Republic of Macedonia. The troop-contributing countries were Argentina, Australia, Bangladesh, Belgium, Brazil, Canada, Colombia, the Czech Republic, Denmark, Egypt, Finland, France, Ghana, Ireland, Jordan, Kenya, Luxembourg, Nepal, the Netherlands, New Zealand, Nigeria, Norway, Poland, Portugal, the Russian Federation, the Slovak Republic, Spain, Sweden, Switzerland, Tunisia, the Ukraine, the United Kingdom, the United States and Venezuela (UNDPI, 1993b: 16–17 and UNDPI, 1993a: 43). As mentioned above, approximately 300 US troops were added later to the FYROM component. By September 1993 UNPROFOR had incurred fifty-one fatalities out of a total of 548 casualties (Boutros-Ghali, 1993c: para. 450). The annual cost of UNPROFOR was estimated at about US$ 1,020 million. As at 30 April 1993, outstanding contributions amounted to approximately $325 million, for the period ending on 30 June 1993 (UNDPI, 1993c: 29).[23]

In parallel to the peace-keeping activities, the United Nations General Assembly, following the recommendation of the Security Council, on 22 May 1992 admitted to UN membership the republics of Croatia, Slovenia and Bosnia-Herzegovina. With regard to the new Federal Republic of Yugoslavia (Serbia and Montenegro) the Security Council, through its resolution 777 (1992) of 19 September 1992, expressed the view that this state could not automatically continue the UN membership of the former Socialist Federal Republic of Yugoslavia. The Council recommended to the General

Assembly that the Federal Republic of Yugoslavia should apply for UN membership and that it should not participate in the work of the General Assembly. The General Assembly agreed with the Security Council recommendation through its resolution 47/1 of 22 September 1992. Later, on 29 April 1993, it further decided, again on the recommendation of the Security Council (resolution 821 (1993) of 28 April 1993), that the Federal Republic of Yugoslavia should not participate in the work of the Economic and Social Council. On 8 April 1993 the General Assembly, acting on the recommendation of the Security Council contained in its resolution 817 (1993) of 7 April 1993, admitted to UN membership the 'former Yugoslav Republic of Macedonia', under this provisional name, pending a settlement of the difference over the name of this state (UNDPI, 1993b: 31).

In the meanwhile, the International Conference on Former Yugoslavia, successor to the EC's Conference on Yugoslavia, had been convened in London on 26–28 August 1992, under the joint chairmanship of the UN Secretary-General Boutros Boutros-Ghali and the UK Prime Minister and then President of the Council of Ministers of the EC, John Major. The co-chairmen of the Conference's Steering Committee, Cyrus Vance and Lord Owen (who succeeded Lord Carrington as EC mediator), were assigned the task of preparing the basis for a settlement of the conflict. Based at the UN Office in Geneva, they were to direct the six working groups of the conference, namely those on Bosnia-Herzegovina, on Humanitarian Issues, on Ethnic and National Communities and Minorities (including a special group on the former autonomous province of Kosovo), on Succession Issues, on Economic Issues and on Confidence and Security-Building and Verification Measures. An Arbitration Commission and a small secretariat were also established in the framework of the Conference (UNDPI, 1993b: 19). Thereafter, efforts to bring about a conflict settlement by peaceful means in former Yugoslavia (the peace-making part) proceeded on the basis of the principles adopted at the London conference and by means of the machinery set up.

Especially regarding Bosnia-Herzegovina, the co-chairmen of the Conference's Steering Committee held a series of difficult talks with the parties concerned, namely the predominantly Muslim government of Bosnia, the Bosnian Serbs and the Bosnian Croats. On 4 January 1993, in Geneva, the co-chairmen submitted to the parties a comprehensive package including a set of constitutional principles as well as a map dividing the country into ten provinces and a peace agreement. The peace talks continued in New York, by means of the good offices of the Security Council, in an attempt to overcome the objections to some aspects of the deal expressed by the parties. By 25 March 1993, the Bosnian government and the Bosnian Croats had signed four documents relating to the constitutional principles, the peace agreement, the revised provincial map and the provisional agreement on interim governmental arrangements respectively, while the Bosnian Serb side declined to sign the latter two documents. On 17 April 1993, the Security Council, through its resolution 820 (1993), commended the peace plan for Bosnia-Herzegovina, welcomed the full acceptance of it by two of the Bosnian parties and called on the remaining party to proceed in the same way. It was also decided that the sanctions regime imposed against the Federal Republic of Yugoslavia (Serbia and Montenegro) would be strengthened nine days after the date of adoption of the resolution, unless the Bosnian Serbs accepted in full the peace plan and ceased military operations in Bosnia-Herzegovina. The deadline elapsed without any positive move from the Bosnian Serb side and, as a result, the sanctions came into force at midnight on 26 April 1993. The sanctions would be reconsidered only after unconditional acceptance of the plan (UNDPI, 1993b: 21–2).

According to resolution 820 (1993) of the Security Council, the Secretary-General reported on 26 April 1993 on the preparations made for the implementation of the peace plan once it had been accepted by all parties. The Secretary-General indicated that the operation would exceed the capacity of the UN Secretariat and of UNPROFOR. NATO had signalled its willingness to cooperate and consultations were initiated in that direction. Preliminary studies by NATO experts had indicated that about 60,000 to 75,000 troops would be required for implementation of the various aspects of the peace plan. The UN would maintain overall political and strategic control through its Secretary-General under the authority of the Security Council (UNDPI, 1993b: 22). At a further meeting in Athens on 1–2 May 1993, the co-chairmen of the International Conference Steering Committee, Cyrus Vance, Lord Owen and Thorvald Stoltenberg (appointed to succeed Vance), tried to persuade the Bosnian Serbs to sign the remaining two documents of the peace plan. The meeting was attended by the leaders of the three Bosnian parties as well as by the presidents of Croatia, the new Federal Republic of Yugoslavia and of the constituent republics of the latter, that is, Serbia and Montenegro. Dr Karadzic, the leader of the Bosnian Serbs, finally signed the documents, but indicated that they would have to be approved by the Bosnian Serb 'Assembly'. However, on 5 May, the 'Assembly' rejected the plan, despite strong international pressure to the contrary. A referendum on the peace plan was then held among the Bosnian Serbs (UNDPI, 1993b: 22–3).[24] The referendum also resulted in a negative vote and the peace plan collapsed, in spite of statements to the contrary by important international actors.[25]

Efforts for a peaceful settlement soon focused on a new proposal by Thorvald Stoltenberg and David Owen which provided for the division of Bosnia-Herzegovina into three autonomous republics according to ethnic composition. Each one of these republics could unilaterally secede from the union if it so decided by referendum two years after the settlement.[26] The plan was acceptable to the Bosnian Serbs and the Bosnian Croats, while the

Muslims of Bosnia and the Bosnian Government seemed reluctant to agree to it. Among other things, they asked for access to the Adriatic through special arrangements with Croatia. Although negotiations in this respect were progressing well, the predominantly Muslim Bosnian Parliament virtually rejected the plan by asking for more land to be surrendered by the Serbs, the victors on the ground.[27] Internal fighting which broke out soon afterwards within the Muslim camp was a sign of further degeneration of the situation.[28]

The conflict in former Yugoslavia has been marked by massive violations of human rights and of international humanitarian law, especially within the territory of Bosnia-Herzegovina. The practice of 'ethnic cleansing', that is the systematic elimination or harassment and displacement by the ethnic group controlling one area of the members of other ethnic groups inhabiting the same area, was condemned by the representative organs of the international community (see, inter alia, Security Council resolutions 764 (1992) of 13 July 1992 and 771 (1992) of 13 August 1992 as well as General Assembly resolutions 46/242 of 25 August 1992 and 47/121 and 47/147 of 18 December 1992) (UNDPI, 1993b: 25–6).

A Special Rapporteur was appointed by the UN Commission on Human Rights in order to conduct a first-hand investigation of the human rights situation in former Yugoslavia, in particular within Bosnia-Herzegovina, to identify acts that constitute war crimes and to make recommendations towards ending human rights violations and preventing similar occurrences in the future. Tadeusz Mazowiecki, the former Prime Minister of Poland, who was appointed Special Rapporteur, conducted several missions to the former Yugoslavia and in his subsequent reports confirmed that human rights violations were perpetrated by all parties to the conflict with victims on all sides, though the situation of the Muslim population was found to be particularly tragic and the conduct of ethnic Serbs was judged to be the worst (UNDPI, 1993b: 26–7).

On 6 October 1992, the Security Council dealt with human rights violations in its resolution 780 (1992). In response to a request contained in this resolution, the Secretary-General established an impartial Commission of Experts to examine the evidence of grave breaches of the 1949 Geneva Conventions and other violations of humanitarian law in former Yugoslavia (UNDPI, 1993b: 28–9 and Boutros-Ghali, 1993c: para. 453). Moreover, the establishment of an International Tribunal was decided by the Security Council through its resolution 808 (1993) of 22 February 1993. The Tribunal would prosecute persons responsible for serious international humanitarian law violations in the territory of former Yugoslavia since 1991 (UNDPI, 1993b: 29). The Statute of the Tribunal was approved by the Security Council by resolution 827 (1993) of 25 May 1993 (Boutros-Ghali, 1993c: paras.454–5). In a related move, on 8 April 1993 the International

Court of Justice issued an Order of provisional measures calling upon the Federal Republic of Yugoslavia (Serbia and Montenegro) to take all necessary measures to prevent genocide by groups within its control against the Muslim population of Bosnia-Herzegovina or against any other group (UNDPI, 1993b: 29–30).

In order to protect the lives of civilians, in particular of Muslims threatened by Bosnian Serb military or paramilitary units, the Security Council, acting under Chapter VII of the UN Charter, adopted resolutions 819 (1993), on 16 April 1993, and 824 (1993), on 6 May 1993, through which Srebrenica, Sarajevo and the towns of Tuzla, Zepa, Gorazde, Bihac and their surroundings were declared 'safe areas'. UNPROFOR was strengthened by an additional fifty military observers to monitor the humanitarian situation in the above areas (UNDPI, 1993b: 16). By resolution 844 (1993) of 18 June 1993, UN members were encouraged by the Security Council to assist UNPROFOR in protecting the declared safe areas, acting nationally or through regional organizations or arrangements, in close coordination with the UN Secretary-General.[29]

The ambassadors of the NATO countries meeting in Brussels in September 1993 decided to approve initial contingency plans according to which approximately 50,000 additional troops would be sent to enforce a future peace plan agreed in relation to Bosnia-Herzegovina. Washington was reported to favour carrying out the operation under NATO command, while the European Allies insisted on UN preponderance.[30] The Security Council voted unanimously in early October 1993 to authorize six more months of peace-keeping by UN troops in former Yugoslavia.[31]

CONCLUSIONS AND COMMENTS

As already stated, UN peace-keeping in the Mediterranean region has represented a very large proportion of overall UN peace-keeping efforts, especially during the Cold War years. Centred mainly around the Arab–Israeli dispute, it was an attempt to contain a conflict that potentially could lead to a generalized war, superpower intervention and confrontation, and even nuclear war. Other focal points of UN peace-keeping in the region have been the cases of domestic/intercommunal conflict in Cyprus and Lebanon. A post-Cold War addition to the picture has been the complex situation that resulted from the dissolution of former Yugoslavia. The latter case is currently occupying centre stage, more so after the positive turn the Arab–Israeli dispute took in late 1993. The Lebanon case seems to have been settled too, while the Cyprus question remains unanswered, despite commendable attempts by the Secretary-General and the Security Council to put pressure on the parties in the direction of expediting the settlement process.

The situation in former Yugoslavia has been a testing ground for the efficiency and relevance of several international organizations. The CSCE tried its luck there too, as did the EC/EU, NATO and the WEU, in addition, of course, to the UN. The shortcomings of each and all of these organizations were amply demonstrated through this process. Perhaps most disappointing has been the performance of the European institutions, namely the EC/EU, WEU and the CSCE, which have proved themselves incapable of dealing with the situation without external (UN and US) assistance. The UN came to the rescue of the Europeans' failing attempts at dealing with the conflict. For quite some time international intervention limited itself to the protection of international humanitarian assistance efforts, an important but not central or decisive task.[32] Ultimately, it seems to be the situation on the ground, among the warring factions, that actually conditions the outcome. The proposed solution, namely the creation of a Bosnian state consisting of three 'ethnically clean' components, for the Bosnian Serbs, the Bosnian Croats and the Muslims respectively, demonstrates the clear military advantage won on the ground, mainly by the Bosnian Serbs and at the expense primarily of the Muslims. How long will such a settlement, if finally adopted, last? Will it allow – in practice – for peaceful change, for example, for secession and union of the Bosnian Serb part with Serbia and/ or of the Bosnian Croat part with Croatia? Only time will tell. Of course, any settlement in former Yugoslavia will require, for its implementation, a large international mobilization, be it of UN and/or NATO troops, as well as bewildering logistics and a great deal of political will.

In the case of Cyprus, where the UN role has been and still is indisputably central, the situation has dragged on for many years, with almost-reached agreements finally rejected by one party or the other. It is a clear-cut example of the negative repercussions that the deployment of peace-keepers can have. The absence of immediate confrontation freezes the situation and establishes a state of affairs that seems satisfactory to some actors. These actors then favour the prolongation of this state of affairs and participate in a 'slow motion' peace-making process for the sake of appearances only.[33] If it was not for the cost of the operation, especially to the troop-contributing countries, this might remain unnoticed and continue for ever. However, the UN's clout, previously non-existent due to Cold War divisions, has not been made use of yet, even though it has been rediscovered in a renewed great power unity in the post-bipolar world. Perhaps this is because Cyprus has no oil (cf. Iraq–Kuwait), and thus it is of no great importance to international political economy, as many people have come cynically to believe. Having said this, one must admit that, even without oil, the new – more complicated – 'Cyprus type' situation in former Yugoslavia, especially Bosnia-Herzegovina, seems to be attracting a great deal of attention, for the time being, at least.

The situation in the Middle East, regarding the Arab–Israeli conflict, was always a game for grown-ups, too serious for the UN to play any substantive role. Its contribution was limited to post facto peace-keeping, ceasefire verification, humanitarian assistance, and, of course, the adoption of those early resolutions regarding the partition of Palestine. The mutual recognition of Israel and the Palestine Liberation Organization (PLO) and the Declaration of Principles they signed in Washington on 13 September 1993, regarding the initial granting of limited autonomy to the Gaza Strip and Jericho, clearly signify a breakthrough. This was the result of secret negotiations, conducted in parallel to the official peace talks, with Norwegian mediation. In any case, the United Nations does not seem to have played any central role in achieving the settlement.[34]

What does all this indicate about the future of the UN and of international peace-keeping? Clearly, in the post-Cold War world, the United Nations is asked to perform a multitude of tasks:

> ... [T]oday's operations are not 'peace-keeping' in the traditional sense. ... Today, United Nations operations may take place where there is no peace to keep. New forms of assertive action may be required. United Nations forces protect relief shipments, provide services for victims, respond to refugee needs, enforce embargoes, remove mines and seek to confiscate arms. Beyond military-related steps, United Nations operations now involve a large civilian dimension: monitoring elections, public safety, information and communication, institution-building, and the restoration of infrastructure and administrative services. Peace-keeping today is quantity- and quality-wise different from the past.[35]

Proposals have been made by Boutros-Ghali through his report *An Agenda for Peace* and subsequent documents for the strengthening of the role of the UN in preventive diplomacy, peace-making, peace-keeping, peace enforcement and post-conflict peace-building (Boutros-Ghali, 1992; Boutros-Ghali, 1993c; Kostakos, 1993). Generally speaking, the Secretary-General advocates a more rationally organized machinery and modus operandi for the world body in the post-bipolar era. Would this, if adopted and implemented, bring about a faster and 'cleaner' settlement of international disputes? Having the countries (virtually all countries now, following the end of Cold War restrictions) earmark troops for UN service – one of the Agenda proposals – in one form or another and improving financial and logistical support would certainly facilitate the deployment of international forces in conflict areas, thus rendering international intervention more timely and effective. What is more important, however, is conflict prevention and all that this entails, i.e. information gathering and analysis, early warning, confidence-building measures, and so on. Post-conflict peace-building is equally important as it can contribute to preventing conflict recurrence. The UN machinery as well as its moral authority should be greatly enhanced in this respect, in order to be able to bring about real and lasting solutions to conflicts without major military operations, by or even only with the sanction of the UN, which cost a lot in lives and money, and also in UN legitimacy among the world's peoples.

In any case, finding solutions to conflicts deeply rooted in history and complicated by ethnic, religious, political, economic and other factors, is not an easy job. The United Nations, expressing the will and duty of the international community, is forced and bound to do so. The limited means made available to it by its member states often complicate things further. In this respect, the proposals made in *An Agenda for Peace* are again relevant. The creation of a 'United Nations Peace Endowment Fund' of, initially, US$1 billion, should be seriously considered, as should the financing of peace-keeping operations from the defence rather than the foreign affairs budgets of states (Boutros-Ghali, 1992: paras. 69–74 and para. 48). This would make more money available, more easily, and would make clearer the new meaning of defence – that is, collective support of international peace and security, in a broad interpretation of the terms (including natural and man-made disaster relief, for a start).

The lack of a clear 'cosmo-theory' regarding the peaceful functioning of the post-Cold War world, certainly hinders the role of the aspiring peace-makers. Nevertheless, the world body is making a great effort, although it is clear that not everything can be expected to be done by it alone. In the case of the Mediterranean region, the establishment of a Conference on Security and Cooperation in the Mediterranean (CSCM), similar to but distinct from the CSCE, has already been proposed (Nikolaou, 1993 and Aliboni: 47–8). Although the record of the latter in conflict resolution is not that good, attempts at self-help can only be encouraged, when, of course, they remain in the framework of and in harmonious coordination with broader and more comprehensive arrangements (Toscano, 1993: 56–7). However, the question remains whether a regional initiative, in order to be meaningful, requires a minimum degree of homogeneity between the states, peoples and traditions in a given area, which in the case of the Mediterranean as a whole may not be there yet (Nikolaou, 1993: 198–9).

When the situations in former Yugoslavia and in Cyprus reach a positive conclusion – one should not, of course, hold one's breath in expectation – there will still be a lot to be done for peace and security in the region. Interest may well shift from the Mediterranean proper to its periphery, already in a shambles: the Caucasus and the former Soviet Union in the north and east, of course the Gulf in the east, Somalia and the Sudan in the south and east, the Western Sahara in the south and west, and so on. Of course, one should not forget other spots of great international concern around the globe (Mozambique, Angola, El Salvador, and others, already there or yet to come). There is a lot to be done before this world of ours is saved 'from the scourge of war' (see preamble to the Charter of the United Nations).

NOTES

1. Based on the information provided in the following publications: United Nations Department of Public Information (1990), *The blue helmets: a review of United Nations peace-keeping*, New York, (second edition), Appendix II, 419–49; *Peace-keeping information notes*, (update no.1) United Nations Department of Public Information, New York, (1993); and Thomas G. Weiss and Jarat Chopra (1992), *United Nations peace-keeping*, The Academic Council on the United Nations System (ACUNS), USA, 61–4. As shown in the latter publication, attempts at peace-keeping are not confined to United Nations forces only – see *ibid.*, 65.

2. See similar difficulties in delimiting the 'Mediterranean region' experienced by Roberto Aliboni (1991), 'European security across the Mediterranean', *Chaillot Papers*, 2, (March), Paris: WEU Institute for Security Studies, 2–3.

3. Excerpt from General Assembly resolution 998(ES-I) quoted in *The blue helmets*, op. cit., 46.

4. See *United Nations News*, PR 169/93, United Nations Information Centre, Athens, 1 September 1993.

5. See *United Nations News*, PR 61/93, United Nations Information Centre, Athens, 11 May 1993 and report of the Secretary-General in UN Doc. A/47/1001 of 20 August 1993.

6. See report of the Secretary-General in UN Doc. S/25492 of 30 March 1993.

7. *United Nations News*, PR 161/92, United Nations Information Centre, Athens, 24 September 1992.

8. See report of the Secretary-General in UN Doc. S/25492 of 30 March 1993.

9. The first veto to be cast since 31 May 1990, when the US vetoed a draft resolution on the situation in the occuppied Arab territories, as stated in *United Nations News*, PR 72/93, United Nations Information Centre, Athens, 12 May 1993.

10. See *United Nations News*, PR 72/93, United Nations Information Centre, Athens, 12 May 1993. See also the Greek newspaper *Eleftherotypia*, 12 May 1993, 11 and *ibid.*, 13 May 1993, 3.

11. Resolution 831 (1993) given in *United Nations News*, PR 87/93, United Nations Information Centre, Athens, 28 May 1993.

12. See report of the Secretary-General in UN Doc. A/47/1001 of 20 August 1993, especially paragraphs 13, 33–4, 40 and 42; *United Nations News*, PR 103/93, United Nations Information Centre, Athens, 14 June 1993; and the Cypriot newspaper *Fileleftheros*, 15 September 1993.

13. See UN Press Release GA/8498 of 14 September 1993.

14. See report of the Secretary-General in UN Doc. A/47/1001 of 20 August 1993, para. 9 and *The blue helmets*, op. cit., 439.

15. See UN Docs. S/23780 of 3 April 1992 and S/24472 of 21 August 1992.

16. See reports of the Secretary-General in UN Docs. S/24830 of 23 November 1992 and S/26438 of 14 September 1993.

17. See text of the letter of the president of the Security Council to the secretary-general dated 20 September 1993 in *United Nations News*, PR 199/93, United Nations Information Centre, Athens, 21 September 1993.

18. By March 1993, 3.8 million people were receiving assistance in the whole of former Yugoslavia, of which 2.28 million in Bosnia-Herzegovina, according to the

Office of the UN High Commissioner for Refugees – see Boutros Boutros-Ghali, *Report on the work of the Organisation from the forty-seventh to the forty-eighth session of the General Assembly*, United Nations, New York, September 1993: para. 449.

19. See *The United Nations and the situation in the former Yugoslavia*, United Nations Department of Public Information, Reference Paper: 7 May 1993, United Nations, June 1993: 13–14 and reply received from NATO to the UN Security Council invitation to regional arrangements and organizations to study ways and means of improving cooperation with the United Nations in the framework of Chapter VIII of the UN Charter, in UN Doc. S/25996 of 15 June 1993: 18–19.

20. See reply received from WEU to the UN Security Council invitation to regional arrangements and organizations to study ways and means of improving cooperation with the United Nations in the framework of Chapter VIII of the UN Charter, in UN Doc. S/25996/Add.1 of 14 July 1993, 3.

21. *The United Nations and the situation in the former Yugoslavia, op. cit.*, 9–10. It has been proposed that the mandate of UNPROFOR should be clearly divided into three independent mandates, one for the Republic of Croatia, another for Bosnia-Herzegovina and a third one for the former Yugoslav Republic of Macedonia. This has been particularly asked for by the government of Croatia, which would like to reassert its authority over the UNPAs as well as other areas within its territory known as 'pink zones', not formally recognized as UNPAs but largely populated by Serbs. See 'Letter dated 30 July 1993 from the Permanent Representative of Croatia to the United Nations Addressed to the Secretary-General', UN Doc. S/26220 of 2 August 1993 and *The United Nations and the situation in the former Yugoslavia, op. cit.*, 3–5 and 10–12.

22. See *United Nations News*, PR 111/93, United Nations Information Centre, Athens, 21 June 1993.

23. For some interesting aspects of UNPROFOR financing see Rosalyn Higgins (1993), 'The new United Nations and former Yugoslavia', *International Affairs*, 69, 3 (July), 478–9.

24. See also 'Make Serbs Cooperate', *International Herald Tribune*, 10 May 1993, 6.

25. See 'Peace Plan Now "Dead", Bosnian Serb Leader Says', *International Herald Tribune*, 17 May 1993, 1 and 4; 'Russia Backs Peace Plan Regardless of Bosnia Vote', *International Herald Tribune*, 17 May 1993, 4; and 'US to Push for Accord among Allies on Balkans', *International Herald Tribune*, 18 May 1993, 1 and 6.

26. 'Le nouveau plan de paix ouvre la voie à l' éclatement de la Bosnie-Herzégovine', *Le Monde*, 18 September 1993, 1 and 4.

27. *International Herald Tribune*, 30 September 1993, 1 and 8. After the reported concessions by the Serbs, about 31 per cent of the territory of Bosnia-Herzegovina would go to the Muslims, 17 per cent to the Bosnian Croats and 52 per cent would remain under the Bosnian Serbs – see *ibid*.

28. 'Bosnie: Musulmans contre Musulmans à Bihac', *Le Monde*, 6 October 1993, 6.

29. *United Nations News*, PR 113/93, United Nations Information Centre, Athens, 21 June 1993.

30. See the Greek newspaper *Kathimerini,*, 16 September 1993.

31. See 'UN Extends Peace Unit and Warns Serbs', *International Herald Tribune*, 6 October 1993, 8.

32. For a critique of these 'ancillary functions' assigned to UNPROFOR, instead

of enforcement tasks – of a ceasefire at least - see Rosalyn Higgins, op. cit., 465–83, especially 468–70.

33. See also Roberto Toscano (1993), 'Peacekeeping in the New International Situation', *The International Spectator*, Vol. XXVIII, 1 (January–March) , 53–4. Of course, premature withdrawal, for whatever reason, may open the way to renewed hostilities, as the case of UNEF I demonstrates.

34. See the Greek newspapers *To Vima*, 12 September 1993, 26–7 and *Kathimerini*, 19 September 1993, 29.

35. 'Secretary-General Says Peace-Keeping, Development and Democratization are Great Tasks and Priorities of United Nations', *United Nations News*, PR 37/93, United Nations Information Centre, Athens, 17 March 1993, 1–2.

REFERENCES

Aliboni, Roberto (1991), 'European security across the Mediterranean', *Chaillot Papers*, 2 (March), Paris: WEU Institute for Security Studies.

Boutros-Ghali, Boutros (1992), *An agenda for peace: preventive diplomacy, peacemaking and peace-keeping*, UN Doc. A/47/277–S/24111 17 June.

Boutros-Ghali, Boutros (1993a), 'UN peace-keeping in a new era: a new chance for peace', *The World Today*, 49, 4 (April).

Boutros-Ghali, Boutros (1993b), 'An agenda for peace: one year later', *Orbis: a journal of world affairs*, 37, 3 (Summer).

Boutros-Ghali, Boutros (1993c), *Report on the work of the Organisation from the forty-seventh to the forty-eighth session of the General Assembly*, New York: United Nations, (September).

Goulding, Marrack (1993), 'The evolution of United Nations Peace-keeping', *International Affairs*, 69, 3 (July).

Heraclides, Alexis (1991), *I Aravo–Israelini antiparathesi* [*The Arab–Israeli confrontation*], Athens: Papazissis Publications [in Greek].

Kostakos, Georgios (1993), 'The United Nations in the service of peace: presentation of and commentary on the new proposals of the Secretary-General', in Y. Valinakis, G. Kostakos and S. Dalis (eds), *Epetirida amyntikis & exoterikis politikis '93*, Athens: Hellenic Foundation for Defense and Foreign Policy (ELIAMEP) [in Greek].

Nikolaou, Yannis S. (1993), 'Political cooperation and security in the Mediterranean – the limits of and the preconditions for dialogue in the framework of a CSCM', in Y. Valinakis, G. Kostakos and S. Dalis (eds), *Epetirida amyntikis & exoterikis politikis '93*, Athens; Hellenic Foundation for Defense and Foreign Policy (ELIAMEP) [in Greek].

Souter, David (1984), 'An island apart: a review of the Cyprus problem', *Third World Quarterly*, (July).

Toscano, Roberto (1993), 'Peacekeeping in the new international situation', *The International Spectator*, XXVIII, 1 (January–March).

United Nations Department of Public Information, 1990, *The blue helmets: a review of United Nations peace-keeping*, New York (second edition).

United Nations Department of Public Information, (1993a), *Peace-keeping information notes*, New York (update no. 1).

United Nations Department of Public Information (1993b), *The United Nations and the situation in the former Yugoslavia*, Reference Paper: 7 May 1993, United Nations (June).

United Nations Department of Public Information (1993c), *United Nations peace-keeping*, New York (August – data effective 31 May 1993)

PART TWO
EXTERNAL RELATIONS

5
Echoes from the Past: Greece and the Macedonian Controversy

Kyriakos Kentrotis

One direct result of the revolutionary changes in the political and social system of the East European countries since 1989 has been a revival of forgotten nationalist dreams and territorial claims. These developments have turned the Balkans into a disaster area, fully justifying the region's old nickname of 'the powder-keg of Europe'. No sooner did one of the basic factors of post-war stability, the USSR, begin to totter, as revolutionary changes shattered its socio-political foundations, than a chain reaction of forces was initiated in Eastern Europe. The immediate outcome has been an endeavour to establish a new status quo – not, usually, by peaceful means.

Those who are familiar with the situation in the Balkans are well aware that the harsh nationalist and religious strife which at present is ripping apart the once united Yugoslavia is nothing new. It existed in latent form even before the Second World War ended. But the communist regime covered it over with a thin veneer and relegated it to the margins of history.

After Yugoslavia's federal structure collapsed, Europe was shocked by the civil conflict that suddenly convulsed the former union. From mid-1990 onwards, one republic after another began to demand and consolidate its independence, and was sucked into the maelstrom of war: Slovenia first of all, followed by Croatia, and then Bosnia-Herzegovina.

The Former Yugoslav Republic of Macedonia (FYROM) is a special case. It has escaped war so far, but in September 1991 it began in its turn to demand independence and international recognition. As a direct consequence, the so-called Macedonian Question flared up again. It is an issue that has produced many moments of tension, and has always been at the hub of the political and social agitation and diverse realignments on the map of the Balkans.[1]

THE BASIC PARAMETERS OF THE MACEDONIAN QUESTION

After the peace treaty was signed at Bucharest in 1913, the broader geographical area of Macedonia became directly linked with the course of events in the nation states of Greece, Serbia, Bulgaria, and, later, Albania. From this point onwards it was to be a source of discord, the arena in which the national dreams of the Balkan countries collided. Macedonia's crucial geopolitical position and the ethnic mix of its population (a result of some five hundred years of subjugation to the Ottoman Empire) are the main reasons why the whole issue is so complex. They are also the basic resultant of the national claims of the Balkan peoples, and the conflicting interests of the Great Powers. Early in the nineteenth century, when the Ottoman Empire was beginning to decline and the Balkan Christians' efforts to create and expand their own nation states were at their height, the Macedonian Question was a constant factor in the ethnic and military confrontations in the sensitive area of south-eastern Europe.

For scientific observers and world opinion, particularly in the West, many aspects of Balkan politics remain incomprehensible. This is clearly illustrated by the general reaction to Greece's insistence that the Former Yugoslav Republic of Macedonia change its chosen name. Such an unprecedented demand and the discussion surrounding it strike West European ears as preposterous to the point of absurdity.[2] The spirit of the modern age dictates that if one wants to be a realist in the twentieth century, one must conduct oneself with an eye to the economy, or at least try to legitimize one's stance on the basis of economic factors. The nationalist aspect of the self-determination of a national and cultural entity is regarded as a feature of the last century.[3]

Events in former Yugoslavia, however, daily underline the fact that if one is living in this southern part of Europe one is obliged to take all such 'outdated' notions and aspirations into account. The history of the Balkans is primarily the history of the peoples who have inhabited the region for centuries, and their nation states complete the image of the peninsula through their continual disputes and conflicts, in their efforts to achieve national integration each in accordance with its own perceptions and ideals. The Balkan mind sees nothing strange in dreams of yesteryear. Particularly for someone who was born when the present state of affairs in former Yugoslavia was not even a speck on the horizon, it is even more difficult to rise above nationalistic ideology.

One fact, the fundamental parameter of the Macedonian Question, which must be stressed above all others, is that the word 'Macedonian' is an adjectival adjunct, which in ancient Greek denoted a plains-dweller.[4] It has always signified a purely geographical provenance. Furthermore, after the ancient Macedonian kingdom of Philip and Alexander had been overthrown, and particularly after Slavonic tribes had arrived and settled on the Balkan Peninsula in the seventh century AD, neither an independent and sovereign Macedonian state nor any such concept as Macedonian nationality ever existed, until the end of the Second World War. It was in the twentieth century that all this took on a new dimension, through the catalytic presence and influence of communist ideology in the Balkans.

A HISTORICAL REVIEW

The Balkan countries and Turkish-held Macedonia (1870–1919)

The Macedonian Question essentially came into being in the nineteenth century. The whole region of Macedonia was under Ottoman occupation at that time and it was a century convulsed by national uprisings. The Christian peoples of the Balkans were trying to achieve a national renaissance and were breaking away from the decaying Ottoman Empire. Towards the end of the nineteenth century there began a keen race between Greeks and Slavs over who would succeed the Ottomans in Macedonia. The population of the region at this time was approximately one third Muslim and two thirds Christian. The Christians were more or less united until the middle of the nineteenth century, when the Ottomans began deliberate efforts to sunder them. In 1870, the Sultan recognized the Bulgarian Church's independence from the Oecumenical Patriarchate of Constantinople, and this, together with the Russo-Turkish War of 1877–8, enabled the victorious Russia to force the Sultan to accept, under the Treaty of San Stefano (3 March 1878), an independent Great Bulgaria. It included most of Macedonia and Thrace and had a catalytic effect on the further evolution of the Macedonian Question.

These unexpected developments provoked an immediate reaction from the other Great Powers, which eventually managed to impose a new settlement of the Eastern Question at the Congress of Berlin in 1878. The Treaty of San Stefano was revoked and two Bulgarian states came into being: the southern part of Great Bulgaria was detached and renamed as the autonomous province of 'Eastern Rumelia', still subject to the Sultan. The geographical area of Macedonia also remained a province of the Ottoman Empire until 1913. San Stefano was henceforth to embody the great dream of Bulgarian nationalism; and the warring Bulgarians, Greeks, and Serbs were now engaged in an ongoing nationalist and religious struggle to achieve ethnic and cultural homogeneity in Macedonia.[5]

At the end of the nineteenth century, the whole of geographical Macedonia formed three horizontal linguistic zones. The north zone, which now corresponds to two-thirds of the Former Yugoslav Republic of Macedonia and half of Bulgaria's Pirin Macedonia, was densely populated by speakers of Slavonic, mostly Bulgarian. The south zone, which now comprises two-thirds of the Greek part of Macedonia, had a dense Greek-speaking population. The zone in between was inhabited by a mixture of Slavonic-, Vlach-, Greek-, and Albanian-speakers. As far as Greece's national idea was concerned, the south and middle zones corresponded historically to the Macedonian kingdom of antiquity, which, together with their ethnic composition, bolstered Greek hopes to have them incorporated into the Greek state.

The Bulgarians in their turn wanted to exploit the dense presence of Slavonic-speakers all over Macedonia to support their own irredentist aspirations in the region. A leading part in achieving their national goals was to be played by the Internal Macedonian Revolutionary Organization (IMRO);[6] and the Bulgarian presence and influence throughout Macedonia, particularly in the controversial middle linguistic zone, was considerably strengthened by means of education and the Exarchal Church. This combination was regarded as the best counterweight to the Greek Patriarchal influence in the region, in an effort to offset the losses inflicted by the Treaty of Berlin. The chief aim of the Bulgarian strategy was to awaken the notion of self-defence in the Bulgarian-speaking population of Macedonia and Thrace, which would urge them to demand and achieve a degree of political autonomy within the Ottoman Empire; subsequently they could be annexed by Bulgaria.

To begin with, the Bulgarians' activity was strongly anti-Turkish in tone, and it culminated in the Ilinden uprising of 1903.[7] Though short-lived, this minor revolt provoked the Turks into massacring a considerable proportion of Macedonia's Slavonic-speaking population. The confrontation subsequently developed into an undeclared Greek–Bulgarian war lasting until 1908, at which point the Greek government decided to help the enslaved Macedonian Greeks to resist both their Turkish conquerors and the activities of the Bulgarian revolutionary organizations. Spiritually united with their fellows in Macedonia, the people of metropolitan Greece managed to prevent Macedonia's capitulation to Bulgarian influence. An important part was also played by the revolution of the Young Turks (1908), whose messages of legal and civil equality for all the Empire's subjects helped to bring the four-year guerrilla war in Macedonia to an end. Although a significant proportion of the local population did not speak Greek, they were strongly committed to the Oecumenical Patriarchate and to Greek ideology, and this proved favourable for the ultimate fate of the Greeks in the region.[8]

While the rivalry between Greeks and Bulgarians was raging in Macedonia, a number of attempts were made to draw up a statistical record of the ethnic composition of the local population. It cannot be denied that both the methods used and the criteria on which they were based were designed to serve the national ends of the interested parties. The Bulgarians tended to take spoken language as their criterion, while the Greeks focused on national consciousness or ecclesiastical adherence (Patriarchal or Exarchal). Perhaps the most objective census was carried out by Hilmi Pasha in 1904 for the Ottoman authorities:[9]

Vilayet of Thessaloniki	Greeks	373,227	Bulgarians	207,317
Vilayet of Monastir	Greeks	261,283	Bulgarians	178,412
Vilayet of Kosovo (Skopje)	Greeks	13,452	Bulgarians	172,005

After the Balkan Wars, the area of Macedonia awarded to Greece (34,603 sq. km. or 51.57 per cent) included most of the vilayets of Thessaloniki and Monastir, with the exception of a few northern provinces, which now belong to the Former Yugoslav Republic of Macedonia (25,714 sq. km. or 38.32 per cent) and Bulgaria (Pirin Macedonia, 6,789 sq.km or 10.11 per cent). In fact, the area awarded to Greece corresponds to the 'historical Macedonia' of antiquity, apart from two tiny pockets on the northern border. The movements and exchanges of populations that occurred between 1912 and 1925 had a considerable effect on the region's ultimate ethnic composition.[10] After the Balkan Wars (1912–13) and the First World War, the Greek component of Macedonia's population swelled greatly. Both during the wars, when Greeks and Bulgarians on both sides of the Greek–Bulgarian border relocated of their own accord, and after the Greek–Bulgarian agreement on a mutual exchange of populations in 1919, the Greek part of Macedonia acquired a high degree of ethnic homogeneity.[11] The situation was even further clarified after the compulsory exchange of populations between Greece and Turkey on the basis of the Treaty of Lausanne (1923). This provided for the mass departure of the Muslims and much of the pro-Bulgarian element from Greece and their replacement in Macedonia by Greek refugees from Asia Minor, the Black Sea, Thrace, Bulgaria and Russia. Hence, statistics produced by the League of Nations in 1926[12] showed the Greek element as representing 88.8 per cent of the population of Macedonia, the Slavonic- and Bulgarian-speaking element as 5.1 per cent, with the remainder being made up chiefly of Muslims and Jews.

During the inter-war period,[13] the territory of the Former Yugoslav Republic of Macedonia became part of the newly established 'Kingdom of the Serbs, the Croats, and the Slovenes' and in 1918 it was named 'Southern Serbia'. Subsequently, when the Kingdom became 'Yugoslavia' in 1929, Southern Serbia became one of the country's nine *banovine* (provinces), a part of Serbia with a Serbianized Slavonic population. It was now called 'Vardar Banovina', after the River Vardar (Axios in Greek), which flows through Macedonia and into the Gulf of Thessaloniki.

The ethnic character of the Slavonic population of Vardar Banovina during the inter-war years was clearly described in a study conducted by

British scientists for the Foreign Office: 'The Morava valley and much of Macedonia in particular were inhabited by Slavonic populations of an intermediate ethnic character, which could become specifically Bulgarian or non-Bulgarian according to whether they were incorporated in a Bulgarian or non-Bulgarian state.'[14]

The communist movement and the Macedonian Question (1920–49)

The inter-war period, particularly after the Treaty of Lausanne, saw the start of a new phase in the Macedonian Question. The nationalistic disputes and claims of the interested Balkan countries were further complicated by the admixture of the newly established Balkan communist parties' ideological and class concepts.[15]

The Soviet Union and its powerful Communist Party had already emerged onto the world's political scene and had led to the birth of similar movements in the Balkan countries. On the initiative of the Bulgarian Communists, the Balkan Communist Federation (BCF) was established in Sofia in 1920; it was recognized by the Comintern and its members were bound by its decisions.

Bulgarian influence in the BCF was very strong, both because of the history of the Socialist movement in Bulgaria, and because the Bulgarian communists (such as the Secretary, Georgi Dimitrov, for instance, and Vasili Kolarov) wielded enormous power within the Comintern. Between 1922 and 1924, the BCF bowed to Comintern pressure and adopted as its fundamental aim the establishment of 'a united and independent Macedonia and Thrace', which would derive from the union of the three geographical regions of Greek, Yugoslav, and Bulgarian Macedonia. While the communist parties of both Yugoslavia and Greece were obliged to fall in with this decision, they never promoted it with great zeal, and this proved to be a source of friction in the Comintern. In 1934 the Comintern passed a resolution recognizing the existence of a 'separate Macedonian nation'.[16] In 1935, however, when the communist parties were forced to decide how they would oppose the emerging menace of Fascism, the communist parties of Greece and Yugoslavia seized their chance to pull out of the binding decisions made in the 1920s on the Macedonian Question.

The Second World War signalled new and unexpected developments. Bulgaro-Macedonian nationalism flared up once more as Bulgaria occupied the greater part of Yugoslav Macedonia after the Nazi invasion of Yugoslavia in April 1941. The local people hailed the Bulgarian troops as liberators, and in the early days of the occupation pro-Bulgarian feeling ran high.[17] The local communists even preferred to join the party of their Bulgarian 'brothers', rather than the Yugoslav Communist Party. However, the pro-

Bulgarian atmosphere was soon clouded by the high-handedness and mis-government of the Bulgarian occupation forces, and the local population became increasingly dissatisfied; though this did not mean that they began to question their national consciousness.

Furthermore, Tito's partisan movement, which had already made a very dynamic appearance in the region, was unable to make any progress in Yugoslav Macedonia until the autumn of 1943, when the war began to take an unpromising turn for the Axis powers. It was only then that the Yugoslav Communist Party managed to establish the Communist Party of Macedonia and to organize some degree of resistance there. To counter Bulgarian influence, Tito revived the Comintern's old watchword of a 'separate Mace-donian nation', with the aim of liberating all the people of Macedonia through the framework of a united confederation of the south Slavonic peoples, including the Bulgarians.[18]

On 29 November 1943, the Anti-fascist Council for the National Libera-tion of Yugoslavia met for the second time, in Jaice in Bosnia-Herzegovina, and decided that post-war Yugoslavia would also include Macedonia as one of its federal republics. The Yugoslav communists thus managed to reverse the trend and to force their Bulgarian comrades, who had been handling the Macedonian Question hitherto, to back down considerably and accept Tito's catalytic role as a leader.

On 2 August 1944, the first meeting of the Anti-fascist Council for the National Liberation of Macedonia[19] created the 'People's Republic of Mace-donia' in the framework of Yugoslavia's federal structure. This was the cornerstone of Tito's hegemonic plans eventually to annex the administrative areas of neighbouring Greek and Bulgarian Macedonia in the name of international communist solidarity. He even had Stalin's approval, for the Soviet dictator had already implemented a similar policy in 1940, when he had created a separate Moldavian nation to the detriment of Romania.[20] Prior to 1944, no historical source and no ethnographical map had ever mentioned the existence of a Macedonian nation. Never before had the present territory of the Former Yugoslav Republic of Macedonia, either as a state entity or as an administrative unit, borne the name 'Macedonia'. The Yugoslav area of Macedonia was to become the 'Macedonian Piedmont' for the unification of all three parts of geographical Macedonia.

Subsequently, with the civil war raging, the situation in Greece did not develop favourably for the Yugoslav plans. These included the creation of a Slavo-Macedonian 'Popular Liberation Front' and support for the Greek communist partisans. A more dynamic policy was then launched against Bulgaria with the intention of integrating Bulgarian, or Pirin, Macedonia into the People's Republic of Macedonia. By 1946 Yugoslavia had managed to secure a status of cultural autonomy for Pirin Macedonia, with the direct sanction and approval of Stalin. In fact, in August 1946 the Bulgarian

communists initially agreed to Macedonian unification, with the People's
Republic of Macedonia as the main resultant, as part of federal Yugoslavia.
They received in exchange the promise that the Soviet Union and Yugoslavia
would support the Bulgarian demand for an outlet to the Aegean at the
Paris Peace Conference.[21]

After the Bled accords between Yugoslavia and Bulgaria in August 1947,
Yugoslav infiltration of Pirin Macedonia was left at the stage already agreed
upon, namely that the area would continue to enjoy cultural independence.
The Bulgarians gained nothing from Paris, and consequently Pirin's integration into the People's Republic of Macedonia remained a desideratum. It
may in fact have been the subject of the secret protocols accompanying the
agreement, as may the question of Greek Macedonia; but the relevant
sources are not yet available to historians.

Tito's ambitions were beginning to exceed the bounds of communist
legitimacy and Stalin was obviously irritated. In February 1948, both the
Yugoslav and the Bulgarian communists were summoned to Moscow, where
the Soviet leader severely criticized and censured both the proposed federation of southern Slavs and the continuing support for the Greek partisans,
for he believed that the communists had already lost the battle in Greece.

The ensuing rupture between Tito and Stalin led to Yugoslavia's expulsion from the Cominform in June 1948, which gave Bulgaria the chance
to dissociate itself from the Yugoslav policy on the Macedonian Question.
As another result of the new developments, Bulgaria immediately put a
stop to Yugoslav–Macedonian cultural infiltration of Pirin Macedonia.

After Greece's civil war ended in 1949, a few dozen Slavonic-speakers
(the so-called Macedonians from 'Aegean Macedonia'/'Egejska Makedonija')
fled to Yugoslavia and other East European countries. A great wave of
emigration to the New World followed, between 1950 and 1970, chiefly
from the western part of Greek Macedonia, and in fact it received considerable support from the Greek state. This explains why most of the
Slavo-Macedonian and pro-Bulgarian associations in Canada, Australia, and
the United States consist of émigrés from Greek Macedonia.

The Macedonian Question in its present form (1950–93)

In the early 1950s, Tito's policy focused on two key aims: i) to cultivate
and consolidate the 'Macedonian' identity of the population of Yugoslav
Macedonia in an effort to foil the rival Bulgarian influence; and ii) to lobby
for the rights of so-called 'Macedonian' minorities in the neighbouring
countries. In fact, the latter was a fundamental feature of the period when
Tito was at the helm of Federal Yugoslavia.[22]

The keen interest shown both by Belgrade and by the local government
in Skopje in the 'Macedonian' minorities in the neighbouring countries led

to much more friction and tension between Yugoslavia and Bulgaria than between Yugoslavia and Greece. Indeed, relations between Belgrade and Athens became considerably more relaxed after Greece, Yugoslavia, and Turkey signed the Balkan Pact of 1953–4, which meant that the West would support Yugoslavia's anti-Soviet policy.

In contrast to the central government in Belgrade, the local leaders of the People's – later Socialist – Republic of Macedonia always maintained a distinctly resentful attitude towards Greece. The Macedonian part of the Greek state had inevitably become the focus of their post-war irredentist dreams. Their efforts consisted in building up all the ingredients of a solid and substantial national ideology, such as historical roots, language and church. At the same time, they also began to swell the arsenal of the 'Macedonian' national ideology with the requisite irredentist aspirations. The latter were a basic component of all Balkan national ideologies after the creation of the nation states in the nineteenth century.[23]

The republic's historians[24] sought their new 'Macedonian' irredentist dream chiefly in the historical tradition and the cultural identity of their Balkan neighbours, in an attempt to develop a 'Macedonian' consciousness in the country. This they achieved both by appropriating any and every available foreign element they could lay their hands on, and by casting doubt on the provenance of these. However, the historical myth of the unification of the whole of geographical Macedonia was vital if 'Macedonism' was to be noised abroad, particularly in the New World, where there were a great many émigrés from the whole of Macedonia.

The theory of a 'Macedonian nation' took on almost psychotic proportions in Tito's Yugoslavia and the Socialist Republic of Macedonia. Both Bulgaria and Greece refused to acknowledge the existence of a separate Macedonian nation. Bulgaria regarded the Republic's local Slavonic population as Bulgarian through and through; and charged that its identity had been deliberately Serbianized in the inter-war period, and that, after the Second World War, it had been instilled with 'Macedonian' ideology on a purely anti-Bulgarian basis. For its own part, Greece rejected the existence and artificial perpetuation of a thirteen-century-old 'Macedonian' nation, because historical sources mention only Bulgarians, or Slavs generally. It was only in the framework of post-war Yugoslavia, under the known socio-political circumstances, that 'Macedonian' ethnicity had been fabricated and encouraged; an ethnicity for 'state and administrative purposes', so to speak. The Muslims of Bosnia-Herzegovina are a similar case: the Croatian Tito's immediate aim was appreciably to reduce the antagonistic Serbs' territorial and political strength by granting certain population groups political autonomy and stressing their ethnic individuality.

The Slavonic-speaking émigrés from Macedonia not only accepted 'Macedonian irredentism', but were the basic vehicle by which the concept spread all over the world. It was chiefly thanks to these Slavonic-speaking communities abroad that world opinion was made aware of the Slavo-Macedonians' irredentist aspirations throughout the period of post-war bipolarity. In the late 1960s, indeed, strong nationalist trends began to emerge, which were often very different from the official ideology of the metropolitan centre, Skopje. This is illustrated, for instance, by the fact that, whereas the Skopje parliament did not adopt the sixteen-rayed sun of Vergina as the emblem of the republic's flag until August 1992, the symbol had already been appropriated and exploited by Australia's Slavo-Macedonian nationalistic circles as long ago as 1983.[25]

Following the constitutional reforms in Yugoslavia in 1974, Belgrade's grip on the federal republic began to weaken. Skopje immediately started to follow an independent line on the Macedonian Question, which diverged somewhat from Belgrade's official policy. Indeed, the local leaders in Skopje frequently appeared to be sweeping the federal government in Belgrade along the byways of extreme nationalism, so that Yugoslavia's bilateral relations with its Balkan neighbours took a sudden nose-dive. As a result, relations between Belgrade and Sofia were very strained between 1978 and 1982, on account of the Macedonian Question and various issues pertaining to the interpretation of Macedonian historiography.[26]

Throughout the 1980s, and until Yugoslavia disintegrated in 1991, its federal and local political cadres became dangerously vociferous in their nationalist and irredentist claims against Greece and Bulgaria. International bodies and various scholarly conferences gave Yugoslavia's representatives the chance to accuse their neighbours of violating the human rights of the 'Macedonian minorities' in Greece, Bulgaria, and Albania.

In November 1990 the first free elections were held in the Former Yugoslav Republic of Macedonia (FYROM).[27] The undisputed winner was the extremist nationalist IMRO-DPMNU (Internal Macedonian Revolutionary Organization – Democratic Party of Macedonian National Unity). Both its name and its manifesto refer directly to the organisation of the same name that was active at the end of the nineteenth century. Nor is it a coincidence that a report published by the US Department of State in 1991 describes IMRO-DPMNU as a terrorist organization modelling itself on the old IMRO.[28] Its main election poster showed the whole of the geographical region of Macedonia, accompanied by the words: 'Take Macedonia's destiny in your hands.' Its Founding Charter of 17 June 1990 explicitly emphasizes 'the need for the Macedonian people's spiritual, political, and economic unification', and states its keen interest in 'those sections of the Macedonian people who are living in servitude in Greece, Bulgaria, Serbia, and Albania'.[29] Furthermore, at the close of the party's First National Conference in Prilep (6–7 April 1991), it was resolved that 'the next conference will be held in Thessaloniki.'[30]

PROPAGANDA AND THE MACEDONIAN QUESTION

Those aspects of the FYROM's policy, both at home and abroad, which lie at the heart of the tensions with Greece, are as follows.

i) The undermining of the history of geographical Macedonia, chiefly by disputing the uninterrupted Hellenic presence and influence in the region. After the official birth of the 'Macedonian state' on 2 August 1944, its intellectual leaders launched a systematic campaign for international recognition of the 'Macedonian nation'. Their aim was twofold: first, to establish the unbroken historical continuity of the 'Macedonian nation' after the first Slavonic tribes appeared in the Macedonian region in the seventh century AD; and second, to cast doubt on or nullify the historical and cultural presence of the neighbouring peoples – the Greeks, the Serbs and the Bulgarians.

Finding themselves unable openly to appropriate the history of ancient Macedonia, the FYROM's historians then resorted to questioning the ancient Macedonians' Hellenic origin.[31] They maintained that only the ruling class accepted the domination of Hellenic culture and thought, which came from southern Greece. In the course of time, the indigenous population gradually intermingled with the Slavonic tribes that came into the region, and thus created a people of Slavonic origin, which has lived there ever since.

The outdated notion that the Macedonians were not Greek was completely demolished by the archaeological investigations and excavations in and around Vergina in the 1970s and 1980s. The fact that the ancient Macedonians used the Greek language is attested by the vast number of finds from tombs and inscriptions, all of which, without exception, bear only Greek names. One very clear illustration of the continuity of the Greek language over more than twenty-six centuries is given by a ring of the sixth century BC, which was found at Sindos and is now on display in the Archaeological Museum in Thessaloniki. It is inscribed 'ΔΩΡΟΝ' (gift),[32] a word that can be seen in any souvenir shop in Greece today. Ever since 1944, when the foundation of the People's Republic of Macedonia added an ethnic and national dimension to the purely geographical term 'Macedonia', Slavo-Macedonian historians have been doing their level best to cloud the whole issue as much as possible.

ii) The systematic cultivation of a spirit of vindication and the consequent promotion by the FYROM of territorial claims against Greece. This policy has been pursued either directly, through official statements by political leaders and declarations by local parties, or indirectly, through the circulation of historical maps of a united Macedonia and the systematic use of Slavonic names for the Greek towns, cities, and villages of northern Greece.

iii) *The constant and escalating accusations against Greece of systematic viola-*
tions of the basic human rights of the so-called 'Macedonian minority' in 'Aegean
Macedonia'. In the case of Greece in particular, the self-styled 'Macedonians' who are demanding their rights so vociferously are a handful of
known individuals.[33] It is due, in fact, to the naivety of successive Greek
governments that these people have managed every now and then to step
into the limelight and denounce to the world the Greek administration and
judiciary's policy against them. Skopje is particularly willing to promote
and disseminate their views about 'Macedonian minorities' in the Balkans.
It seizes every possible chance to make its views known through international fora (e.g. the Conference on Security and Co-operation in Europe),
scholarly conferences, exhibitions, university circles, the mass media both
at home and abroad, newspapers, periodicals, encyclopaedias, and history
and geography textbooks.

iv) *The periodical appearance and activity of Slavo-Macedonian extremist and*
paramilitary organisations, which encourage subversive activities against the
Greek state through statements, proclamations, calendars, and propaganda
leaflets. A typical example is the 'Macedonian National Liberation Army'.
It made its appearance in the 1980s, when it began sending autonomist
propaganda to the Greek authorities, embassies abroad, newspapers, and
private individuals. Its logo is a map of 'Great Macedonia' with Thessaloniki
('Solun') as its capital. The MNLA also uses a picture of Alexander the
Great or the above-mentioned map with the Statue of Liberty and an armed
'Macedonian warrior'. Clearly, these phantom freedom fighters make their
American origin obvious in order to spread the emotional appeal of Mace-
donian irredentism to as wide an audience as possible.

Greece and the Macedonian Question

In an effort to secure prospects for lasting peace and cooperation in the
wider area of the Balkans, at the meeting of the EC Foreign Ministers on
16 December 1991 Greece laid down three conditions for recognition of the
Former Yugoslav Republic of Macedonia:

— the provision of constitutional and other adequate guarantees that the
   FYROM has no territorial claims;
— the cessation of all hostile propaganda promoting territorial claims; and
— a change of name to one that carries no implication of territorial claims.

The main indicator of the FYROM's expansionist aims is its 1991 constitution, the preamble to which specifically affirms that it is based upon
'the statehood and legal traditions of the Krushevo Republic [1903] and the
historic decisions of the Anti-fascist Assembly of the People's Liberation of

Macedonia [1944]'. It was these decisions that signalled the birth of the People's Republic of Macedonia in the framework of federal Yugoslavia. They specifically proclaim the freedom and the unification of all the 'Macedonian brethren' beyond the artificially created borders of the twentieth century Balkans. If one investigates how the post-war generations in the FYROM have been educated over the past forty-seven years, it is clear that they have grown up and been instilled with the notion that only part of Macedonia has been liberated, the part that comprises the Socialist Republic. The remaining areas in Greece, Bulgaria and Albania are still unredeemed and will have to be liberated at some future date.

Throughout the post-war period, Skopje's leaders have abused the name of Macedonia to an incredible extent. They have seized every possible opportunity to turn it from a simple geographical term into the ethnic definition of a single state – a state whose chief characteristic, be it said, is the catalytic presence of ethnic, linguistic, and religious minorities, none of which can be completely identified with Slavonic culture and irredentist ideology. According to the latest census, carried out on 31 March 1991, the republic's second largest ethnic group (the Albanians) accounts for 21.1 per cent of the population, or 427,313 inhabitants out of a total of 2,033,964.[34] The Albanians' political leaders, however, vigorously dispute this and claim a figure somewhere between 35 per cent and 40 per cent. Certainly, many Albanians did not take part in the 1991 census.[35] The official census figures also include 4.79 per cent Turks, 2.73 per cent Romanies, and 2.17 per cent Serbs. Particularly since the republic of Skopje seceded from Yugoslavia, not only the Albanians, but all the other minority groups as well, have been steadily accusing the state and the administration of systematic discrimination against them.

Through a deliberate confusion of the two meanings – ethnological/ historical and geographical/administrative – of the term 'Macedonia', there has been an ongoing attempt for the past fifty years, in the heart of the Balkan Peninsula, to establish and legitimize a policy of arrogating any and every useful historical factor relating to 'Macedonism'. It is done in the name of a people's inalienable right to self-determination and its will to decide its own future.

It is inconceivable to the Greeks that the name of Macedonia should be used exclusively to designate one independent state, whose sovereign rights are confined to a single part of the broader geographical region of Macedonia. Not only would it cause confusion but, above all, the name carries clear implications of historical claims. The territory of the present 'Republic of Macedonia' does not cover the whole of geographical Macedonia; if the republic is nonetheless allowed to monopolize the whole of Macedonia and all things Macedonian, it will become a powerful destabilizing factor in the Balkans.

If the FYROM joins and is accepted by the world community under its constitutional name of the 'Republic of Macedonia', the next step will inevitably be the creation of a state entity that is a Macedonian national centre. Its primary concern will then legitimately be to elect itself the protector of the extra-territorial administrative areas of the same name in Greece and Bulgaria. If the inhabitants of Skopje's multi-ethnic republic acquire the right to define themselves as 'Macedonians' in an official context, then the Greek Macedonians will automatically lose their historical right to use the terms 'Macedonian' and 'Macedonia' to define themselves and their own geographical origin. The constitution of the 'Republic of Macedonia' actually provides for just such an eventuality; article 49§1 explicitly states: 'The Republic cares for the status and rights of those persons belonging to the Macedonian people in neighbouring countries.'

As far as the national flag of the 'Republic of Macedonia' is concerned, it consists of the emblem of the ancient Greek Macedonians, the sixteen-rayed sun, on a red field. The emblem was brought to light sixteen years ago during excavations in and around Vergina in Greek Macedonia. Since then the Vergina finds have been displayed in archaeological exhibitions all over the world as an integral part of Greece's cultural heritage. Meanwhile, the Vergina sun itself has already been adopted as a Greek cultural symbol, either as a logo or as a trademark, by countless cultural associations, scholarly institutions, banks and companies both in Greece itself and wherever Greeks live all over the world.

The decision of the FYROM's parliament in August 1992 to put a Greek cultural symbol on this multi-ethnic republic's flag was made in no sudden surge of philhellenic sentiment. Early in 1991, President Kiro Gligorov had stated that his republic laid no claim to ancient Macedonia and the ancient Macedonians; but the new flag starkly vindicated Greece's fears for present and future peace and stability on the Balkan Peninsula. In fact, it might not be very far from the truth to suggest that the FYROM put the Sun of Vergina on its flag quite deliberately in order to have a ready-made 'concession' to hand in future negotiations. To appear to give way on this point would increase the international community's sympathy and admiration for the FYROM's leaders; while the new republic would actually be 'giving back' something which even its own people never really regarded as belonging to them.

Each of these cases constitutes a cultural assault using the skilful ploys of piracy, which prove, to paraphrase a famous Chinese proverb, that 'an emblem speaks a thousand words'. Once the new state achieves recognition under its constitutional name of the 'Republic of Macedonia', it will be able to lay claim to all things Macedonian, including the history and culture of the people in the geographical area of Macedonia; and, what is more, it will be legally entitled to do so.

As a full member of both NATO and the EU, Greece is concerned above all that peace and stability be consolidated in the Balkans with absolute respect for existing national borders, which are guaranteed by international treaties and further protected by the system devised by the CSCE. Greece has repeatedly stated that it has no territorial claims against the FYROM. Indeed, it has promised assistance on several occasions, both on a bilateral level and in the framework of the EU, so long as the republic can make itself politically and economically viable.

The inhabitants of the Former Yugoslav Republic of Macedonia have the inalienable right to establish their own independent state and to define themselves as they wish. Objectively speaking, Greece is the only power in the region that can be relied upon to give the nascent republic economic and defensive support. Greece has no reason to fear its, undeniably weak, neighbour at the moment, for, alone and armed only with its irredentist dreams, the FYROM can pose no threat to Greece's territorial integrity. But what no one can control or guarantee (and this is precisely where Greece's fears lie) is the possibility that this mini-state may one day be used as a basis for claims against Greece.

After all, the whole region's history is rife with political and military interventions by non-Balkan nations: typical examples are Tsarist Russia in 1878, the Central European powers in 1917–19, the Axis powers in 1941–4, and the Soviet Union in 1946–9. As for the Balkan countries, whose sights have been set on Greece's northern provinces for years, throughout the twentieth century they have exploited the international situation and allied themselves with non-Balkan powers in repeated efforts to achieve their goal. During the First World War, Bulgaria, for instance, tried to annex the Macedonian territory of neighbouring Greece and Serbia on the strength of the Kaiser's expansionist plans, and briefly occupied parts of Greek Macedonia and Thrace. In the Second World War too, Bulgaria allied with Nazi Germany to occupy parts of Greek Macedonia and Thrace again, and also parts of Yugoslav Macedonia. Tito tried to do the same just after the Second World War, with the support of Stalin and the Soviet Union. It is these historical experiences that foster such strong emotions on the Greek side and such fears for the present, and above all the future, of Macedonia and Thrace. The Greeks will not easily forget the traumatic experiences of the twentieth century, when their country was faced so many times with the very real prospect of losing its administrative province of Macedonia. Serious attempts have been made to annex Greek Macedonia to a unified Macedonian state in the framework either of Federal Yugoslavia or of a Balkan Communist Federation under Bulgarian control.

The only precondition laid down by Greece is that the FYROM repudiate the Communist concept of 'Macedonism' and toe the EU line. It would be a dreadful irony if, in the present post-communist era, the

European Union granted a posteriori historical legitimacy to a communist idea. Furthermore, if the EU and the world community as a whole, through the UN, are anxious to recognize the 'Republic of Macedonia' in order to avert the risk of destabilization, they should be aware of the equally great risk of creating another trouble-spot in Greece. In either case, we must remember that, while voluble denials of territorial claims can be of purely momentary duration, the monopolizing of a name and/or a symbol is a claim that can last for ever.

The political developments that have taken place in relation to the Macedonian Question since 8 April 1993, when the republic joined the UN under the interim name of the 'Former Yugoslav Republic of Macedonia', have already effected a change of course. In response to obvious pressure by the US and the UN to resolve the dispute over the name, both sides (Greek and 'Macedonian') seem disposed to mend fences on a political level. Nor is it a coincidence that, after two years of vigorous disagreement within the EC/EU over recognition of the FYROM, the confrontation is at a much lower pitch today. This means that a political compromise, at least, over the republic's name and emblem is on the horizon. There are signs that the Greek side's insistence that 'Macedonia' be completely omitted from the republic's eventual official name is growing less categorical as time goes by. Various alternatives are now being presented for consideration, such as 'New Macedonia', 'Upper Macedonia', and 'Slavo-Macedonia'. On the other hand, there is also the possibility that the 'canton' solution will be accepted. The creation, for instance, of two large cantons, a Slavo-Macedonian one (for the 'Macedonian' 64.62 per cent of the population, according to the 1991 census) and an Albanian one, could mark the start of a peaceful coexistence between the republic's minorities. Besides, the Albanians are steadfastly demanding the right to official status in the new republic, something that the preamble to the 1991 constitution does not provide for: 'Macedonia is established as a national state of the Macedonian people, in which full equality as citizens and permanent coexistence with the Macedonian people is provided for Albanians, Turks, Vlachs, Romanies, and other nationalities living in the Republic of Macedonia.'

After Skopje joined the UN in April 1993 as the 'Former Yugoslav Republic of Macedonia', UN-brokered talks began between Skopje and Athens in an effort to get some confidence-building measures off the ground. These concerned the constitution, the flag, security of borders, propaganda, minority issues and of course the former republic's name. The UN Secretary-General appointed Cyrus Vance and Lord David Owen to act as special mediators and made the end of September the deadline for an agreement on all matters under negotiation. According to the, by then outgoing, New Democracy government in Greece, agreements were in fact reached on all issues apart from the name, on which latter point there had been considerable progress. Specifically, on 14 May 1993 the mediators had presented Athens and Skopje with a draft proposal that fully covered Greece's demands relating to the borders, the flag, the constitution and the irredentist propaganda, and suggested 'New Macedonia' as an acceptable name.

However, the news that early elections would be held in Greece on 10 October 1993 brought the negotiations to a standstill. And the PASOK victory created an entirely new situation, which essentially ended the talks altogether. The immediate upshot was that, just before Christmas 1993, most of the members of the EU, together with other European countries, unilaterally recognized the FYROM (under that name), leading to considerable friction with the new Greek government. It turns out that this widespread recognition was due to a number of factors, the most important being: the electoral victory of PASOK, which had been a constant target of European criticism in the 1980s too; Greece's impending presidency of the EU; Greece's pro-Serbian stance on the Yugoslav crisis; and the fact that PASOK now manifestly embraced US foreign policy over the Yugoslav crisis in general and the Macedonian Question in particular, in the hope of seeing the latter resolved to Greece's benefit.

Above and beyond the possibility and/or necessity of reaching a political compromise for the sake of peace and stability in the Balkans, the historical background to the Macedonian Question still remains very much open to investigation and will continue to occupy the attention of historians for a long time to come. No international conciliatory or political legitimization of 'Macedonism' can hope to bring about a permanent resolution of the problem. Europe is naturally anxious to minimize all the potential sources of war and ethnic strife on its broader periphery. It does not want anything to undermine its progress towards unification, and is keen to avoid the pressures of the various American interests in Eastern Europe. The conflict between European integration and the larger European nations' strategic and economic interests in the Balkans considerably limits the chances of finding a solution to the specific issue of the Macedonian Question. But this does not mean that Greece's and the other Balkan countries' progress towards Europe should provide an excuse for yet another superficial cover-up of the historical dimensions of the Macedonian Question. The conflict between the 'vital interests' of various third parties and the 'historical rights' of the Balkan peoples has always been a fact of life on the Balkan Peninsula.

NOTES AND REFERENCES

1. Concerning the Macedonian Question generally, see: Barker, E. (1950), *Macedonia: Its Place in Balkan Power Politics*, London; Kofos, E. (1964), *Nationalism and Communism in Macedonia*, Thessaloniki; Palmer, S. Jr. and King, R. (1971),

Yugoslav Communism and the Macedonian Question, Hamden; Kolishevski, L. (1979), *Aspekti na makedonskoto Prasanje* (Aspects of the Macedonian Question), Skopje.

2. When the EC was debating whether or not to recognize the Former Yugoslav Republic of Macedonia, articles in Western newspapers and periodicals adopted an openly hostile stance towards Greece's expressed position. A few examples: *Frankfurter Allgemeine Zeitung*, 25.11.91, 28.11.91, 16.3.92, 24.3.92, 9.4.92, *The Independent*, 17.3.92, *Financial Times*, 4.3.92, *Boston Globe*, 12.3.92, *Die Presse* (Vienna), 21.3.92, *Washington Post*, 16.5.92.

3. Weizsäcker, E.U. (1990), *Erdpolitik*, Darmstadt, 4–5.

4. Andriotis, N. (1991), *The Federative Republic of Skopje and its Language*, Thessaloniki.

5. Adanir, F. (1979), *Die Makedonische Frage*, Wiesbaden.

6. Perry, D. (1988), *The Politics of Terror. The Macedonian Revolutionary Movements, 1893–1903*, London.

7. Lapé, L. (1973), *The Epic of Ilinden*, Skopje.

8. Dakin, D. (1966), *The Greek Struggle in Macedonia 1897–1913*, Thessaloniki.

9. Dakin, 20 (note 63).

10. Ladas, S. (1932), *The Exchange of Minorities: Bulgaria, Greece, Turkey*, New York; Pentzopoulos, D. (1962), *The Balkan Exchange of Minorities and its Impact upon Greece*, Paris.

11. Fifty-three thousand Bulgarians left Greece and 16,000 Greeks left Bulgaria, Ladas, op. cit., 122–3.

12. Kofos, op. cit., 47.

13. Sfetas, S. (1992), *Makedonien und interbalkanische Beziehungen 1920–1924*, Munich.

14. Public Record Office, Foreign Office 371/33128, R1650/1650/7 (4 Dec. 1941), 'Bulgarian Irredentism', Study by Foreign Research and Press Service, Balliol, Oxford.

15. Sfetas, op. cit., 287–457; Papapanagiotou, A. (1992), *To makedoniko zitima kai to valkaniko kommunistiko kinima 1918–1939* (The Macedonian Question and the Balkan Communist Movement 1918–1939), Athens.

16. Kondis, B., Kentrotis, K., Sfetas, S. and Stefanides, Y. (1993), *Resurgent Irredentism. Documents on Skopje 'Macedonian' Nationalist Aspirations (1934–1992)*, Institute for Balkan Studies, Thessaloniki, 23–4 (henceforth: *Documents*).

17. *Documents*, 24-6.

18. *Documents*, 28–9.

19. The University of Cyril and Methodius/Institute for National History (1985), *Documents on the Struggle of the Macedonian People for Independence and a Nation-State*, Skopje, 429–33

20. Siupur, E. (1993), 'Von Bessarabien zur Republik Moldau – die historischen Wurzeln eines Konflikts', *Südosteuropa*, 3-4: 153–62.; *Documents*, 48–9. It is worth noting that, after 1917, the Bolsheviks had created a separate Byelorussian nation, in order to weaken Russia.

21. *Documents*, 56–7.

22. Veljanovski, N. (1992), *Drzhavnopravniot Razvoj na Makedonija* (The State and Legal Development of Macedonia), Skopje.

23. *Documents*, 60–3.

24. Dimitar Vlahov, Hristo Andonovski, Dancho Zogravski, Lazar Mojsov, Dragan Tashkovski, Slave Dimovski, Krste Bitovski, Hristo Poplazarov, Mihailo Apostolski, Todor Simovski, Ivan Katardziev, Risto Kirjazovski, Stojan Kiselinovski, Alexandar Trajanovski.

25. *Macedonia Weekly Herald* (Australia), 15.9.1983.

26. Bulgarian Academy of Sciences/Institute of History (1978), *Macedonia. Documents and Material*, Sofia; Troebst, S. (1983), *Die bulgarisch–jugoslawische Kontroverse um Makedonien 1967–1982*, Munich.

27. Timovski, B. and Stefanovski, S. (1991), *Izbori '90. Politichkite partii vo Makedonija* (Elections '90. Political Parties in Macedonia), Skopje, 6–39.

28. US Department of State (1991), *Patterns of Global Terrorism:1990*, 18.

29. Article 6 of the Foundation Charter of VMRO (1990), Skopje.

30. *Politika Express* (Belgrade), 9.4.1991.

31. Institut za Nacionalna Istorija (1969), *Istorija na Makedonskiot Narod* (History of the Macedonian Nation), Vol. I., Skopje, 79; Macedonian Academy of Sciences and Arts (1993), *Macedonia and its Relations with Greece*, Skopje, 13–14.

32. Martis, N. (1984), *The Falsification of Macedonian History*, Athens, 137.

33. Ch. Sidiropoulos, N. Tsarknias, A. Boulis, St. Anastasiades, T. Pasois, Ch. Pritskas, P. Voskopoulos. The first three in particular very frequently appear in public as representatives of the 'minority', mainly in international fora and in Australia. In the 10 October elections, Anastasios Boulis (a.k.a. Tasko Boulev) stood as an independent candidate and garnered a grand total of 369 votes.

34. Statistical Office of Macedonia (27.12.1991), Skopje, 14–15.

35. Perry, D. (1992), 'The Republic of Macedonia and the odds for Survival', *Radio Free Europe /Radio Liberty, Research Report*, 46: 12–19; Parvanov, A. (1992), 'Albanian Syndrome in the Republic of Macedonia', in Institute of Balkan Studies at the Bulgarian Academy of Sciences, *National Problems in the Balkans*, Sofia, 140–58.

6

Coping with Chaos: Turkey and the Bosnian Crisis

Philip Robins

Since 1989 Turkey has found itself at the centre of the tumultuous changes that have taken place in the international system. The Balkans has been no exception. To its west, Turkey has experienced regime change in all the former communist states, often resulting in markedly different policies being pursued towards itself, as in the case of Bulgaria. It has also experienced the disaggregation of the former Yugoslavia, resulting ultimately in a bloody war, the multiplication of small states, and, hitherto, a period of instability. Set alongside conflict in the Caucasus, the opening up of Central Asia, the Iraq crisis and its consequences, and the uncertain future of Russia, the volatility of the Balkans has transformed the context in which Turkey is located.

That Turkey should be considered a Balkans actor must be firmly asserted from the outset. The fact that it does not geographically lie in the Balkans means that those who deal with the area are often apt to omit it from their analysis. For a student of international relations, the only criterion of importance in considering the issue is whether Turkey and Turkish policy is taken seriously by the central actors in the Balkans; in other words, whether the actions and pronouncements of Turkey have an effect on the politics of the area. This chapter will establish that in the successor states to the former Yugoslavia, together with Albania, Greece and Bulgaria, this is indeed the case. This contention will be supported by historical, demographic, economic and diplomatic evidence. The overall picture to be presented will be that of Turkey as one of only two middle powers (the other being Italy), located at the periphery yet casting its shadow over a fragmented sub-system of small states.

This chapter principally seeks to explore the relationship between Turkey and the former Yugoslavia since the break-up of the latter. The emphasis is on the effects of the Yugoslav crisis on Turkey and Turkish policy, and how Ankara has developed and implemented policies on the issue. Relations between Turkey and other Balkan states will only be considered as and when relevant. A predominantly thematic rather than a chronological approach will be adopted to facilitate analysis, although all major developments will be covered. The chapter will conclude by describing the effect which the Yugoslav crisis has had on Turkish foreign policy in general.

1. THE DOMESTIC DIMENSION

A Bosnian lobby?

It is frequently asserted that Turkey has a special interest in the fate of Bosnia. When doing so, journalists and commentators often begin by invoking domestic factors in support of this contention. The three arguments most often used are demographic, confessional and historical. The first is the most tangible. Though numbers are inevitably disputed it is beyond question that many Turkish citizens today are of Balkan origin. One leading foreign writer on Turkey has estimated that as many as one fifth of a population exceeding 60 million hail from the Balkans.[1] Many of these migrated eastwards as the Ottoman Empire's Balkan presence waned. Moreover, a significant number of Turkish citizens are identified as being of specifically Bosnian extraction. Most estimates for this figure range between two and four million, though some have been prepared to put the figure as low as one million,[2] while others claiming the upper figure have estimated that, with intermarriages and their offspring, there are as many as sixteen million Turks with a direct familial link to Bosnia.

Having established that the Turkish population of Bosnian origin is a substantial one, commentators go on to assert the coherence, self-consciousness and influence of this constituency. Frequent mention is made of the existence of the Istanbul suburb of Yenibosna (New Bosnia).[3] The community of Bosnian extraction in Turkey is often described as prosperous and well-to-do. It is regarded by at least some Turkish diplomats as a well-organized constituency with influence over the political leadership of the country.[4] In the absence of systematic research on the influence of these communities, such assertions are largely intuitive and anecdotal. The nature of Turkish policy towards the Bosnian question, as will be shown, suggests either that the influence of such a constituency is vastly over-estimated, or that the constituency is a mature one, placing the interests of Turkey, soberly calculated, ahead of emotion or the nostalgia of old ties.

The factors of confession and history are more nebulous than that of demography. With regard to the former, it is simply asserted that because the overwhelming population of Turkey is Muslim it will feel sympathy for the Muslim populations of the Balkans, and in particular the Muslims of Bosnia. This view tends to distort the self-identity of Turkish elites in particular. While most Turks do not deny their religious origin and an increasing number are becoming personally devout, the ideology of secularism remains very strong. Consequently, being Turkish and secular remains a much stronger part of the identity of Turkish elites than that of being Muslim. Action is therefore not demanded in the name of Muslim solidarity. Where the confessional dimension is of importance is in the perception of the actions of the West. The West is regarded as an aggregate of Christian states that are indifferent to suffering if sustained by Muslims.[5] This is offered as a general explanation for the West's perceived lack of political will to stop the killing in Bosnia. As one Western official observed in exasperation, it is the Turks that have the 'crusades mentality'.[6]

As far as history is concerned it is often asserted that because the Balkans were once provinces of the Ottoman Empire there is a residual concern on the part of the Ottoman successor state and its citizens with the fortunes of its former domains. This may or may not be true; it is unlikely, however, that a policy could be developed and supported solely on this basis, especially in such a serious troublespot as Bosnia. Furthermore, successive governments in Ankara stretching back to the foundation of the modern Turkish state have been keen to reassure these former provinces, with varying degrees of success at different times, that Turkey does not harbour ambitions to recreate the Ottoman Empire.

Though commentators have been quick to point to domestic factors in support of Turkey's involvement in the Bosnian question there has been little evidence of this in practice. In particular, public opinion does not appear to have been openly mobilized in support of an assertive, let alone a unilateral, approach towards the issue. Indeed, there has been a marked lack of public concern beyond a general sympathy for the victims of the strife. Perhaps the best example of this was the demonstration in Taksim Square, Istanbul in February 1993, which was organized under the ambiguous slogan of 'Turks to Bosnia'.[7] In the event only some 20,000 people turned up, well below the numbers expected by the organizers. One reason posited as to why many more did not turn out was that President Ozal had tried to use the event for domestic political gain. While this is undoubtedly true, what is of key interest is that the main parties felt able to boycott the event without provoking a popular backlash over Bosnia. Moreover, Turks chose domestic party politics in preference to the Bosnian issue as the critical determinant of whether they would participate. As a result, the rally only attracted ultra-nationalists and Islamists.

A second example of the limited interest of public opinion over Bosnia was the period between January and September 1993. After an extended phase of great diplomatic activity, Turkey was virtually inert on the question during this eight-month period.[8] The fall-off in activity was in part caused by the sudden death of President Ozal, the need to choose a new head of state and the consequent need to find a new leader of the True Path Party and Prime Minister once Suleyman Demirel announced his candidacy as a replacement for Ozal. Between mid-April and the end of June Turkey was preoccupied by its own domestic politics. Once again, the political parties perceived there to be no cost in concentrating on internal politics at a time of continuing conflict in Bosnia. Moreover, there was no accumulation of public pressure to return to an active role over Bosnia once these domestic political issues were resolved. As one Turkish columnist remarked in early August: 'Bosnia has simply disappeared from the minds of the people ruling Turkey. Public opinion has forgotten the issue – or has been made to forget'.[9] It was therefore the end of the summer before Ankara resumed an active diplomatic role.

The lack of public mobilization in the Bosnian case is hardly surprising. The Turkish people rarely demonstrate strong views over foreign affairs. Responsibility for policy-making is consistently left to government elites, especially the Ministry of Foreign Affairs. Public opinion has continued to be a relatively marginal force, even since 1989. There have, however, been exceptions. The most notable is the Cyprus issue. The most recent example of public opinion being a critical factor over Cyprus was in summer 1992, when a campaign by Turkish newspaper columnists close to President Denktas[10] succeeded in relieving pressure from Ankara on the Turkish Cypriot leader for fear on the part of the Turkish government of a backlash among the Turkish public.[11] To a lesser extent, public opinion was important during the Gulf crisis of 1990–91, especially in persuading President Ozal that it would be imprudent to send a contingent of Turkish troops to be part of the multinational forces active in Operation Desert Shield in Saudi Arabia. At no time has public opinion in Turkey shown itself to be as agitated over Bosnia as it has been periodically over Cyprus. There has in turn as yet been no concerted pressure on decision-makers from the Turkish public.

Criticism and alternatives

The lack of organized public concern over Bosnia cannot be attributed either to ignorance or to the lack of alternative policy proposals. Bosnia became a subject of intense political debate in Turkey after the first two months or so of the conflict in the former Yugoslavia spreading to that republic; that is, once it was clear that the Bosnian Serbs were making spectacular gains at the expense of the Bosnian government. Subsequently, Bosnia was often the subject of intense political debate both in the Turkish press and also on television. Bosnian politicians were frequently to be seen on television in Turkey appealing for help.[12] There was no shortage of gruesome photographs displaying massacre victims in Bosnia. Fly-poster campaigns in the major cities ensured that the brutal realities of the situation were virtually unavoidable.

From May 1992 onwards, the coalition government in Turkey was criticized for aspects of its policy. Criticism came both from the coalition's major rival for power, the Motherland Party, and from the smaller parties, notably the Welfare Party, which, as an Islamist party, uniquely offers the Turkish electorate an alternative world view to the Kemalist consensus of the rest of the Turkish political parties.

The Motherland politicians critical of government policy tended to attack it for being conservative and over-cautious in style, and for lacking substance. For instance, one of the most consistently vocal critics on the matter, Kamran Inan, accused the government of a 'Wailing Wall policy', whereby Ankara's only action was to bemoan the developments in Bosnia in a multitude of foreign capitals.[13] Adnan Kahveci was another leading critic from the Motherland Party. He denounced government policy, accusing it of being 'passive and cowardly ... [and] timid'.[14] Such criticism was not, however, exclusively confined to Bosnia. In this case Bosnia was but the latest example of the new differences in approach between a traditional, cautious, Kemalist style of foreign policy, as implemented under the coalition, and the new, assertive and interventionist policy that had been developed by Turgut Ozal since the late 1980s. Indeed, Inan and the coalition were to clash again on the same basis over government policy towards Azerbaijan in spring 1993.

Criticism of coalition policy by the Welfare Party went much deeper. Islamist politicians were less concerned with issues of style than of what the matter said about the general orientation of Turkish policy. For instance, during the debate on sending Turkish troops to Somalia, Abdullatif Sener implied that Ankara was more interested in executing a US strategic plan than in intervening to end strife and starvation, and compared the positive decision with Turkish inaction on Bosnia.[15] The Welfare Party was generally much more willing to advocate the use of Turkish forces in the Bosnian conflict. For instance, the party leader, Professor Necmettin Erbakan, said that his party would form a rapid deployment force of 10,000 troops to be sent to Bosnia.[16] Otherwise, Welfare was rather short on the details of troop deployments, such as how forces would travel to Bosnia, the nature of the mission, rules of engagement and so on.

Criticism of government policy was not, however, confined to the opposition parties. Coalition performance was also the target of influential deputies from within the ruling parties. Coskun Kirca, the *de facto* leader of the nationalist right wing of the dominant True Path Party, was an early critic of the coalition. At the beginning of May 1992 Kirca criticized the government for not having taken prompter action in seeking a meeting of the UN Security Council to take steps against Serbia for attacks on Bosnian Muslims.[17]

Dissident voices were also heard in the junior coalition member, the

Social Democratic Populist Party (SHP), notably that of Mumtaz Soysal. Professor Soysal emerged in November 1991 as the alternative voice on foreign affairs in the SHP, in contrast to his fellow deputy Hikmet Cetin who was appointed foreign minister in the new coalition. Soysal had argued for a complete revision of Turkish foreign policy in the aftermath of the October 1991 election, the central planks of which would be reduced dependence on the US and the cultivation of a leadership role within the Third World. Soysal's revisionism was probably a key reason why he did not receive the foreign affairs portfolio. Soysal extended his revisionism to policy over Bosnia. By the end of 1992 he was not merely criticizing government policy but advocating a new basis for Turkey's advocacy of Bosnia-Herzegovina. He argued that because the Muslims of the Balkans were converted under the Ottoman Empire, Turkey should declare itself to be the moral protector of these communities. He underlined this view by drawing an analogy with nineteenth-century France, which had demanded a similar role for itself with regard to the Christian communities of the Levant under the Ottoman Empire.[18]

While Turkey's policies towards Bosnia were robustly attacked by many political figures during the first year of the conflict, the succeeding ten months have produced rather less rhetoric. It is therefore an irony that as the coalition has become distracted from Bosnia, by both other pressing policy questions and matters of internal politics, its critics have become similarly distracted. Those who had been most vocal on the shortcomings of Turkey's Bosnia policy seem to have accepted the very limited political gains to be made from seeking to embarrass the coalition on the issue. In other words, after twelve months of persistent criticism, the disparate opposition voices seem also to have come to terms with the fact that Bosnia is not a potent issue in Turkish domestic politics.

Managing the issue

For all the notional concern about Bosnia inside Turkey and in spite of the criticism of a range of Turkish politicians, the issue has not emerged at any time thus far to dominate the domestic political agenda. Much of the credit for this must lie with the Turkish government and the skilful way in which Ankara has set about managing a delicate issue. In doing so, it adopted a three-pronged approach. First, the Turkish government, at least in the early months of the conflict, vigorously pursued the issue in its foreign policy; the charge of apathy or lack of interest could not therefore easily be levelled against it. Second, the government organized a domestic aid effort for Bosnia, thereby showing that it was active in terms of humanitarian assistance. Third, Ankara also indicated, rhetorically at least, that it would be willing to contemplate Turkish participation in the use of force in Bosnia;

such a posture thereby helping to parry emotional calls for the immediate commitment of Turkish forces.

Section 3 of this chapter will deal in greater depth with the diplomacy of the Turkish state over the Bosnian issue. Here I wish only to emphasize that a vigorous diplomatic campaign on behalf of the government of Bosnia was an essential part of the strategy of the Turkish government to ensure that public opinion remained reasonably content with its actions on this matter. At this point it is sufficient to note two points. The Turkish government utilized every forum that provided it with a public platform at which to raise the issue. Within Western institutions like NATO, within international organizations such as the CSCE and as part of Islamic institutions, notably the Islamic Conference Organization, Turkey displayed considerable energy. The dynamism of the Turkish foreign policy establishment, led by the Foreign Ministry, helped the coalition government to shrug off the criticism of rival politicians for being cautious and ineffectual.

The second and arguably the most important element of this diplomatic strategy was that it firmly wedded Turkey to a multilateral approach. By doing so, it enabled the coalition government to argue that only through mobilizing the major powers and international institutions could effective action be taken over Bosnia. Moreover, this helped Ankara to veer away from a unilateral effort, being able to argue that it was inappropriate and indeed counter-productive, in addition to being itself of limited utility, in view of such a multilateral strategy. By the same token, Ankara was also able to argue that the apparent immobilization of these institutions was not due to the inactivity of Turkey. This, however, was a somewhat risky furrow to plough, as it inevitably came to imply that the real reason for the lack of decisive intervention was the inactivity of Turkey's closest Western allies.

In retrospect, given the way that the Bosnian tragedy has unfolded, it may seem unconvincing that the Turkish government could keep up this multilateral political alibi for a period of more than one year. However, such a view ignores a number of factors. Turkish government rhetoric was always committed to the pursuit of a solution to the Bosnian conflict; at times it did so excessively, such as in December 1992 when Hikmet Cetin declared that Bosnia was top of Turkey's list of priorities.[19] Turkey did emerge at various stages of its Bosnian diplomatic campaign with something to show for its involvement. This began with the public acknowledgement of its efforts by the Bosnian government; continued with such gestures from its Western allies as appointing a Turkish admiral to command the fleet patrolling in the Adriatic, and including Turkey as a participant in the enforcement of the no-fly zones over Bosnia-Herzegovina; and most recently has resulted in a new willingness on the part of the international mediators to recognize and utilize a role for Turkey in the peace negotiations.[20]

Turkey's humanitarian effort can be divided into two elements: direct aid to Bosnians on the ground; and the provision of sanctuary to large numbers of Bosnian refugees. Initially, the Turkish government was slow to understand the importance of the provision of aid. The coalition government was criticized in early July 1992 for being slow to send relief flights to Sarajevo. One columnist in the Turkish press stung the government by noting that even Greek planes had already resumed flights since the re-opening of the airport.[21] The initial tardiness of the Turkish government in providing aid may have had something to do with the fact that Ankara has always regarded the Western aid effort as a substitute for real political action on Bosnia. Turkey did, however, eventually implement an aid effort. By March 1993, according to Turkish Minister of State Orhan Kilercioglu, Ankara had disbursed $23 million worth of aid in Bosnia-Herzegovina;[22] $11.7 million was disbursed in the first four and a half months of 1993 alone.[23] Turkey felt frustration at the problems of distributing international aid on the ground. Consequently, Ankara backed Washington's controversial decision to use cargo planes to drop aid directly to Muslim areas cut off in eastern Bosnia, a practice which began on 28 February. Part of Turkey's aid was subsequently dispersed in this way.[24]

The Turkish authorities were rather speedier in launching their policy of giving sanctuary to Bosnian refugees. As early as April 1992, Turkey had accepted 2,000 Bosnian refugees.[25] A month later this had risen to 7,000, the bulk of whom were staying with relatives. In May formal provision began to be made for temporary housing in anticipation of the arrival of more refugees, with mayors of three cities offering to take up to 6,000 newcomers in total between them. Unlike most European countries, Turkey did not seriously attempt to put bureaucratic obstacles in the way of Bosnian refugees, which might well have elicited a backlash among Turks of Bosnian origin. By March 1993, the number of Bosnian refugees was estimated to be in excess of 200,000.[26]

It is in the third area of government action that the clever and subtle way in which the coalition managed the Bosnian issue, and even exploited it to achieve policy objectives in other domains, can best be seen. In December 1992, the government chose to approach the Turkish Grand National Assembly (TGNA), again maximizing the profile of such a move, to authorize the sending of troops to Bosnia.[27] The timing of the move, however, had less to do with the Bosnian issue than that of Somalia. The US had asked Turkey to send a contingent of troops to Mogadishu in order to expand the international base of an operation initiated in Washington. Ankara, ever keen to underline its new, post-Gulf crisis partnership with the US, needed to gain broad-based consent for a move that was generally unpopular in the country. The government chose to go to the TGNA under Article 92 of the constitution,[28] linking a vote on troops to Somalia with that of the issue of troops to Bosnia. While the vote on the latter met no opposition, there were forty-four votes cast against dispatching troops to Somalia.[29]

The fact that the government had obtained authorization for a possible troop deployment in Bosnia seemed to expand the options of the Turkish state. It also showed an apparent willingness to deploy troops in support of principle and international legitimacy. This willingness to commit troops on the ground was to contrast a few short weeks later with the determination of the new Clinton administration in the US not to post ground forces to Bosnia.

However, the reality in Turkey was rather different. The wording of the resolution passed by the TGNA stated plainly that any troop deployment would be 'To participate in the Peace Force (UNPROFOR) agreed under UN Security Council Resolution No 743'. In short, the resolution did not countenance unilateral military action. To underline the message, a report from the Turkish military was leaked to the press which concluded that because it had no refuelling capability, Turkish aircraft could only remain over the territory of former Yugoslavia for about five minutes. The Turkish military thereby ended all further speculation that its airforce could mount a military strike against Serbian positions on its own.[30]

Furthermore, the Turkish government must have known that there was almost no chance whatsoever that Turkish troops would be called upon by the UN to take part in UNPROFOR operations in Bosnia. The participation of states party to or geographically proximate to a conflict in peace operations would have been a major departure from UN precedent. The TGNA vote therefore stands up as no more than a gesture in the direction of those in the country who wanted to see Turkey playing a more assertive role in foreign affairs, including the deployment of military power, and a manoeuvre to attain support for the Somalia operation.

2. THE STRATEGIC DIMENSION

Turkish interests and the end of communism

It is strategic rather than domestic factors that most adequately explain Turkey's intense interest in the fate of former Yugoslavia, and the Balkans in general. In the changes that were taking place in the politics of eastern Europe, Turkey saw many new opportunities for advancement. Prior to the late 1980s the communist states of eastern Europe had been perceived in Ankara almost exclusively as military and ideological allies of the Soviet Union. Economic, cultural and social interaction was strictly limited. Periodic tensions were experienced, most recently with Bulgaria over President Zhivkov's assimilationist policies towards its Turkish minority. The downfall of communism in eastern Europe allowed Turkey to set aside its rigid and monolithic treatment of such countries. Bilateral relations began to flourish. Interaction broadened. Turkish entrepreneurs, both large and small, began to explore economic opportunities in former communist countries of the Balkans.

Against such a backdrop, it was almost inevitable that Turkey would become a more active player in the Balkans region.[31] Turkey took part in the conference of Balkan foreign ministers in Belgrade in February 1988. Ankara drew Bulgaria, Romania and, eventually, Greece into its Black Sea Economic Cooperation Project, a multilateral organization that was formally constituted in 1992, but which was first unveiled as an idea in the late 1980s (see Athanassopoulou, this volume). On a bilateral level, Sofia dropped its assimilationist policies, with cooperation over economic and military issues replacing the confrontation that prevailed before.[32] Turkish companies found the Romanian market particularly attractive,[33] while bilateral trade flourished; Bucharest also promised cooperation with Ankara against Turkey's armed oppositionists, the Kurdish Workers' Party (PKK) and the Kurdish organization Dev Sol.[34] Turkey expanded its relations with Albania, dispensing aid from early 1991 onwards and developing diplomatic and military ties. The rapid deepening of Turkey's ties with a number of countries that had recently experienced regime change, and whose economies were ripe for penetration, made Turkey immediately more vulnerable to charges of harbouring hegemonic ambitions, especially from those, most obviously Greece, whose relations with Turkey remained poor.

In fact Turkey has stayed wedded to the idea of the Balkans remaining stable. Such a goal is recognition of Turkey's own interests in view of the fact that its land link with Western Europe runs through the Balkans. By the early 1990s close to 50 per cent of Turkey's total trade was with the twelve states of the European Community. Most of Turkey's exports were visible goods such as textiles. They relied on land transport to reach their Western European markets. Turkey's most important land route to the EC traversed Yugoslavia. Internal stability in and access for Turkish goods through Bulgaria, Greece, Yugoslavia and (since 1991) Romania was therefore essential.

Turkey's commitment to stability in the Balkans, in other words its need for swift and secure transit routes, was underpinned by historical and ideological factors. Since the foundation of the modern state in the early 1920s, Turkey had not been a revisionist power in the Balkans. The regime changes that took place across the region in 1989 gave no reason for Turkey to reconsider this approach. At a time of political change in the region, and against a backdrop of new institutions and economies suffering massive contraction, the continuity in Turkey's approach to the Balkans was of great value. This historical continuity was buttressed by Turkey's Kemalist ideology. Mustafa Kemal Ataturk, the founder of modern Turkey and its dominant political figure for almost the first two decades of its existence, had willingly renounced all claims to the former provinces of the Ottoman Empire. Ataturk was satisfied to consolidate the new state on Anatolia and Eastern Thrace. This clear geopolitical vision continues to provide an ideological bulwark against territorial adventurism to the west of Turkey's borders.

Turkey's commitment to stability in the Balkans, combined with the innate caution of its foreign policy practitioners, led it into a knee-jerk policy reaction when the Yugoslav crisis began to emerge. Together with the US and the EC, Turkey clung on to the status quo of a unitary Yugoslav state, well after it was tenable. Perhaps Turkey found additional succour in the fact that its major Western allies also supported the policy. Once the Yugoslav army, the JNA, had moved forcibly into Slovenia on 26 June 1991 to prevent its secession, and once the fighting had spread to and intensified in Croatia soon afterwards, stability in Yugoslavia was at an end. The new spectre of Serbian expansionism had emerged to change the strategic landscape of the Balkans. The decision of the EC to recognize the independence of Slovenia and Croatia formally legitimized change in Yugoslavia. Turkey was belatedly released from its obligations to the status quo ante. Ankara was therefore free to support the independence of Bosnia-Herzegovina and Macedonia.

Four strategic concerns

Since the war in former Yugoslavia spread to Bosnia-Herzegovina the four main strategic concerns of the Turkish state have been as follows: the desire for stability; anxiety at the erosion of secularism; the fear of precedent; and the impact on regional rivalries.

i) Stability Turkey's desire for stability in the Balkans is as strong now as it was before the conflict broke out in Yugoslavia. The aim of this passion for stability is, however, different. The goal of maintaining the status quo has been replaced by the twin objectives of ending the conflict in Bosnia-Herzegovina, and ensuring that that conflict does not spread to other entities, especially Macedonia. As a territorially non-revisionist power with important economic ties with Western Europe, Turkey has nothing to gain and much to lose from war in the Balkans. With a bloody insurgency taking place in south-eastern Turkey and perennial problems with its neighbours to the north-east and south-east, Ankara would not welcome additional or protracted conflict close to its Balkan borders.

The spread of conflict to Macedonia would be particularly alarming for Turkey. First, it would mark the geographical spread of the conflict in the direction of Turkey, especially in view of the fact that both Greece and

Bulgaria, Turkey's two Balkan neighbours, have potentially explosive relations with Macedonia. Second, were Macedonian Slavs and Albanians to be pitted against each other, which appears to be the most likely scenario for domestic conflict in the republic, Turkey would be in a position of great discomfort. Were the resultant tensions between Macedonia and Albania, arguably Turkey's closest friends in the Balkans, to spill over into conflict, Ankara would be left with some difficult choices to make. Third, the involvement of Macedonia's neighbours (and any combination of Albania, Bulgaria, Greece and Serbia could become drawn in) would offer the prospect of territorial revisionism affecting those Balkan states outside the former Yugoslavia. Turkey in turn could find itself sucked into a generalized Balkans conflagration.

Turkey also wants to see the fighting stop in Bosnia-Herzegovina, but not at any price. Ankara has stated that it is prepared to accept a compromise settlement in the republic provided that it is acceptable to the Bosnian government. In view of the fact that the Bosnian Muslims have suffered most from the civil war and that, from autumn 1993, they began to make limited territorial gains at the expense of the Bosnian Croats, it is less likely that the Bosnian government is going to accept a compromise that enshrines the current division of land, even with minor amendments. In spite of its strong desire to see an end to the fighting, Ankara has adopted such a course because of its perceived need to bolster the Bosnian government as a secularist, non-confessional entity.

ii) Secularist governance   Turkey enjoyed good relations with the Bosnian federal government before the secession of the republic from Yugoslavia. When, for instance, Bosnia was in desperate need of emergency supplies of oil and humanitarian aid it was to Ankara that the Bosnian Vice-Premier, Muhamed Cengic, flew in November 1991.[35] The Bosnian government also approached Turkey to plead its case within NATO and to the EC.[36] The Bosnian Foreign Minister, Haris Silajdzic, canvassed support for the recognition of Bosnia-Herzegovina in Ankara in advance of its declaration by Sarajevo.[37] Turkey responded to such representations by being the second state, after Bulgaria, to recognize the independence of Bosnia, as well as the three other former Yugoslav republics, on 6 February 1992. Once the conflict had spread to Bosnia, the Sarajevo government continued to look to Turkey for advice and advocacy.

In working closely with the Bosnian government, Ankara has been pleased to give support to a state that it identifies as closely resembling itself; that is a secular government in a country predominantly made up of Muslims. In particular, the Turkish government has been gratified at its relationship with President Alija Izetbegovic. In the early 1970s, as an opponent of communism, Izetbegovic was a political figure who couched his opposition in terms of Islam. By the early 1990s he had become essentially a secular politician leading a non-confessional state. For Turkey, Izetbegovic represents one of the great secularist conversions.[38]

Turkey has been concerned at the effect that the battlefield victories of the Bosnian Serbs might have on the Bosnian government. Ankara fears that the lack of political and military success might result in the discrediting of secularism and moderation. Turkish officials have long worried about the fall of the secular administration in Sarajevo and the Islamization of Bosnian politics. In autumn 1993, with the devaluation of inter-confessional ties and the growing importance of the Muslim assembly in Bosnia, some of Turkey's worst fears looked as if they might soon be realized. This steady undermining of the secularism of the Bosnian government has taken place at a time when the other secularist Muslim regimes most closely allied to Turkey were looking increasingly embattled. Azerbaijan sustained a string of defeats at the hands of the Armenians in spring and summer 1993; this resulted in the ousting of the most Kemalist of Azerbaijan's aspiring leaders, Abulfez Elcibey. In the Turkish Republic of Northern Cyprus President Raouf Denktas was coming under increased pressure to make concessions over the future of Cyprus; pressure that in 1993 brought him into greater friction with his domestic opposition. With the movement of political Islam growing in the Arab World and as entrenched as ever in Iran, for Turkey the erosion of the position of its secular Muslim friends is a perplexing sight.

iii) Precedent   When Iraq invaded Kuwait in August 1990, one of the most powerful arguments in favour of reversing the occupation was that a deeply undesirable precedent for inter-state relations in the post-Cold War era should not be created. The Turkish authorities are unanimous in being concerned that the Bosnian situation will likewise create an undesirable precedent. The difference between the two examples is that while the Iraqi invasion was reversed, and the erring state punished materially in the process, the Bosnian situation has not been rolled back. From the perspective of Ankara, a powerful precedent now exists for the grabbing of territory and the virtual annihilation of a territorial state recognized by the United Nations.

For Turkey, the guilty actor over Bosnia is the state of Serbia and its leader, President Slobodan Milosevic. Serbia has been officially labelled as guilty of 'expansionism'; it is held responsible for the 'inhuman acts' against Bosnian Muslims; Serbian officials are held to be 'directly responsible for the events in Bosnia-Herzegovina'.[39] In so doing, Ankara dismisses the notion that the Bosnian conflict is essentially a civil war. It believes that the Bosnian Serbs would not have been able to sustain their war effort without significant and continuing assistance from the state of Serbia.

As far as Turkey is concerned, the dangers inherent in the Bosnian model have already become manifest. Ankara regards the upsurge in the war in and around Nagorno-Karabakh as a direct result of the precedent set in Bosnia. Armenia is perceived as having observed that Serbia has been able to launch and succeed in its expansionist plans. The sanctions against Serbia, which amount to little more than an oft-violated economic embargo, are viewed as being an insufficient deterrent to states such as Armenia. Consequently, the Turks believe, Armenia decided to launch its military campaign not only to secure the whole of Karabakh with linking corridors to Armenia, but to take control of large swathes of Azerbaijani territory. In the wake of Azerbaijan's military weakness, no international check was brought to bear on Yerevan and Armenia emerged without even the economic sanctions imposed against Serbia. According to such an analysis, Ankara similarly dismisses the ability of Azerbaijan's Armenian population in Karabakh to launch and execute such a plan independent of Armenia.

From a Turkish point of view, the prospect of rewarding Serbian aggression by recognizing its control of a disproportionate part of Bosnia-Herzegovina, as prescribed for instance under the Vance–Owen Plan, will make it even harder to dislodge Armenian fighters from Azerbaijani territory. The greater proximity of the conflict in the Caucasus to Turkey, and the potential importance of Azerbaijan as a Turkic ally, make the Karabakh situation of much greater strategic importance to Ankara than that of Bosnia. There must also be the possibility that the Bosnian model will act as an incentive to other states and leaders to use military means to realize their ambitions. The Bosnian example could yet inspire similar actions elsewhere in the Balkans and the Caucasus, or perhaps in the Middle East or Central Asia. In any of these cases such conflict would be taking place in regions where Turkey claims important interests.

iv) Regional rivalries The breakup of Yugoslavia and the war in Bosnia have taken place against a background of old and emerging rivalries in the Balkans. Prior to 1989, Turkey's primary adversary and competitor was Greece, notwithstanding the fact that both countries are formally allies within NATO. This tension manifests itself over such issues as Cyprus, the Aegean, the treatment of minorities and the fear of expansionist designs. Since the end of the Cold War, Athens has become alarmed at the fact that Ankara is taking a greater interest in the Balkans. Greece regards Turkish success in building relations with Albania, Bosnia and Macedonia as an attempt to surround and hence intimidate it. Ankara's further success in improving relations with Romania and Bulgaria is perceived as part of a strategy to isolate Greece. To help stave off such developments, Athens has sought good relations with Serbia.

Since 1989 new tensions have emerged between Turkey and other powers with a direct bearing on the Balkans. Relations between Ankara and Belgrade have been deteriorating since 1990, and acutely so since January 1992, when President Milosevic visited Ankara in a vain effort to dissuade Turkey from bestowing recognition on four of the republics of Yugoslavia.[40] Reference has already been made to the degree of responsibility that Turkey ascribes to Serbia for the conflict in Bosnia-Herzegovina.

Relations have also become difficult between Turkey and Russia since the dissolution of the Soviet Union at the end of 1991. Prior to the end of communism, the two states were in rival ideological and military blocs with their bilateral relations subsumed under the broader strategic considerations of East–West relations. Since the end of this primary cleavage, the particular interests of the two states have come to the fore, resulting in the emergence of a series of bilateral tensions. Turkey has perceived economic and strategic opportunities in Central Asia and the Caucasus which Russia has viewed as a threat to its national interest. These frictions have been exacerbated by renewed differences over access through the Straits and different perceptions over the conflict in former Yugoslavia. While Russia has been sympathetic to Serbia, Turkey has developed improved relations with the Muslim states of the region. In Russia historical resonances of a traditional rivalry with the Muslim, principally the Ottoman, south have re-emerged. Turkey has in turn increasingly perceived ties of confessional solidarity based on the Orthodox Christian faith emerging among Greece, Russia and Serbia.

The presence of this complex cocktail of historical suspicions and antipathies permeates contemporary problems in the Balkans like the war in Bosnia. It affects perceptions on all sides towards the conflict. Regional rivalries time and again affect policies of individual states towards the conflict. The most public example of this in Turkish policy was the convening of the Istanbul conference on 25 November 1992. Nominally, the conference was presented as being a contribution to the London Conference process, aimed at delivering a message from the region that the international community should do more to end the bloodshed.[41] In practice, the conference ended up as a crude manoeuvre to isolate Serbia and Greece, both of which boycotted the gathering.[42] The convening of the conference proceeded despite the 'strong doubts' of some of Turkey's allies,[43] and was attended by neither of the two international peace envoys, Cyrus Vance and Lord Owen.

3. THE DIPLOMATIC DIMENSION

Having discussed the Bosnian question as a domestic and strategic issue, it is time to look at Turkish foreign policy in practice. This third section will therefore look at Turkish diplomacy towards the Bosnian issue. For purposes of analysis, this section will be divided into four, which, I would contend, reflect the four phases thus far of Turkish foreign policy towards the issue.

The four phases would cast Turkey as: a reluctant actor; a vigorous advocate; a more or less passive bystander; and a mediator.

Turkey as reluctant actor, 1923[44]–April 1992

Earlier on in this chapter reference was made to the fact that from the foundation of the modern state, Turkey renounced claims over the Ottoman provinces of the Balkans. This ultimate act of disengagement was later followed by relatively little interaction between Turkey and the Balkans during the era of communism. Though Turkey's involvement with the Balkans grew quickly with the collapse of communism, it remained, politically, a reluctant actor in the region.

Even as the cohesion of the Yugoslav state began to weaken, Turkey maintained regular relations with Belgrade. Bilateral cooperation was emphasized. Turkey remained fully committed to the protection of the unity and the territorial integrity of Yugoslavia.[45] Frequent bilateral official visits took place. The relationship was at its most auspicious during this difficult period in April 1991, when the chairman of the Presidential Council of Yugoslavia, Borisav Jovic, visited Turkey as the official guest of President Ozal.[46] Jovic referred to 'the desire of the hosts that Yugoslavia should remain a united country'; Turkey proposed that Yugoslavia should be included in the development projects of the Black Sea Economic Cooperation Project; both sides stated that there was no issue between them that could not be resolved peacefully.[47] Controversial in addition to cooperative subjects were also discussed at such meetings. For instance, during the visit to Turkey of the Yugoslav Foreign Minister, Budimir Loncar, in August 1990 the issue of national minorities was addressed; the resulting communiqué rather unrealistically stated that such minorities should be the means to create greater trust, rather than suspicion, in the Balkans.[48]

The two sides were, however, plainly less ill at ease when discussing economic issues. The broadening of economic ties was a non-controversial area into which both parties could channel their desire for good relations. It therefore featured prominently during all such visits between 1990 and 1992. Many of the agreements signed on broader economic matters showed the importance of Yugoslavia for Turkey in its transport and communications strategy. For instance, when the joint economic commission met in July 1990, it ended up by clinching accords on air, rail and road transport matters. As part of the mutual expectation of intensified transport cooperation, the use of Yugoslav rail and road networks by services from Turkey was predicted to rise by 75 per cent and 25 per cent respectively.[49] Contracts were also signed to boost bilateral trade. As late as January 1992 Turkey took delivery of the first consignment of municipal buses from a firm in Belgrade.[50]

In spite of the general reluctance of Turkey to get involved in the

Yugoslav question, Ankara was clearly seen as an important player by the various parties to the problem. As senior members of the Yugoslav state visited the Turkish capital to try to maintain Ankara's support for the union, so did top officials from some of the constituent republics lobby for their own interests. Throughout this process, Turkey remained subject to the diplomacy of others, rather than acting as an initiator. Senior figures from Bosnia-Herzegovina were the first from the individual republics to see the utility of a link with Turkey. Against a backdrop of full scale war in Croatia, Bosnian Vice-Premier Muhamed Cengic paid a one-day private visit to Turkey in November 1991 to discuss the possibility of oil and humanitarian deliveries from Turkey. The beginning of such a relationship clearly alarmed Belgrade, as Tanjug, the official news agency, tried to embarrass Turkey by attributing inflammatory remarks to Cengic, which he vehemently denied, about Germany and Christianity.[51] The fact that Belgrade was unsuccessful in this tactic was revealed a month later when Cengic visited Turkey for twelve days to discuss a variety of different types of cooperation. He concluded the trip by describing Turkey as 'our primary partner' in the future.[52]

Macedonia also invoked the friendship of Turkey. President Gligorov of Macedonia paid a three-day official visit to Turkey as early as July 1991. He was keen to obtain Turkish support as insurance against the disintegration of Yugoslavia. His visit appears to have been a considerable success. The Turkish press, whether accurately or not, quoted officials in Ankara as saying that 'Turkey will protect Macedonia from the countries which would threaten it'.[53] This emerging relationship was further consolidated by a visit from the Macedonian Minister for Foreign Relations, Denko Malevski, in October. He was confidently able to assert that the two entities held 'identical stands on how to deal with the crisis in Yugoslavia'. In particular, he seemed to have won the Turkish Foreign Ministry over to the idea that Yugoslavia should be reconstituted as an alliance of sovereign states.[54]

Though Turkish diplomacy was generally reticent during this period, the one exception was over the question of recognition. While the EC in particular adopted a piecemeal approach to the issue of recognition, the earlier representations of the Bosnian and Macedonian governments to Ankara seem to have paid off; Turkish policy was clearly to treat the constituent republics of Yugoslavia as a whole. By January 1992 the Turkish Prime Minister, Suleyman Demirel, was able to tell the Croatian foreign minister that 'Turkey will not recognize Yugoslav republics individually but in a package'.[55] Thus, while the EC gave full recognition to Croatia on 15 January 1992, but to Bosnia-Herzegovina as late as 7 April, Turkey recognized all four republics on 6 February. However, although the decision of Ankara to recognize the four together reflects an emerging special relationship between Turkey and the governments in Skopje and Sarajevo, the timing of the move reflected the inherent conservatism of Turkey. Ankara was unwilling to run ahead of the EC or the USA in formalizing the breakup of Yugoslavia.

Furthermore, it should be noted that neither recognition nor the outbreak of fighting in Bosnia immediately changed the reticence of the Turkish diplomatic approach. When Muhamed Cengic tried to use his relationship with Turkey to bring in Ankara as a mediator and as an advocate on the Bosnian government's behalf with the USA and France, Turkey's response was disappointing. Ankara responded by sending a fact-finding mission to Belgrade under a Foreign Ministry official. The ministry was reluctant to adopt a new policy until the mission had returned.[56] It was nearly a week later before the first stirrings of Turkey's activist diplomatic engagement began with Foreign Minister Cetin raising the Bosnian issue at the UN, the Conference on Security and Cooperation in Europe (CSCE) and the Islamic Conference Organization (ICO). Even then, Ankara seemed slow to engage diplomatically, with Cetin announcing that only 'if necessary' would Turkey back its 'verbal efforts with written applications'.[57]

Turkey as vigorous advocate, May 1992–January 1993

Section 1 of this chapter showed that the Turkish government was partly galvanized into diplomatic action on behalf of Bosnia in order more effectively to manage the issue at a domestic level. Section 2 stated that strategic calculation on the part of the country's foreign policy elite was an important factor in Turkey's advocacy of the cause of the Bosnian government. After a slow start, by the beginning of May 1992, Turkey was an energetic actor in support of Bosnia within the multinational machinery of which it was a part. For instance, at one point in December 1992 Cetin managed to address the CSCE, the conference on Yugoslavia at Geneva and a NATO Council of Ministers meeting, all in the space of less than three days. Increasingly, however, this period became one of disillusionment as Turkey's allies politely, even sympathetically, heard the passion with which Ankara argued its case only to turn their backs on the sort of substantive action being proposed.

During the first three months of this phase Turkey seemed to find some satisfaction in the international community. Nowhere was this more evident than in Turkey's attitude to the work of the United Nations. For example, Turkey expressed itself satisfied with the chairmanship statement after the Security Council meeting of 24 April, which called for the immediate cessation of the fighting.[58] A truce was signed on 5 May between the Bosnian presidency and the JNA. Though the fighting quickly re-erupted, Turkey welcomed the tougher approach of the international community as the UN introduced sanctions against Serbia and Montenegro on 30 May. May also saw the UN commence its relief missions for Sarajevo. At this time Ankara recalled its ambassador from Belgrade, representing the complete breakdown of what had been for many months a worsening diplomatic relationship with Serbia.[59]

As the fighting intensified, as stories about the displacement of populations and the existence of prisoner camps emerged, and the international community was completely unable to make any brokered ceasefire stick, Turkey became more frustrated with the international diplomatic process. This exasperation helped encourage Turkey to move from supporting the initiatives of others to launching its own integrated plan. Consequently, on 7 August the Turkish government submitted an 'Action Plan for Bosnia Herzegovina' to the Security Council.[60] The plan clearly identified the Bosnian Serb militia, supported by Serbia, as being responsible for the continued conflict. It demanded that Belgrade cease helping the Serb militia. By also stating that the attacks in Bosnia should be considered crimes against humanity, the plan ensured that the perpetrators had no inducement to conform to it. The Action Plan included a major role for international agencies, insisting that the Red Cross should take over Serb-run prison camps and that the UN assume control over the region. Finally, it imposed a deadline on the Serbs to be followed by military action in the form of air raids on the militia and even against Serbia itself if the fighting did not cease within two weeks. From this point onwards, while Ankara remained committed to working within the machinery of the international community, its policy prescriptions became increasingly divorced from the sort of measures that the major external actors were willing to contemplate.[61]

The Action Plan has proved to be Turkey's major diplomatic initiative on Bosnia-Herzegovina. At the London Conference on Yugoslavia, which began on 26 August 1992, Cetin circulated the Action Plan as a conference document.[62] Indeed, as far as the Turks were concerned the plan still appeared to be on the table the following January.[63] But already by the time of the London Conference Turkey's mounting frustrations appeared to have hardened its line. Cetin thus went beyond the Action Plan in his statement to the conference. In particular, he stated that all territory occupied as a result of the conflict should be given up. Furthermore, he maintained that all those who had been expelled should be allowed to return to their own homes.[64] Though this may have been a laudable statement of principle, it completely ignored both the realities on the ground in Bosnia and the politics surrounding the conflict. It is therefore hardly surprising that the subsequent attempts on the part of the international mediators to broker a peace were at great variance with such positions, as Lord Owen and his successive UN-appointed partners addressed reality rather than principle.

The substance of Cetin's speech to the London Conference proved to be but the first of a number of public manifestations of Turkish frustrations with the Western-dominated international diplomatic machinery. The staging of the Balkan Conference in Istanbul on 25 November, apparently against or without the advice of the USA, was a second notable instance. A third example was Turkey's greater diplomatic activity within the Islamic Conference Organization towards the end of 1992 and in early 1993. Turkey tried to use the emergency meeting of the ICO in Senegal in January to hinder the Vance–Owen Plan, which had been unveiled less than ten days before. The vigour with which Ankara pursued the matter at the ICO, of which at the time it held the presidency,[65] was, nevertheless, a shrewd move: it prevented Islamist ideological rivals such as Iran from charging Turkey with being soft on the Bosnian issue because of its strategic alliance with the West. Ironically, it also raised Turkey's importance in Western strategic calculations, as Ankara was viewed as an effective block against the adoption of embarrassing resolutions.

With Ankara's plan for limited intervention clearly moribund, in autumn 1992 Turkey switched tack. The Turkish government now began to argue that, in the absence of military help from the international community, the Bosnian state should not be deprived of the right to self-defence.[66] Indeed, by mid-October Ankara had decided to concentrate its diplomatic efforts on trying to get the UN arms embargo, which hitherto had been applied on all parties to the conflict, revoked in the case of the Bosnian government.[67] By December, Turkey had formulated a simple trinity of demands: for the lifting of the arms embargo; the establishment of safe havens; and limited military intervention.[68] But while Turkey's allies in the West continued to listen to the pleas of Turkish politicians and officials with respect, Turkey remained singularly unable to realize any of its central goals.

Turkey as passive bystander, January 1993–September 1993

The death of President Ozal and the domestic party political turmoil that resulted in Turkey was clearly a major factor in distracting senior figures from the Bosnian question. The loss of Ozal in particular was important. Turgut Ozal had been a prominent advocate for Bosnia during the ICO meeting in Senegal. Ozal had even flown President Izetbegovic to Dakar in his private jet. Furthermore, Ozal had undertaken a controversial visit to the Balkans, including Macedonia and Albania on his itinerary, a matter of just two months before his death. Some reports quoted his enemies as saying that Ozal now saw himself as a 'Balkans crusader'.[69] Though Ozal was by this time on the margins of political power in Turkey, a position that was clearly visible through his increasingly unpredictable actions, Ozal did still have the ability to influence the political agenda. His demise meant that there was virtually no-one left of sufficient stature in Turkey capable of projecting the issue back before the public eye.

The death of Ozal and the period of introspection that followed should not, however, obscure the fact that Turkey by April 1993 had already become a bystander as far as the Bosnian issue was concerned. By January, after months of 'intense lobbying',[70] Ankara had not made any real diplomatic headway. Disillusionment with the West was deepening. For instance, incredulity was expressed at the fact that the Security Council was prepared to give the Serbs thirty days to comply with its no-fly resolution.[71] On 2 January the Vance–Owen Plan, which Ankara profoundly objected to on the grounds that it legitimized the seizure of territory by the Bosnian Serbs, was unveiled by its two sponsors. By the end of January, with the Vance–Owen Plan now dominating the peace process, it had become clear that Turkey was effectively a spectator to the conflict.[72]

The realization that Turkey had been confined to the margins of influence appeared ultimately to have a corrosive effect on the morale of the Turkish diplomatic elite. This perhaps explains why senior Foreign Ministry officials seemed to run out of steam as their political masters became side-tracked by the political vacuum created by the death of Ozal. If a serious loss of morale was indeed significant in subduing the diplomatic activity of the Turkish Foreign Ministry, it appears to have had two additional factors. First, the killing of the Bosnian deputy premier, Hakija Turajlic, in Sarajevo by Bosnian Serbs, moments after seeing off a Turkish Minister of State, Orhan Kilercioglu, in January. Second, the failure of the new American President, Bill Clinton, once in office, to deliver on the interventionist words he uttered during the election campaign. Once Clinton had dropped his plans for intervention in Bosnia following a diplomatic fiasco, there was no longer any realistic chance that the aspirations outlined in the Action Plan and during Cetin's speech to the London Conference would be implemented.

As a result of Turkey's consequent diplomatic inertia, there were only two developments of note regarding Turkey and Bosnia during this period. The first, in April, was the NATO decision that the Turkish air force should participate in the enforcement of the no-fly zone. Eighteen Turkish F-16s subsequently flew to Vicenza in Italy to be part of 'Operation Clear Skies'.[73] However, this was in reality nothing more than a formal gesture towards Turkey on the part of its Western allies, as Turkish planes remained part of a second group of NATO countries with their aircraft on permanent standby. Turkey had been put on 'the team sheet', but, due to its geographical proximity and controversial profile in the Balkans, it had little chance of taking the field.[74] The second was a decision by the ICO to send a delegation of foreign ministers to major international capitals to lobby on behalf of the Bosnian government. This ultimately ceremonial gesture did not even achieve the symbolic success of the inclusion of Turkish aircraft in Operation Clear Skies.

Turkey as mediator, September 1993-

Turkey emerged from its prolonged period of *de facto* disengagement from the Bosnian question apparently purged of its maximalist inclinations. Instead, Ankara appeared to adopt a much more modest strategy. Rather than forlornly appealing for the international community to take sweeping action over Bosnia, the efforts of Ankara appeared to be more focused on specific and limited diplomatic aims. Foremost among these was the objective of reforging the anti-Serb alliance of the Bosnian government and the Croats and, as a necessary precursor of this, bringing an end to the fighting between Bosnian Muslims and Croats. The seeds of this role were planted with the visit to Ankara of President Franjo Tudjman at the end of April. As a result, a joint governmental goodwill mission was put together and dispatched to Bosnia. Though the Tudjman visit made little substantive difference, it was of important symbolic value. Croatia had acknowledged that Turkey was a major regional player, and one with which Zagreb was eager to strike up good relations. Turkey had therefore established the credibility necessary to begin a mediation effort.

It was, however, to be some months before Turkey emerged as an important mediator. In fact it was not until mid-September that Turkey took on a role as active mediator in the Bosnian Muslim–Croat fighting. Interestingly, Ankara did not take the initiative, but only responded following the urging of both the Bosnian and Croatian governments. When Cetin paid a lightning visit to Zagreb in September, he was keen to make the point that his involvement was only at the invitation of the Bosnian and Croatian governments.[75] The fact that Turkey was a reluctant mediator may have reassured Croatia that Turkey did not have a political prescription that it would seek to thrust upon the Croats. The recent battlefield reverses for the Bosnian Croats at the hands of government forces gave the Croats an extra incentive to accept Turkey's good offices. Nevertheless, when Cetin declared that Turkey 'did not intend to impose its views on anyone' both parties (though of course not the Serbs) appeared to accept such a statement at face value.[76]

Ankara's approach to the mediation effort began by drawing attention to the futility of the Croat–Muslim fighting, when the strategic enemy of both sides continued to be the Serbs. This view appeared to be more a function of Ankara's antipathy towards Belgrade than a realistic appraisal of the Croat–Muslim conflict. It was because the Bosnian Croats were weaker than the Serbs and continued to occupy a disproportionate amount of territory that the Bosnian government forces, now better trained and stiffened by mercenaries, turned their guns on them. Despite this apparently flawed analysis, Ankara did seem to play a useful role in exploring the boundaries of a potential compromise between the two new warring parties.

For example, Turkey took up the Bosnian demand for an outlet to the Adriatic Sea with Croatia.[77] The practical usefulness seemed to re-invigorate Turkey's foreign policy-makers, and three months later Ankara was still active in painstakingly trying to bring the two parties closer together.

The role played by Turkey immediately boosted Ankara's credibility on a wider plane. The two international mediators were the first to appreciate Turkey's new, more practical involvement. Thorvald Stoltenberg and Lord Owen were quoted as saying that Turkey was 'playing a key role in seeking a rapprochement between Bosnia's warring Muslims and Croats'.[78] This in turn led some Western countries to consider a Turkish role in Bosnian peace-making. Following a Turkish–EC Association Council meeting in Brussels on 8 November, Turkey was asked by some EC foreign ministers to explain the details of a Franco-German peace proposal for ending the fighting to the Bosnian government.[79] Such a request is symptomatic of the fact that many Western diplomats believe that Turkey might have an important role to play in achieving a comprehensive peace settlement. However, there are also clear limitations to any Turkish role. Ankara has no potential whatsoever for interceding with Serbia. Turkey's role with the Bosnian government is only likely to be of limited utility; Ankara's influence with Sarajevo would probably only be critical if a comprehensive deal was close at hand.[80]

CONCLUSION

The outbreak of a new conflict in the Balkans has, as was the case with earlier crises, not left the world untouched. The difference with this particular war in Bosnia-Herzegovina is that it has not drawn outside powers into a wider conflict; the world has learnt to live with slaughter in Bosnia. The same is true with regard to Turkey. Turks have been appalled at the killing in Bosnia, even to the point of perceiving dark conspiracies to be at work. Turkey certainly has good reasons for wanting an end to conflict in Bosnia, based on *raison d'état* as much as humanitarian sentiment. The impact of the Bosnian crisis on Turkish public opinion and hence on policy has, however, been consistently over-estimated. As with much of the rest of Europe, Turkey has been able to live with the consequences of the fighting on the ground. At no time during the conflict have some of the basic tenets of Turkish foreign policy – from its Western orientation, to its commitment to multilateralism to its distrust of foreign adventures – come anywhere close to being overturned.

More broadly, the events of the last three years in what was Yugoslavia have shown that Turkey is a Balkan power. Ankara considers that it has interests in the Balkans; Balkan states, and entities that aspire to statehood, consider Turkey to be an important potential ally or obstacle to their ambitions. While the events in Bosnia are important for Turkey, the real centres of gravity for Turkish interests in the region are to be found further to the south and east. It is Albania and Macedonia that Turkey has identified as being the most strategically important states in the region. It is with Romania and Bulgaria that bilateral relations have improved most rapidly. It is Greece that is regarded as the old, unreconstructed rival; Serbia that is viewed as the new threat to order. Should the present conflict cease to be contained in Croatia and Bosnia, and spread down through the Balkans, Turkey would very quickly find itself much more directly affected than has hitherto been the case.

NOTES AND REFERENCES

1. Andrew Finkle in *The Times*, 12 December 1992.

2. Interview with a senior Turkish official, 17 September 1992.

3. For example see *Turkey Confidential* No. 26, February 1992, 10.

4. Interview with senior Turkish diplomat, 23 November 1993.

5. *Turkey Confidential* No. 31, September 1992, 12.

6. Interview with senior Western diplomat, 19 November 1993.

7. See *Turkish Probe* Vol. 2 No.14, 16 February 1993.

8. An article entitled 'Turkey Back in the Bosnia Equation' refers to 'an absence of nearly five months from the diplomatic scene'. See *Turkish Probe* Vol. 4, No. 44, 21 September 1993.

9. Cengiz Candar in *Sabah*, 1 August 1993, reprinted in *Turkish Daily News* (*TDN*), 2 August 1993.

10. The most notable was Mumtaz Soysal; see his columns in *Hurriyet*, for example 24 July 1992 and 8 August 1992. Others included Professor Erol Manisali, for instance writing in *TDN*, 27 July 1992.

11. The Turkish government appeared to put considerable pressure on Denktas at the instigation of the US to accept a 'non-map' of the island under a peace plan put forward by UN Secretary-General Boutros Boutros-Ghali.

12. Kemal Kirisci, 'New Patterns of Turkish Foreign Policy Behaviour', unpublished paper presented at conference on 'Change in Modern Turkey: Politics, Economy, Society' at University of Manchester, 5–6 May 1993, 15.

13. *TDN*, 1 December 1992.

14. *TDN*, 28 July 1992.

15. British Broadcasting Corporation, Short Wave Broadcasts, Middle East (henceforth BBC/SWB/ME), 11 December 1992.

16. *TDN*, 18 February 1993.

17. *TDN*, 9 May 1992.

18. See *Financial Times*, 11 January 1993.

19. *TDN*, 22 December 1992.

20. For example, note the visit to Turkey of Lord Owen and Thorvald Stoltenberg 'as it emerged that Ankara is playing a key role in seeking a rapprochement between Bosnia's warring Muslims and Croats', *Guardian*, 16 September 1993.

21. Mehmet Ali Birand in *Sabah*, 7 July 1992, reprinted in *TDN*, 8 July 1992.

22. BBC/SWB/ME, 29 March 1993.
23. *TDN*, 17 May 1993.
24. *TDN*, 11 March 1993.
25. *TDN*, 27 April 1992.
26. BBC/SWB/ME, 29 March 1993.
27. See *Newspot* No. 92/25, 17 December 1992.
28. This states that: 'The power to authorise the ... send[ing of] Turkish Armed Forces to foreign countries ... is vested in the Turkish Grand National Assembly'.
29. BBC/SWB/ME, 10 December 1992.
30. *Turkish Probe* Vol. 1 No. 5, 15 December 1992.
31. For a recent discussion of Turkey's new relationship with the Balkans, see Gareth Winrow, *Where East Meets West: Turkey and the Balkans* (Institute for European Defence & Strategic Studies, London) 1993.
32. On 6 May 1992 the two countries signed a Friendship, Cooperation and Security Treaty. A more specific agreement on military cooperation, the Edirne Document, was concluded in November 1992. A bilateral trade protocol was signed in Ankara in March 1993. A Military and Technical Cooperation Agreement was signed in the same month.
33. According to Romanian statistics there were about 2,000 Turkish companies (many of them, one assumes, very small) operating in Romania by autumn 1993. *TDN*, 7 September 1993.
34. *TDN*, 29 April 1993.
35. BBC/SWB/EE (Eastern Europe), 18 November 1991 and 20 November 1991.
36. BBC/SWB/EE, 20 November 1991.
37. BBC/SWB/EE, 3 January 1992.
38. Interview with senior Turkish official, Ankara 22 April 1993.
39. *TDN*, 28 May 1992.
40. For the failure of Milosevic's mission, see the *Guardian*, 24 January 1992.
41. Hikmet Cetin quoted in *TDN*, 26 November 1992.
42. Turkish diplomats admitted at the time that the isolation of President Milosevic was a direct aim of the conference. Interview with senior Turkish diplomat, 25 November 1992.
43. *The Times*, 24 November 1992.
44. Though earlier dates could have been taken, 1923, and more particularly the Treaty of Lausanne, has been selected as it marks the securing of the international status of the modern state of Turkey.
45. For example, see one of the first statements of the Turkish foreign minister, Safa Giray, after the creation of the Yilmaz government in June 1991; a statement which actually took place against a background of increasing violence in Slovenia. *Newspot*, 4 July 1991.
46. For a commentary on the visit of the Yugoslav head of state see *Newspot*, 25 April 1991.
47. BBC/SWB/ME, 13 April 1991.
48. BBC/SWB/EE, 8 August 1990.
49. BBC/SWB/EE, 2 August 1990.
50. BBC/SWB/EE, 23 January 1992.
51. See BBC/SWB/EE, 20 November 1991.

52. BBC/SWB/EE, 20 December 1991.
53. *Hurriyet*, 12 July quoted in BBC/SWB/EE, 19 July 1991.
54. BBC/SWB/EE, 18 October 1991.
55. BBC/SWB/EE, 14 January 1992.
56. *TDN*, 18 April 1992.
57. *TDN*, 24 April 1992.
58. *Newspot*, 7 May 1992.
59. *Newspot*, 21 May 1992.
60. Unpublished plan formally dated 7 August 1992.
61. For details see *Newspot*, 13 August 1992.
62. *Newspot*, 10 September 1992.
63. *Turkish Probe* Vol.1 No. 9, 12 January 1993.
64. For Hikmet Cetin's London Conference speech see *Newspot*, 10 September 1992.
65. Turkey held the presidency of the ICO for eighteen months, relinquishing it in April 1993.
66. *TDN*, 29 October 1992.
67. *TDN*, 21 October 1992.
68. For example see *TDN*, 17 December 1992.
69. *Turkish Probe* Vol. 2 No. 15, 23 February 1993.
70. *Turkish Probe* Vol. 1 No. 9, 12 January 1993.
71. *Turkish Probe* Vol. 1 No. 10, 19 January 1993.
72. *Turkish Probe* Vol. 1 No. 11, 26 January 1993.
73. *Daily Telegraph*, 19 April 1993.
74. Interview with West European diplomat, 19 November 1993.
75. *TDN*, 27 September 1993.
76. *Turkish Probe* Vol. 4 No. 45, 28 September 1993.
77. Ibid.
78. *Guardian*, 16 September 1993.
79. *Turkish Probe* Vol. 4 No. 52, 18 November 1993.
80. Interview with senior Western diplomat, 19 November 1993.

7
Turkey and the Black Sea Initiative

Ekavi Athanassopoulou

On 25 June 1992, the heads of eleven states (Albania, Armenia, Azerbaijan, Bulgaria, Georgia, Greece, Moldova, Romania, Russia, Turkey, Ukraine) gathered in Istanbul and signed the Black Sea Economic Cooperation Declaration. The brainchild of the late Turkish President Turgut Özal, it was another indication of Turkey's shift towards regionalism as a response to the post-Cold War developments. This shift, however, does not constitute a break with Ankara's traditional Western-oriented foreign policy. On the contrary, it should be seen as a new card in Ankara's hands, intended to reinforce Turkey's relations with both the United States and Western Europe.

For almost half a century, Turkey's membership of NATO and its association with the European Community have provided the basic framework for the country's foreign relations. Since 1945 Turkey has sought integration with the West on grounds of security and because of economic and ideological considerations. The dismantling of the Iron Curtain may have erased the first of these considerations, but the other two still remain very much alive.

The end of the Cold War at first appeared to undermine Turkey's position in the Western world since its role as a warrior on the borders of the Soviet Union was over. Ankara's feeling of uncertainty was further increased, as was pointed out by the Turkish Foreign Minister, Hikmet Çetin, when the European Community – with which the Turks have a long-standing association agreement – rejected Turkey's application for membership in 1989 (Ilkin, 1993: 53). Not only was the Community reluctant to accept Turkey as one of its members, but also political and economic developments in Eastern Europe and the Community itself meant that Turkey ran the risk of being pushed to the bottom of the European agenda. It was in this context – and given the winds of change around its borders with the former Soviet bloc – that Turkey became active in establishing formal ties in all fields with Russia, the Turkic republics of Central Asia and the Black Sea states. Thus, Ankara sought to secure its relationship with the West through a new role, that is, of a regional stabilizing power in the centre of an area of actual and potential conflicts – a role that Western Europe and the United States welcomed as they saw Turkey particularly as a counterweight to Iran's influence. The new Turkish President, Süleyman Demirel, stated on more than one occasion that the underlying factor in Turkey's new diplomatic activities was not to develop an eastern alternative. As he put it when still prime minister, 'we may be a bridge to Asia but we do not pretend to be the voice of Asia. On the contrary, for our closest neighbours we represent the voice of Europe' (*Guardian*, 23 November 1992).

Nevertheless, there was also an element of opportunism in Ankara's new approach to the region. The Turks, like others, were well aware of the economic potential of these countries. The decline in Turkish exports to the Middle East since the second half of the 1980s increased Turkey's need for new markets. In the first half of the 1980s Turkish trade with the Middle East was on the rise. The oil-producing countries of the Middle East accounted for 16 per cent of Turkish exports in 1979 and 44 per cent in 1983. Since the mid-1980s, however, there has been a reverse trend and exports to the area have fallen to 20 per cent (Akagül and Vaner, 1993: 25). Both government and opposition were attracted by the idea of Turkey becoming the economic – and in the case of the Turkic states the political – centre of the area. In Özal's words:

we are at a point where we should not lose sight of other possible alternatives [to the European Community]. Turkey cannot have all its eggs in one basket. I don't say that to challenge the EC or Europe. This is not at all the case. But we should consider every alternative. Turkey must react quickly and show an interest in regional developments. Not after the events have taken place, but at an opportune moment (Ilkin, 1993: 53).

Thus, Turkey's initiative in launching the idea of Black Sea economic cooperation – 'a new "Great Silk Road" under modern conditions', as Özal described it (*Foreign Broadcast Information Service* (*FBIS*), *Soviet Union*, 26 June 1992: 5) – has to be seen in the light of the above mentioned considerations. Demirel stressed on the day of the Declaration's signature that it was 'a sign of Turkey's prestige and also a sign that Turkey must be treated with respect and attention' (*FBIS*, *Western Europe*, 26 June 1992: 12).

The ambitious scheme was put forward in 1990 before the dismantling of the Soviet Union. A preliminary report by the Turkish Ministry for Foreign Affairs was discussed in an exceptional meeting with the participation of representatives of the Turkish private sector and it was decided to go ahead with the initiative (Elekdag, 1992: 23). In December 1990 representatives of the Soviet Union, Bulgaria, Romania and Turkey met in Ankara and agreed to examine proposals on the free movement of capital, goods, services and labour across their borders. After the breakdown of the Soviet Union, the Black Sea successor states (Russia, Ukraine, Georgia, Moldova) together with Armenia and Azerbaijan took their place in the discussions, and in 1992 Greece and Albania[1] were also invited to participate. Greece had intended to be only an observer but finally it agreed to become a member due to Romania's and Bulgaria's insistence, on the grounds that Athens would provide the link with the EC (Akagül and Vaner, 1993: 18).

The final Bosphorus Declaration of June 1992 was a short, subdued document. It merely expressed the good will of the participants to promote bilateral and multilateral economic cooperation and also made specific reference to cooperation in the fields of transport, energy, science and technology, without putting forward a concrete plan to this end. In fact, it was less ambitious than the agreement envisaged in 1990 (Hale, 1992: 5). Thus, in place of free movement of labour, the declaration spoke only of free movement of businessmen, and instead of the establishment of free trade the signatories agreed to contribute 'to the expansion of their mutual trade [...] by continuing their efforts to further reduce or progressively eliminate obstacles of all kinds, in a manner not contravening their obligations towards third parties'.

If the original concept had already been watered down by the time of this final announcement, it was no surprise that one year after the Bosphorus Declaration little headway had been made to coordinate policies for its implementation. Although in December 1992 it was decided to establish a permanent secretariat along with a Black Sea trade and development bank and a regional statistics centre – all essential for the development of the project – everything still remained on paper by the end of 1993. In fact, during the second meeting of foreign ministers in Istanbul, on 17 July 1993, Russia made it clear that it did not have the capacity, for the moment, to proceed with the idea of the Bank. Russia along with Turkey and Greece was expected to have a 16.5 per cent share in the initial capital. Therefore, its contribution would be a prerequisite for the establishment of the bank since in December 1993 it was agreed that this would be established only after 50 per cent of the capital had been made available. Obviously there was little chance of the other countries providing the necessary capital. Moreover, Greece and Bulgaria boycotted a meeting in February 1993 where it was agreed to set up a Consultative Parliamentary Assembly. A majority of the other participant states approached the Assembly sharing the attitude of an Armenian MP, who stated that 'participating in this Assembly does not benefit my country, but it does not harm it, either' (*Hayk*, 26 June 1993).

There is no doubt that progress regarding the institutional aspect of the agreement was bound to be slow since the member states were lacking the necessary experience. However, the real difficulties of putting the idea into practice were to be found elsewhere. Not only were the majority of the member states in the midst of economic chaos, but also Georgia, Azerbaijan, Armenia and Moldova were in a state of war. The newly independent states had no modern infrastructure in terms of telecommunications or financial services to facilitate contacts. Moreover, conditions of security along their roads were uncertain. Turkish lorry drivers were constantly assaulted for money before they were allowed to continue their journeys. The situation was unsafe, particularly in Georgia but also in southern Russia, Ukraine and Azerbaijan. The fact that only Greece and Turkey had convertible currencies (or virtually convertible in the case of Turkey) complicated commercial agreements and capital movements. Barter trade was the prevailing mode of exchange between Turkey and the Black Sea states. Turkey usually provided the technology and machinery, and the other country the raw materials and labour (*International Herald Tribune*, 13 July 1992). At some point, Ankara proposed the creation of a payments union, but apparently this could result in a serious leakage of hard currency from Greece and Turkey.

Efforts by the eastern European states to deregulate their economies and liberalize their trade and exchange systems depend on two interrelated elements: their ability to persist with their reforms and the availability of foreign investment. The Turkish Export Credit Bank (Exim Bank) opened a credit line to the former republics of the Soviet Union but it was obvious that Turkey, a heavy borrower itself, could do little in this direction. Turkey's external short-term borrowing rose by 797.6 per cent in the first ten months of 1992, compared with 1991 (*Middle East Economic Digest*, 29 January 1993: 32). As Demirel pointed out in his opening address at the Istanbul summit, 'there is a need for financial power. Currently the region's financial resources seem to be more modest than their aims. There is a need for foreign resources' (*FBIS, Western Europe*, 26 June 1992: 3). Until now, however, the West and the Japanese have been cautious about extending credits and loans to the area and there are no signs that their attitude is about to change. Thus, Ankara is 'unlikely to quickly find others ready to pay for its cherished would-be role as a bridge' between Western financial centres and these states (*Middle East International*, 10 July 1992: 12). Not to mention the fact that all the countries involved in the agreement are competitors in the international financial markets.

There is also the question of commitments to third parties. Greece is a member of the European Union and Turkey is supposed to establish a full customs union with it in 1996. Consequently, both countries will be able to lower trade walls only to the level that Brussels permits. Moreover, some Black Sea countries are already seeking separate agreements with the EU. The declaration acknowledges the problem and states that the agreement will be implemented in a manner not contravening the obligations of the participants towards third parties. Thus, in effect, the Black Sea initiative could be no more than a trade agreement which in the best case could become a poor cousin of the European Free Trade Association (EFTA). Ankara is aware of the structural difficulties. Nevertheless, the idea is, according to Turkish Foreign Ministry sources, to create a basic framework for discussion, 'a medium for businessmen and basically let them carry on without too many bureaucratic barriers' (*Middle East Business and Banking*, January 1991: 6). Turkey, with a potential for exports in consumer and agricultural goods, along with telecommunications, construction and tourism services, expects to be in an advantageous position in this market of 320 million consumers (Mehmet, 1991: 34). The interest of the Turkish private sector in merchandise trade with the area has been developing. Turkish companies have already made their presence felt in Romania. Turkey comes eighth in terms of direct, foreign investment and third in terms of the number of firms operating there (Planche, 1993: 136). Turkish trade with Bulgaria and Albania has increased dramatically. In 1990–91 Turkish exports to the two countries increased by 578 and 282 per cent respectively (*Eleftherotipya*, 10 July 1992). Economic relations with Russia have also been expanding. Russia exports gas to Turkey for hard currency. In return, Moscow is obliged to import Turkish goods and contracting services up to an offset value. The rest of the gas income is recycled to pay back credit facilities extended by Ankara. According to Turkish estimates, by the year 2000 a five-fold increase to $10,000 billion in trade between the two countries is to be expected (*Middle East Economic Digest*, 24 September 1993: 24). At the same time, a significant amount of commercial activity with the Black Sea countries is conducted by 'suitcase traders' who visit Turkey in millions (Bilici, 1993: 169–83).

The ultimate aim, endorsed by all participants, is to alleviate political differences and achieve regional stability through economic cooperation. (*Middle East Business and Banking*, January 1991: 6). For the time being, however, all the states are seeking to secure their own economic interests. This was demonstrated in the negotiations for a pipeline to transport oil from Kazakhstan and Azerbaijan. On environmental grounds, Ankara opposed the proposals for a Black Sea terminal either in Russia or in Georgia. Instead it insisted on a Mediterranean terminal on Turkish territory, enraging the Russians and particularly the Georgians, who were desperate to overcome their economic bankruptcy (*Petroleum Intelligence Weekly*, 29 March 1993: 9). Moreover, Turkey announced plans to introduce a toll in the Bosphorus which, if implemented, would put a further strain on the trade of the Black Sea states, since this is mainly carried through the straits (*Financial Times*, 18 August 1992).

One really wonders how conducive to economic cooperation the atmosphere can be when most of the member states are at each other's throats. In fact, the *modus vivendi* of the area is rivalry and not cooperation (Migranyan,

1992: 11–14). Ankara's initiative was based on the idea that Moscow had retreated politically behind its borders, so Turkey – being the strongest country in the area and backed by the West – could step in as an economic coordinator. However, it was wishful thinking to write Russia off. During 1992–93, Moscow showed that it was far from abandoning its interests in territories long ruled by the Tsarist and Soviet empires (Rahr, 1992; de Tinguy, 1993). Nevertheless, due to the fact that it did not have the means to oppose or to substitute Turkey's activity in the area, it preferred co-operation to confrontation with Ankara. This did not mean that Russia was willing to see the Turks exerting increasing influence in the most sensitive area – due to oil and security considerations – of its 'near abroad'. In fact, the Russians made it more than clear that they did not welcome Turkey's interference in the area. It is sufficient to remember the statement of the CIS military commander, back in 1992, that any intervention by Turkey in Azerbaijan would lead to a third world war. At the same time, Russia sought to include Iran in the regional game. An agreement on cooperation between the two countries was signed and Moscow agreed to sell three submarines to Tehran (*Middle East Economic Digest*, 11 December 1992: 10). Political developments in Azerbaijan undermined the only serious link that Ankara had in the area and made it clear that Russia was still the boss. (Today Turks are not allowed to enter Azerbaijan without a visa.) The Russian Defence Minister, Pavel Grachev, during his visit to Ankara after Aliyev assumed power, even gave 'table-thumping warnings' that Turkey should keep out of 'our' Azerbaijan (*The Independent*, 1 July 1993). Moreover, Moscow appeared to have won the competition for the oil pipeline, since according to an agreement signed on 21 November 1993, Azerbaijan agreed to the transportation of its oil to world markets via Russia (*Briefing*, 29 November 1993: 10–11).

Most of the other member states also have reasons to oppose Turkey's bid for regional power – although some are desperate for solutions to overcome their economic crises. Greece has a long-standing dispute with Ankara over the Aegean and the question of Cyprus, while Turkish policy in the Balkans has become a new source of friction between the two countries. Moreover, Athens itself wishes to play a leading economic and political role in the Balkans (*Kathimerini*, 23 January 1991). Lately, a rapprochement has been taking place between Bulgaria and Turkey. However, the existence of a sizeable Turkish minority in Bulgaria will continue to be a source of tension between the two countries. (Nikolaev, 1993; Ilchev and Perry, 1993). The same can be argued about Moldova with its minority of Gagauz Turks, to whom Ankara has promised moral and material support (*Russia and the Successor States Briefing Service*, April 1993: 17). Ukraine, for the time being, sees Turkey as a counterweight in its present relations with Russia; yet in the long run Kiev will be apprehensive about Ankara's possible political influence in the Crimea. Armenia would feel threatened by any consolidation of Turkish power and Georgia would not be pleased, either, to be squeezed between Russia and a strong Turkey. However, such considerations are unlikely to preoccupy Georgia in the near future, until domestic stability has been achieved. Thus, it was not a surprise that the Black Sea agreement was met with apprehension in Western circles. A Western diplomat called it 'an old-Arab style confabulation where the host country makes such a fuss that the others are afraid not to come in case they would lose out' (*The Independent*, 26 June 1992).

In the light of the above, Turkey's Black Sea initiative does not appear to have a greater chance of success than the Economic Cooperation Organization (ECO).[2] The emergence around Turkey's borders of economically desperate and politically weak states is just one factor out of many that could leave Turkey in a position to play a key role in regional affairs. The same holds true regarding Central Asia, despite the fact that Turkey has cultural links with the Turkic republics (*Le Monde*, 9 January 1993; *International Herald Tribune*, 5 August 1993). It should be remembered, however, that those states chose to be represented abroad by Russia and not by Turkey, and until recently Turkey represented abroad only Azerbaijan. The Turks themselves have realised that there are as many risks and responsibilities as opportunities deriving from the new *raison d'état* around their borders. This has been amply demonstrated in Turkey's attitude regarding the Nagorno-Karabakh conflict. Despite Özal's rhetoric, Ankara was careful not to get involved in a conflict that might endanger its relations not only with Russia but also with the West (*Financial Times*, 7 May 1993). There is also the question of Turkey's domestic situation. Ankara, faced with serious economic difficulties – during the second quarter of 1993 the external debt was $59 billion, and inflation reached 60 per cent – and internal security problems (the Kurdish uprising), and with the Islamic movement on the rise, has been hardly in a position to concentrate its efforts on an active policy in the area. In 1992 the Turkish press gave prominence to Turkey's relations with the former Soviet republics. Today, attention is rightly focused on domestic developments. Of course, no one is denying that Turkey will have a role to play in the Black Sea area. Turkish banking, telecommunications and the construction sector are trying to establish their presence there. Nevertheless, Ankara today realises that this role will be much more modest than the one envisaged at the start of the 1990s.

NOTES

1. It should be noted that the Black Sea agreement does not have any geographical limitations. Currently Tunisia and Poland – along with the European Bank for Reconstruction and Development – have been accepted as observers.

2. Established under the name of Regional Cooperation and Development Organization in 1965 between Turkey, Iran and Pakistan, it changed its name in 1985. In 1992, Azerbaijan, Uzbekistan and Turkmenistan were admitted as new members (Kazakhstan, Kyrgyzstan and Tajikistan were given the status of observer) after Turkey's attempt to revitalize it.

REFERENCES

Akagül, Deniz and Vaner, Semith (1993), 'Peut-il se constituer un sous-ensemble regional autour de la mer noire?', *Cahiers d' Études sur la Méditerranée Orientale et le Monde Turco–Iranien*, 15: 9–49.

Bilici, Faruk (1993), 'L'Arménie, la Turquie et le Marché Commun de la Mer Noire', *Cahiers d' Études sur la Méditerranée Oriéntale et le Monde Turco–Iranien*, 15.

de Tinguy, Anne (1993), 'La Russie a-t-elle une politique à l'égard de son sud?', *Cahiers d' Études sur la Méditerranée Oriéntale et le Monde Turco–Iranien*, 15: 77–105.

Elekdag, Sükrü (1992), 'KEIB'in Türkiye açisindan önemi, Türkiye'nin Dis Ekonomik Iliskilerinde Yeni Ufuklar', *Istanbul Sanayi Odasi, Arastirma Dairesi*, 6: 21–30.

Hale, W. (1992), 'Turkey, the Black Sea and Transcaucasia', paper presented to the Conference on Transcaucasia Boundaries: Geo-Politics and International Boundaries, Research Centre, School of Oriental and African Studies: 1–17.

Ilchev, Ivan and Perry, M., Duncan (1993), 'Bulgarian ethnic groups: politics and perceptions', *Radio Free Europe/Radio Liberty Research Report*, 2, 12: 35–41.

Ilkin, Selim (1993), 'Les tentatives de cooperation économique en mer noire', *Cahiers d' Études sur la Méditerranée Orientale et le Monde Turco-Iranien*, 15: 51–75.

Mehmet, Özay (1991), 'Beyond glasnost and the Gulf War: Turkish foreign policy and economic relations at a crossroad', *International Girne Conferences: Turkey's Relations with the Soviet Union and East Europe*: 32–45.

Migranyan, Andramik (1992), 'The Soviet Union has gone off in all directions', *The Current Digest of the Soviet Press*, XLIV, 43: 11–14.

Nikolaev, Rada (1993), 'Bulgaria's 1992 census: results, problems and implications', *Radio Free Europe/Radio Liberty Research Report*, 2, 6: 58–62.

Planche, Anne (1993), 'La Roumanie et la coopération autour de la Mer Noire', *Cahiers d'Études sur la Méditerranée Orientale et le Monde Turco–Iranien*, 15.

Rahr, A. (1992), 'Atlanticists versus Eurasians in Russian foreign policy', *Radio Free Europe/Radio Liberty Research Report*, 1, 22: 17–22.

Journals and periodical publications

Briefing, Eleftherotypia, FBIS Daily Reports, Financial Times, Hayk, International Herald Tribune, Kathimerini, Le Monde, Middle East Business and Banking, Middle East Economic Digest, Middle East International, Petroleum Intelligence Weekly, Russia and the Successor States Briefing Service, Guardian, The Independent

8

Malta's Post-Cold War Perspective on Mediterranean Security

Stephen C. Calleya

In spite of its limited territorial dimensions, Malta's strategic relevance in the central Mediterranean has led the country to pursue a comprehensive approach to security in the region. The importance that Malta attaches to Mediterranean security is highlighted by the prominent role it has played in institutions such as the Conference on Security and Cooperation in Europe (CSCE). Malta, together with Cyprus, Spain, Italy and the former Yugoslavia, insisted upon the eleventh-hour insertion of the Mediterranean clauses in the Helsinki Final Act (CSCE 'Final Act', 1975 and Grech, 1993: 45–57). Malta's proposal at the CSCE Follow-up Meeting in Helsinki, namely that the CSCE should declare itself the regional arrangement for peace-keeping in terms of Chapter VIII of the UN's Charter, was endorsed by the Helsinki Summit II, and is another example of Malta's Mediterranean security concern.

Moreover, as a member of the United Nations, Malta inspired the concept of the common heritage of mankind in so far as the Law of the Sea is concerned. More recently, when Malta held the presidency of the General Assembly in 1990, it advocated the need to revitalize the concept of collective security under the auspices of the United Nations.

This chapter offers an assessment of Malta's perspective on Mediterranean security following the end of the Cold War. This will include an examination of the security implications that are attached to Malta's application to become a full member of the European Union. A review of Malta's viewpoint regarding trans-Mediterranean security initiatives in the 1990s follows. In the analysis, an attempt is made to determine the extent to which Malta's post-Cold War foreign policy objectives are complementary to the concept of establishing a trans-Mediterranean security forum.

MALTA'S FOREIGN POLICY OBJECTIVES IN THE 1990s

Malta's foreign policy initiatives in the 1990s have envolved amidst a rapidly changing and uncertain international background. The demise of the Soviet

Union, the collapse of Cold War deterrence thinking, and the process towards European union have ushered in a much more nebulous and challenging period in international relations. Whereas the bipolar Cold War arrangement provided a kind of *sancta simplicitas* – predictable parameters – for policy-makers, the multipolar post-Cold War world is proving to be far more fluid, volatile and uncertain.

The Mediterranean region is an area whose varied security parameters cannot be easily reconciled in a single strategic equation. Its politico-military characteristics differ drastically when one shifts the analytical lens from the eastern to the western sector of the basin or from the northern to the southern shores. In addition, its geographical proximity to a large number of great powers and the plethora of potential crises in the vicinity contribute to the complex environment with which the actors involved in the region must contend.

Malta emerged from the Cold War as a non-aligned and neutral country. Located between two distinct security complexes, Europe and the Middle East (Buzan and Roberson, 1993: 131–47), Malta has had to define its security policy accordingly. The year 1987 marked a sea-change in Maltese politics. After sixteen years of Socialist leadership, the Nationalist Party emerged victorious in the general elections. Malta's policy of neutrality and non-alignment was already earmarked for a period of transformation when the newly elected Maltese government announced that foreign policy endeavours would thereafter focus upon nurturing better political and economic ties with the West.

In what ways does this policy differ from the previous one? First, in contrast to the international roles Malta adopted during the Cold War, both as a British colony and an independent country, Malta's current external relations are more determined by its historical and geographical dimensions. The heart of Malta's foreign policy agenda since the early 1990s has centred upon the unique regional security role it can play in the Mediterranean theatre. This is exemplified in the proactive stance Malta has taken in the trans-Mediterranean security debate, as will be discussed shortly. Secondly, Malta's perspective on security now includes new instruments of socio-economic and environmental cooperation. These have been added to the traditional political and military facets of security. Third, and perhaps most significantly, realizing that its policy of neutrality and non-alignment was quickly being superseded by international developments, Malta committed itself to the goal of participating in a common foreign and security policy within the framework of the European Union.

Malta first concentrated its diplomatic resources upon redefining its relationship with Libya. A special effort was made to eliminate the maverick reputation the country had acquired during its flirtation with the Qadhafi regime during the 1970s and early 1980s. The Treaty of Friendship and

Cooperation between Malta and Libya was amended shortly afterwards, with the section relating to cooperation in security questions being deleted, in agreement between the two parties concerned (*Agence Europe*, 1993a: 3).

Once the Cold War glacier began to melt, Malta decided that it could play a more active role in regional security – a security defined essentially in terms of cooperation at the regional level (De Marco, 1993b: 4). The Fenech Adami administration has consistently cited European Union membership as Malta's foremost foreign policy goal. Accordingly, Malta submitted its EC application in July 1990. In the following three years, while the European Community's Commission prepared its Opinion Report on Malta, the Fenech Adami administration relaunched Malta's foreign policy objectives as part of a wider process of developing and adopting *communitaire* attitudes.

The rationale behind this fundamental shift is that inclusion of the European Union in pan-Mediterranean security initiatives will augment the resources required to make them effective. Malta adheres to a European common foreign and security policy as stipulated in the Maastricht Treaty because it considers that the communitarization of Mediterranean security issues will ultimately serve as a confidence-building measure in the region. But this should not overshadow the fact that Malta already participates in a series of programmes launched by the European Community in the Mediterranean which aim at a greater reciprocal understanding among the inhabitants of the basin.

These ventures include the MED-Urbs programme, with ECU 5.5 million, a cooperation project involving municipalities and local authorities of the Mediterranean and MED-Campus, with ECU 6.5 million, an inter-university collaboration scheme. Both programmes are already operating on an experimental basis. On 1 June 1993 the MED-Media project, which promotes cooperation between institutions and companies working in this sector, was inaugurated. In October 1993 the Vice-President of the European Investment Bank (EIB), Alain Prat, and the World Bank Vice-President, Caio Koch-Weser, confirmed their commitment to the implementation of an enhanced Mediterranean Environmental Technical Assistance Programme (METAP II) between 1993 and 1995. An ardent advocate of environmental security in the region, Malta welcomed the second cycle of the programme which will feature: a broadened geographic scope; larger-scale operations; enhanced efforts in the area of improving water quality, urban environmental management and the development of domestic infrastructures. By the end of 1993 a training support scheme, namely MED-Invest, with a start-up budget of ECU 10 million, was also scheduled to be launched (*Agence Europe*, 1993b: 9–10).

Full EU membership will nevertheless bring about a qualitative change in Malta's Mediterranean relations. Whether Mediterranean security initiatives actually benefit from this development will depend entirely upon

Malta's ability to fulfil both its European and Mediterranean security commitments. The more Malta is perceived to support common European security and defence objectives, the less enthusiastic non-member Mediterranean states might become about participating in Maltese-inspired trans-Mediterranean initiatives, such as the Council of the Mediterranean. As a full member of the European Union Malta would therefore have to carefully balance its foreign policy agenda to ensure that its European security dimension complemented its trans-Mediterranean security objectives.

Despite the complexity of implementing such an external programme, the possibility of realizing such a policy is clearly viable. Malta's Minister of Foreign Affairs, Guido De Marco, has already emphasized that there is no need for Malta to amend its constitution prior to European Union accession because Malta's neutrality, based on the principles of non-alignment, in no way contradicts the chapter dedicated to a common foreign and security policy in the Maastricht Treaty. Indeed, Article J.4, paragraph four, stipulates that the introduction of such a policy shall not prejudice the specific character of the security and defence policy of certain member states (Maastricht Treaty, 1992, Title V, Article J.4., and Calleya, 1993: 14). Given its unique geo-strategic location, Malta can convincingly claim that its trans-Mediterranean security relations are conducive to the Union's long-term objective of integrating further the European, North African and Near Eastern shores of the Mediterranean.

MALTA'S ROLE IN TRANS-MEDITERRANEAN SECURITY

Malta's application to join the European Union is therefore not an abandonment of its Mediterranean security dimension, but an extension of this philosophy. Within this European parameter, Malta endorses the policy of increasing security interactions between Europe and the Middle East. Its participation in international institutions such as the Council of Europe, the United Nations and the CSCE has already demonstrated this strategic aim.

An analysis of Malta's track record in Mediterranean affairs since the end of the Cold War will determine whether its commitment to the region has waned in recent years. This review will discuss Malta's position on the various Mediterranean security proposals that have been presented since the collapse of the Berlin Wall, including the concept of establishing a Conference on Security and Cooperation in the Mediterranean (CSCM), and the attempt to set up a Western Mediterranean Forum. Malta's own blueprint for the creation of a Council of the Mediterranean (CM) will also be examined.

From its inception, Malta has been a fervent proponent of the Italian–Spanish proposal for the creation of a CSCM (Fernández Ordóñez, 1990: 1–8, Martinez, 1991; Ministry of Foreign Affairs, Rome, 1990). Launched officially at the CSCE's Palma de Mallorca meeting in September 1990, the 'Italian–Spanish Non-paper on CSCM' advocates a general debate on the security issues in the region. The initiative's long-term objective is to enhance the possibility of institutionalizing a new security forum in the Mediterranean that would embrace all the actors with influence and interests in the region.

To date the Italian–Spanish CSCM proposal has not got beyond the drawing board. Critics of the plan, which include France and the United States, indicate the complexity of issues that a conference encompassing a region extending from Iran to Mauritania would have to address. Serious doubts have also been cast upon the applicability of a Helsinki-type process tailor-made to deal with the problems in Europe during the Cold War (Ghebali, 1993: 97). Due to this lack of consensus at the Palma meeting, the report issued at the end declared that a CSCM arrangement, inspired by the CSCE, could only take place when circumstances permitted (Palma Report, 1992).

In spite of the indifference manifested towards the 1990 CSCM project, the concept of the Conference retains its appeal. A series of CSCM-style systems has since been initiated, with Malta participating in all of them. The Western Mediterranean Forum originally comprised France, Italy, Portugal and Spain on the European side, and the five members of the Arab Maghreb Union (UMA): Algeria, Libya, Mauritania, Morocco and Tunisia. Proposed by France, the 4+5 process was officially launched at foreign ministerial level in Rome on 10 December 1990. Malta became a member of the Western Mediterranean Forum in 1991, and thus the '4+5' became known as the '5+5' process.

The process consisted of a flexible structure of dialogue, consultation and cooperation. Ministerial meetings were to be held at least once a year. Working groups were set up to tackle issues that included international financial resources for development, food self-sufficiency and desertification problems, debt, migration flows and cultural heritage. Although the process was supposed to embrace the concept of security in its broadest sense through the integration of political, economic, cultural, human and eco-logical factors, it actually concentrated most of its resources on the economic aspects of West Mediterranean relations (Ghebali, 1993: 97–9).

The Rome gathering was followed on 26–27 October 1991 by a minis-terial meeting in Algiers where the following proposals were put forward: the creation of a Mediterranean data bank in the fields of industry and commerce, a Mediterranean financial bank, and a Eureka-type western Mediterranean programme for science and technology (Ghebali, 1993: 98).

After a productive start, events of both a national and international character led to the indefinite postponement of the follow-up meeting that was scheduled to take place in Tunisia at the start of 1992. Attempts made throughout 1993 by the 5+5 members to find resolutions to both the Algerian situation and the Libyan–Lockerbie impasse proved futile. As a result the 5+5 talks remain dormant (Pace, 1992: 5).

The next CSCM-type meeting to take place was the Málaga Conference on 15–20 June 1992, which was organized by the Inter-parliamentary Union, a Geneva-based institution. The main difference between this meeting, the Italian–Spanish project, and the 5+5 process, is the representative criteria that the former set up: only parliamentarians from riparian Mediterranean states were entitled to the status of full participants. As a result, countries such as Portugal, the United States, Russia and Britain were excluded. The Palestinians were included as 'associate participants', which led to Israel's withdrawal. Yugoslavia and Algeria also failed to send delegations due to the domestic turmoil they were experiencing.

The conference, entitled 'Regional Stability', adopted by consensus a final document that was divided into three parts. The security section suggested the sketching of a charter handling trans-Mediterranean relations; the creation of a regional centre for crisis management and the peaceful settlement of disputes; the ratification of a set of land-based confidence-building measures; and a series of rules with the objective of transforming the Mediterranean into a denuclearized area. The second chapter focused upon the goals of co-development and partnership, while the third section dealt with issues of human rights and was a carbon copy of the CSCE mechanism dealing with the human dimension. The final document also incorporated a preamble which emphasized that the conference's main purpose was to launch a pragmatic process of cooperation which would gradually gain in momentum and facilitate the settlement of conflicts in the region (Ghebali, 1993: 100–101).

A COUNCIL OF THE MEDITERRANEAN

Aware of the obstacles that must be overcome before a CSCM process can be realized, Malta proposed another trans-Mediterranean security arrangement that complements the CSCM, namely the Council of the Mediterranean (CM). Malta's Minister of Foreign Affairs, Guido De Marco, officially launched the proposal at a symposium in Tunisia in November 1992 (De Marco, 1992: 5 and 14). He envisaged a forum that could be established upon the model of the oldest institution in Europe, the Council of Europe. Facilities would be created to involve all the parties concerned, including the EU, UMA and Arab League, in a continuous dialogue towards the solution of problems affecting the area: 'It is my government's view that the Mediterranean Sea should not be a divide, but through the rich diversity present in all Mediterranean countries, can be harmonised by structures for an ongoing dialogue to serve mutual interests' (ibid.).

De Marco reiterated this proposal at the Third Conference on Mediterranean Regions organized by the Council of Europe in Taormina in April 1993 (*Agence Europe*, 1993a: 5). As guidelines for membership of the Mediterranean Council he listed adherence to the principles of the UN Charter, respect for the dignity of the human person and the rule of law, and respect for the establishment and development of representative institutions.

When outlining the structure of the proposed Council, De Marco conceived of the appointment of a Committee of Ministers: a general assembly with consultative powers where representatives of Mediterranean states could form a Parliamentary Assembly of the Mediterranean. This pillar would be supported by a secretariat intended to coordinate activities of the Council in the political, economic, social, environmental and cultural fields (De Marco, 1992: 14).

Although the establishment of a CSCM remains a priority for representatives from the southern Mediterranean coast, support for the CM initiative among the ministers at the Taormina conference was widespread. Malta's Foreign Minister described the reception received so far as equivalent to what the French call *approfondissement*, that is, an in-depth consideration of the proposal. He added that the multitude of problems in the Mediterranean, namely the Greek–Turkish–Cypriot triangle, the Israeli–Syrian–Lebanese–Palestinian issue, Egyptian fundamentalism, Libya's uncertain future, political instability in Algeria, and the conflict in the former Yugoslavia, are all forcing the leaders of the region to focus upon matters in their own backyard without realizing that their domestic difficulties can occasionally be symptoms of ailments that lie outside their own jurisdiction (Calleya, 1993: 14).

Nevertheless, prospects for the Maltese proposition in the medium to long term remain good for a number of reasons. First, the breakthrough in Arab–Israeli relations in the last quarter of 1993 provides the prerequisite starting point for trans-Mediterranean security efforts to stand a realistic chance of success. Any attempt at institutionalizing discourse and dialogue is certain to founder without the participation of all the countries with an influence and interest in the Mediterranean littoral.

Second, as a non-rigid security arrangement, the CM has the advantage of not only being an exercise in preventive diplomacy, but also an operation in positive diplomacy. As a forum for discussing common interests and common concerns, the CM has the potential to become a bridge of common understanding. Indirectly, it could promote the notion of a Mediterranean identity in an area where such a concept is certainly lacking (Calleya, 1993: 14).

Thirdly, given the diversity of the region, pan-Mediterranean dialogue has a realistic chance of being maintained and strengthened if it is initially limited to non-sensitive issues of concern. The recommendation to imitate the successful example of the 1976 Barcelona Convention for the protection of the Mediterranean Sea is therefore another factor in the CM's favour. Initially the Council could convene to discuss issues such as energy, transport, communications and culture. A more comprehensive debate could then follow. Its primary task would be to find solutions to problems that include economic deprivation, ethnic friction, population explosion, migration, environmental degradation, intolerant fundamentalism, and outright conflict (De Marco, 1993a: 6).

The fact that Malta has proposed the initiative also gives the CM a certain edge. Although the Maltese are Europeans, they are very close to the Arab world. As a micro-state, Malta is also trusted by all the parties concerned as no country can claim that Malta has any ambitions other than cooperating in a regional security process.

The final factor in the CM's favour is the fact that the proposal fits in perfectly with the new spheres of cooperation that the European Union has outlined in its Euro-Maghreb partnership document (Commission of the European Communities, 1992 and *EC Bulletin*, 1992: 65–6). Specific EU cooperation projects to assist in the development of poor rural and suburban regions of large urban centres, identified as principal migration sources, are one example of this phenomenon. The EU's aim of eventually creating a free-trade area with the Maghreb is another.

A more recent CSCM-type meeting was the CSCE Mediterranean Seminar held in Malta in May 1993. The gathering was open to both CSCE members and non-member Mediterranean countries at a ministerial level. The seminar debate revealed that a significant number of non-European Mediterranean states maintain a marked interest in keeping the links, dialogue and cooperation with Europe active within the framework of the CSCE. Requests for more regular consultations were put forward and an interest was expressed in being associated in a more permanent structured relationship (CSCE Mediterranean Seminar, 1993: 4).

Deliberations focused upon the political, social, economic and humanitarian factors behind demographic trends and migration, and accelerated economic cooperation was deemed a priority. In this respect, the seminar heard calls for the further opening up of European markets to exports of manufactured commodities; the financing of projects in the field of agriculture; support for private-sector operations through the encouragement of joint ventures between European companies and companies in non-participant Mediterranean states; and support for macro-economic and sectoral reforms in these countries (CSCE Mediterranean Seminar, 1993: 5). Participants also emphasized the priority that should be attached in international cooperation to cross-sectoral requirements such as protecting the environment and enforcing international law. The very fact that the meeting was not expected to produce an agreed text provided delegates with the unique opportunity to discuss problems pertaining to the Mediterranean without the inhibitions normally associated with a negotiated text (CSCE Mediterranean Seminar, 1993: 1 and Grech, 1993).

Evidence that the concept of creating a pan-Mediterranean security arrangement is still resonant is provided in the continuous pledges of support made during 1993 for a CSCM within the framework of the CSCE: during talks in Algiers between the European Community and Algeria in March; in Taormina at the third conference on Mediterranean Regions organized by the Council of Europe in April; and at the European Parliamentary plenary session on security in Strasbourg at the end of May (De Marco, 1993c: 1). In addition, at its meeting in Sydney in the last quarter of 1993, the IPU decided that a conference on the subject of a CSCM would be held in Malta during 1994.

CONCLUSION

The year 1987 witnessed a sea-change in Maltese politics. The new Nationalist government was determined to reinstate Malta as a more active regional player in Mediterranean affairs. It aimed to achieve this by demonstrating its commitment to the goal of European Union. Malta's motives for wanting to join the European Union are essentially twofold. First, only an integrated institutional framework like the one provided for by the EU can provide the multidimensional security policy that Malta seeks to establish in the Mediterranean. Second, the EU offers a solid and proven institutional structure for multilateral cooperation which is essential if a common foreign and security policy is to be implemented in the region.

Malta's application to join the European Union therefore should not be regarded as an abandonment of its efforts to promote stability and peace throughout the Mediterranean. Instead, it is better to describe Malta's EU membership bid as an extension of this philosophy. Despite the limited practical results that have been achieved through the security proposals in the Mediterranean since the end of the Cold War, the CSCM-type meetings have at the very least been positive as an exercise in advancing towards consensus. Malta's participation in these initiatives at the same time as its EU application was being reviewed, demonstrates the priority Malta assigns to the trans-Mediterranean security dimension of its foreign policy agenda.

Malta's track record since becoming independent, and especially in the last five years, has illustrated its ability to contribute to security initiatives in the region. As a member of the United Nations, the CSCE and the 5+5 process, Malta has confirmed its competence to contribute constructively to the international security debate. As an advocate of the CSCM, and a proponent of a Council of the Mediterranean, Malta has also certified its continued effort to stabilize the Mediterranean region. By adopting a 'Euro-Med' balanced foreign policy agenda, Malta has found a way of maximizing its position in international relations. This in fact has become the hallmark of Malta's foreign policy in the post-Cold War world of the 1990s.

REFERENCES

Agence Europe, (1992), 'EP/Malta', 30 December, 3.

Agence Europe, (1993a) 'Council of Europe/Mediterranean', 9 April, 5.

Agence Europe, (1993b) 2 June, 9–10.

Buzan, Barry and Roberson, Barbara Allen (1993), 'Europe and the Middle East: drifting towards societal cold war?', in Ole Waever, Barry Buzan, Morten Kelstrup and Pierre Lemaitre, *Identity, Migration And The New Security Agenda In Europe*, London: Pinter, 131–47.

Calleya, Stephen C. (1993), 'Malta's Foreign Policy Objectives For The Nineties', *Sunday Times* (Malta), 14 November, 14.

Commission of the European Communities (1992), 'The Future Relations Between The Community and the Maghreb', Sec (02) 401 final, 30 April.

CSCE (1975) 'Final Act', Helsinki.

CSCE Mediterranean Seminar (1993), 'Chairman's Summary', Valletta, 17–21 May, 4.

De Marco, Guido (1992), 'De Marco calls for the setting up of a Council of the Mediterranean', *Sunday Times* (Malta), 22 November, 5 and 14.

De Marco, Guido (1993a), 'Méditerranée, Quel Avenir?', *Malta Review of Foreign Affairs*, special issue for the CSCE Mediterranean Seminar, May: 6.

De Marco, Guido (1993b), 'Malta and the EC', *Malta Review of Foreign Affairs*, 3, July: 4.

De Marco, Guido (1993c), 'Malta Insists On Early Start To Accession Talks With EC', *The Times* (Malta), 24 September, 1.

EC Bulletin (1992), 'Guidelines for a New Partnership with the Maghreb', 4: 65–6.

Fernández Ordóñez, Francisco (1990), 'The Mediterranean: Devising a Security Structure', *NATO Review*, 38, October: 1–8.

Ghebali, Victor-Yves (1993), 'Toward a Mediterranean Helsinki-Type Process', *Mediterranean Quarterly*, 4, 1, Winter: 97.

Grech, John Paul (1993), 'The CSCE Mediterranean Seminar – A Further Attempt?', *Malta Review of Foreign Affairs*, 3, July: 45–57.

Maastricht Treaty (1992), Title V, Article J.4., Provisions on a common foreign and security policy.

Martínez Report (1991), 'European Security and threats outside Europe – the organization of peace and security in the Mediterranean region and the Middle East', Assembly of the Western European Union, Doc. 1271, 13 May.

Ministry of Foreign Affairs, Rome (1991), '*The Mediterranean and the Middle East after the War in the Gulf: The CSCM*'.

Pace, Roderick (1992), 'And Now A Council of the Mediterranean', *Sunday Times* (Malta), 29 November, 5.

Palma Report (1992), 'Proposals for an integrated security in the Mediterranean', June.

PART THREE
DOMESTIC DEVELOPMENTS

9

No Peaceful Revolution: Political Change in Italy

Gianfranco Pasquino

There is no peaceful revolution in contemporary Italian politics. It is not a revolution because, at least so far, there has not been any significant change in the political class, in the distribution of political and economic power, in the institutions, in the regime. It is not peaceful because there is indeed a major and violent power struggle going on. This power struggle has already produced the assassination of two important and courageous judges, Giovanni Falcone and Paolo Borsellino, and their escorts, respectively in May and July 1992, and the explosion of cars transformed into bombs in Rome, Florence, and Milan in the summer of 1993 – not to mention other incidents of this kind prevented by the police and unknown to public opinion. Finally, resorting to another indicator, the so-called Italian revolution is not peaceful since the major scandal, dubbed *Tangentopoli* (Kickbacksville), has also produced almost twenty suicides, some of them 'excellent', that is, involving the deaths of politicians and important managers and financiers. No serious analyst could expect the peaceful demise of a regime and its protagonists who have controlled political power for forty years.

In the past, the risks of degeneration of the political system constructed during the First Italian Republic were denounced, most notably by the former Secretary of the Communist Party (PCI), Enrico Berlinguer (1922–84). Of course, Berlinguer was not believed since many thought that his words were just the product of a partisan view. Throughout the 1980s, when a sequence of five party coalition (*pentapartito*) governments suceeded each other, the phenomena of political corruption multiplied at the same time as organized crime extended its presence and power, not only in southern regions, but also, though in different forms, in some northern sanctuaries, e.g. the city of Milan, where the stock market is located. Weakened by a succession crisis and deliberately isolated by the governing Socialist Party, the communist opposition was unable to control and to denounce. Moreover, the economic conditions of the country, facilitated by the overall Western economic recovery, improved.

Now we know that the improvement was artificial. It took place largely at the expense of the state deficit. It served to finance an enlarged patronage system, to buy the consensus of many social groups. In sum, there was a lot to be questioned and criticized in democracy Italian-style, in sharp contrast with the enthusiastically optimistic view propounded by Joseph La Palombara (1987). Scholars could find a lot to be analysed and explained. Politicians could identify and suggest a lot to be changed. Only politicians in the government were inclined to find special reasons to be complacent and arrogant. Whether the Italian political transformation will in the end amount to a revolution remains to be seen. Before making prophecies about the extent of concrete changes, and their success in transforming Italian democracy, it is advisable to trace the deep roots of the Italian problem.

ONCE UPON A TIME: *PARTITOCRAZIA*

There is almost complete agreement that the dominant component of the Italian political system has been the party system. The First Republic, according to a respected historian (Scoppola, 1992), was the republic of the parties. Even though this view is now disputed, most scholars would stress that Italian parties have to be credited for their ability to bring and sustain democracy in a very difficult context, within strictly defined 'confining conditions' (to use Otto Kirchheimer's 1965 suggestive terminology). Those confining conditions were truly strict. Italy was and remained a border country between the Western and the Eastern camps until the collapse of the Berlin wall. This meant, on the one hand, that the Italian Communist Party could never become a credible governmental alternative. Perfectly aware of this limitation, its leaders played the political game in order to acquire power at the local level, to represent, orient and channel political protest into their powerful party organization, and to extract sizeable resources at the national level by creating and exploiting some consociational devices.

On the other hand, the Christian Democrats were aware that they could not be replaced by a coalition excluding them and including the Communist Party. Nevertheless, they had to steer a difficult course between the often reactionary tendencies of the Catholic Church and the electoral imperative to attract some popular support. Never a cohesive and disciplined party, always obliged to enter into a governmental coalition with minor centrist parties, the Christian Democrats were flexible enough to exploit all the opportunities for consociational agreements with the PCI. Their factionalized party and parliamentary group and their contentious governmental coalitions necessitated this outcome. Anyway, they were on the strong side. Obviously, minor centrist parties, the Liberals (PLI), the Republicans (PRI), and the Social Democrats (PSDI) extracted the resources indispensable for their electoral and political survival almost exclusively when joining an alliance with the Christian Democrats (DC).

As to the Socialists (PSI), they found themselves in the most difficult position. Organizationally and politically, the Communists were far stronger, though internationally they were not an acceptable ally. Therefore, if the Socialists wanted to govern the contradictions of Italian socio-economic development, for a short time characterized by a 'miracle' (1959–64), they were obliged to enter into a coalition with the Christian Democrats. However, the DC could never be a reformist party. Hence, the Socialists were bound to lose votes unless they were capable of compelling the Christian Democrats to enact some socio-economic reforms. This task proved to be beyond the political strength and imagination of the Socialists, who experienced a couple of splits (1947 and 1964) that reduced their electoral strength and led to an electoral decline up to 1976. They revived only under the leadership of Bettino Craxi, their newly elected secretary. Then, however, an entirely different story was going to be written.

The stability of the Italian party system and the strength of the parties were made possible and facilitated by the proportional electoral system. The peculiar variety of PR adopted in Italy saved all the parties in existence after the first national elections in 1948 bar one, the Monarchists, who merged in the 1960s with the neo-fascists. It also made it very easy for splinter parties to maintain their electoral and parliamentary positions and for new minor parties to acquire access to parliament. Moreover, thanks to preference voting for individual candidates, each voter could use three to four preference votes and enter into an exchange relationship with individual candidates and party factions. More precisely, powerful outside groups could organize the casting of these votes and influence the election of their favoured representatives. As a consequence, governing parties were, more or less willingly, fragmented into several factions enjoying different bases of support. This was especially true of the Christian Democrats and to some extent of the Socialists.

However, precisely because it worked as a channel for group representation, preference voting was considered useful by the Christian Democrats. Their party was a successful collection of factions representing diverse and often conflicting interests. Through a skilful policy of intermediation, those interests were never allowed to go completely unsatisfied. One way or another, through individual DC factions, they continued to enjoy access to the governmental sphere and this was good enough for most of them. The dominant characteristic that Hine (1993) rightly attributes to the Italian political system – bargained pluralism – was, in fact, first created and implemented by the DC. It was only thanks to the 1991 referendum, opposed by the DC and the PSI, and after a bitter political and electoral confrontation, that preferences were reduced to only one. By then, DC party factions had already changed profoundly and the party as such had become fundamentally a gathering, an assemblage of powerful parliamentarians, former ministers and ministers-to-be.

Proportional representation was not just an electoral formula. It quickly became the dominant principle for allocating power and several types of political and socio-economic resources. For different reasons, the Christian Democrats and the Left had converged on the creation, staffing and enlargement of a state sector of the economy in the 1950s and 1960s. This public sector was also meant to provide plenty of clientalistic resources. From then on, everything, from governmental office to positions as managers and administrators of state companies, and even menial jobs in those companies, was assigned according to some proportional criteria. Not knowledge and competence, but political loyalty and party affiliation became the exclusive criteria to be utilized for what was known as the procedure of *lottizzazione* in the area of *sottogoverno*. Criticizable, and even criticized, though for a long time only by a minority of Italian opinion-makers, *lottizzazione* was a device very consistent with proportional representation in a party system that could not enjoy the benefits of rotation of power between different coalitions.

Lottizzazione mirrored the power of the various governmental parties while it almost completely excluded the Communists and the neo-fascists. However, the communists were taken into serious consideration when the offices to be allotted were in the political–constitutional arena: members of the Higher Judicial Council and judges of the Constitutional Court. More recently, communist journalists were given, so to speak, Channel Three of the TV broadcasting system. As a consequence, communist criticisms lost some vigour and credibility.

Obviously, *lottizzazione* also represented a conservative device. It reproduced and to some extent amplified the power and the following of the parties in government, at the national as well as the local level. Above all, the lack of alternation deprived the country in many areas of the energies, the knowledge, the representation and the capabilities of one-fourth to one-third of Italians, those voting for and represented by the Italian Communist Party. *Lottizzazione* further reduced the pool of available Italians to serve in public positions to those affiliated to and/or chosen by the four or five governmental parties or, better, by the victorious factions within those parties. Of course, from a systemic point of view, this sub-*lottizzazione*, so to speak, was even worse. It involved more actors, it required more spoils, it entailed more potential and actual tensions and conflicts, and it further reduced the level of performance. That a reaction against this state of affairs was inevitably in the making cannot and should not surprise anybody. If surprise is in order, it may derive only from the late timing of the explosion of criticism. Of course, many criticisms had been made difficult and suffocated by the very fact that Italian political parties monopolized all political and governmental offices and intervened in many socio-economic arenas, that of information included.

All things considered, therefore, Italy may be defined as a case of party government (Pasquino, 1987). Decisions were made by elected party officials; policies were decided within parties which acted, more or less cohesively, to enact them. Officials were recruited and held accountable through parties (Katz, 1987: 7). It was, however, party government by default, since, due to the weakness of Italian society, no other organizations could replace Italian parties and no real challenge was ever addressed to them. Moreover, it was just a demi-party government because of the lack of even the theoretical possibility of alternation.

Were Italian parties so strong because they represented Italian society and its voters in an almost perfect way or were there other reasons for their success in keeping all political, and much socio-economic, power in their hands? It would be an exaggeration to deny any representational capability to Italian parties. At least the two major ones – the PCI and the DC, though politically, ideologically and organizationally very different – were not artificial. They had an organization, recruited members, established real ties with outside groups, selected leaders and elected parliamentarians and local office-holders. They obtained and maintained the political support of their voters and tried to represent and translate their demands, their needs and their emotions into public policies. To a large extent, it is neither preposterous nor polemical to state that the Christian Democrats and the communists needed each other. None the less, at the roots of their existence and persistence there was a real cleavage.

THE COMMUNISM/ANTI-COMMUNISM CLEAVAGE AND ITS DISAPPEARANCE

To an extent that has not yet been systematically explored, Italian parties were in fact the product of some of the cleavages identified and analysed by Stein Rokkan (1970): state/church more than centre/periphery, entrepreneurs/industrial workers more than rural–agricultural/urban–industrial interests. However, following the Second World War, a new cleavage became dominant and subsumed all the others: communism/anti-communism. The new cleavage could be, and was, repeatedly utilized and revived by the Church and by the Christian Democrats. The Church overplayed it in order to maintain the unity of the Catholics, and the Christian Democrats resorted to it in order to attract non-Catholic conservative and moderate voters scared by the persistence of the Communist threat.

The communism/anti-communism cleavage had a varying impact on Italian elections according to the level of domestic and international tension:

extremely high in 1948 and high in 1953; moderate-to-low throughout the 1960s; very low in 1976, when detente seemed to be working, no conflict involved the USA and the USSR, and a new generation of voters entered the political arena; relatively high when the missile issue made its appearance in the 1980s. Finally, the communism/anti-communism cleavage could not be sustained and revived any more after 1989 following the fall of the Berlin wall and the consequent change of name and symbol of the Italian Communist Party. When it was clear that Soviet communism could no longer constitute an international threat and that the PCI, transformed into the Democratic Party of the Left (PDS), no longer existed, then the communism/anti-communism cleavage vanished almost completely.

Not unexpectedly, then, the political identities of all Italian parties had to be reconstructed, in some cases from scratch. Programmes and candidates, coalitions and personalities appeared to matter more than the traditional political identities rooted in a past that could not be resurrected. A classic cleavage resurfaced: the north/south divide. It had never fully disappeared from Italian politics. However, it had been eclipsed by the communism/anti-communism cleavage and by the conscious efforts of the DC and, above all, of the PCI, to present themselves as truly national parties.

Deliberately exploited by the Lega Lombarda, now Lega Nord, the north/south cleavage provides many northern voters with a new, easy, powerful, and widely shared foundation for their political (and pre-political) identity: territoriality. Not to be confused with an ethnic movement, the Lega Nord has efficaciously and unscrupulously utilized different themes already widespread among large sectors of Italian public opinion. The solid and wide basis of the Lega appeal is provided by a strong two-pronged anti-party sentiment against *partitocrazia*, that is, the political monopoly enjoyed by Italian parties and their excesses, corruption, and degeneration, and against Italian parties, accused of no longer being able to provide representation and governability.

On top of this, the Lega Nord has offered: a strong attack on the unitary state and its centralist tendencies not buttressed by effectiveness, fairness or performance; a demand for a federal state or at least for a profound reorganization of the Italian state and the creation of a few, relatively homogeneous macro-regions; a sweeping and insistent criticism of all taxation policies amounting to a sort of threatened fiscal revolt; and pervasive opposition to what the Lega considers excessively permissive immigration policies. Through all this, the Lega Nord is aiming at the reconstruction of a powerful centre-right party to replace both the Christian Democrats and all the minor parties and to attract new voters, possibly even from the left.

Contrary to widespread beliefs, the Lega Nord is not the cause of the collapse of the old political order based upon the communism/anti-communism cleavage and upon traditional political parties. Instead, the very surge of the Lega Nord constitutes the visible by-product of that collapse, enjoying several, though by no means all, of the positive spillover effects. In any case, a realignment of the Italian party system is overdue. It was delayed and postponed by the proportional representation electoral system. It will now be facilitated, accompanied, and in the end consolidated by the replacement of PR by a peculiar single-member majority system, with some proportional clauses added to allow access to parliament to minor parties and groups. However, no stable political realignment will be constructed unless and until Italian institutions too are thoroughly reformed.

THE INSTITUTIONAL QUESTION

The institutional component of the Italian problem has rarely been appreciated, and even more rarely has it been taken seriously and properly analysed. For good reasons, most Italian politicians denied the existence of such an institutional problem until they were squarely confronted with it at the beginning of the 1980s. For less good reasons, most Italian and foreign scholars were very slow in coming to understand the significance and influence of rules, procedures and institutions for and upon the Italian political game and struggle. Interpreting the point of view of many scholars and most Italian politicians, La Palombara (1987, chapter 9) almost denied the very existence of the issue of institutional and electoral reforms and derided its relevance. Neo-institutionalism was not an accepted analytical framework and its utilization is still failing to provide an appropriate and balanced comprehension of the Italian problem (witness, among other factors, the poor reception of the Italian translation of March and Olsen, 1989).

For a long time, the Italian problem was defined with almost exclusive reference to political instability which, for many scholars, was wrongly considered to imply *tout court* democratic instability. In all likelihood, the survival and continuation of democracy in Italy was never at stake except, perhaps, when the founding elections of April 1948 were held. Even then, it is clear that, had the Italian Popular Front (the Socialist–Communist coalition) won the elections, either they would have accepted all the domestic (read: presence of a strong Catholic Church) and international (read: the allocation of Italy to the Western camp) constraints or they would have been soon and quickly ousted. Anyway, from then on, the real problem of Italian democracy cannot be defined in terms of its political instability. By all means, there were several challenges against, and within, the Italian state to make the state machinery weak and the quality of Italian democracy questionable: an attempted conservative coup in 1964, terrorism of the right and left varieties in the 1970s, the mafia and organized crime with their ties to governing politicians from the very beginning although this was especially flagrant in the 1980s. The Italian democratic framework survived and overcame all these challenges and proved to be considerably flexible, resilient and even adaptable. If anything, the problem was not political instability but, especially in the 1980s, political stagnation.

It can now be fully appreciated that the variables and the indicators of the so-called Italian political instability were, first, not well chosen and, second, not carefully applied. Governmental instability, often nothing more than frequent ministerial reshufflings, admittedly concerning the prime ministers themselves, was too often mistakenly considered an indicator of democratic instability. On the contrary, it functioned as the safety valve of a blocked political system. It was a shrewd device to accommodate changes in the strength of political parties, their factions and their leaders. It was a mechanism to shift power and consideration towards some emerging political and socio-economic groups. Finally, especially in the first two decades, that is up to the beginning of the 1970s, it permitted some generational turnover.

On the whole, in Italy there never was political instability as such. There was some governmental instability to be interpreted along the above-mentioned lines. There have been more than fifty governments since December 1945 – fifty two to be precise – and only twenty prime ministers (for a good explanation and documentation, see Hine, 1993). Slightly more than a handful of powerful politicians have monopolized decade by decade the most important governmental offices: Foreign Affairs, the Treasury, Internal Affairs, Justice, Finance, Budget and Planning. Their respective tenure was often longer than the one enjoyed by Her Majesty's Ministers. Their political and ministerial careers have outlasted those of most politicians of the European democracies (with the exception of François Mitterrand's career). Moreover, the variety of Italian governmental coalitions may be reduced, and not just for analytical purposes, to the constant governmental presence of just five parties: DC, PLI, PRI, PSDI, and PSI, and of three major coalitional combinations: centrism (PLI, DC, PRI, PSDI) from 1948 to 1960; centre-left (DC, PRI, PSDI, PSI) from 1962 to 1976; and *pentapartito* (PLI, DC, PRI, PSDI, PSI) from 1980 to 1992, exhibiting an overall exceptional stability and continuity. Was it really political stability or should we, perhaps, utilize a different term and provide a different evaluation?

It was more than political stability and, at the same time, it was less. It was definitely more than political stability. Taking into account the lack of circulation and change in the political class and in the political coalitions, the dominant characteristic of the Italian political system was political stagnation. In fact, taking into account the lack of new policies and political innovation and reforms, it was political immobilism. Only a few public policies of any innovative character were enacted, and with more difficulty implemented, by Italian governmental coalitions, usually at the inauguration of their terms in office. They were the result of mutual commitments and intense bargaining. Most of these policies were just meant to show to voters and supporting groups that governmental parties cared about them. They constituted a response to the problems accumulated or created by the previous governmental coalitions. When good politico-electoral results did not materialize immediately, as was generally the case, the parties began to pass the buck. Naturally, what followed these policies was, for several long years, nothing but bickering inside the governmental coalition itself and party positioning for the next elections.

It was less than political stability because it never worked as a fundamental premise for political innovation, for the approval of those important, in some cases decisive, policies that require time before producing positive effects. Though fundamentally stable, Italian governmental coalitions never functioned on the assumption of asking their supporters and the voters at large for short-term sacrifices in order to produce long-term benefits. They always preferred to reap some selective political and electoral benefits quickly. They never risked their short-term partisan popularity in exchange for long-term systemic gains. The high price paid for all this misplaced and under-utilized political stability became crystal clear at the end of the 1980s, after a decade of enforced and unchallenged political stability.

SYSTEMIC CORRUPTION

Power corrupts, absolute power corrupts absolutely. *Il potere logora chi non ce l'ha.* Power irks those who do not have it. Who is right: Lord Acton, credited as the author of the first sentence, or Giulio Andreotti, who pronounced the second? Until the beginning of the 1990s when the 70-odd year old Andreotti (born January 1919) was for the eighth time prime minister of Italy, allegedly on his way to become the next president of the Italian Republic, many believed that the seasoned and shrewd Italian Christian Democratic politician was, indeed, right. Then, suddenly, the investigation called *Mani Pulite* (Clean Hands) started. All major Italian politicians, those who had governed for ten years or more, in Andreotti's case forty years or more, appeared involved. It is not easy to provide a detailed and comprehensive explanation of the extent, variety and depth of the political corruption that Italian judges have slowly and gradually discovered and uncovered (on this point, see della Porta, 1992 and 1993). The investigations have multiplied, become pervasive, and are by no means ended. Almost no trial has been held so far except for a few politicians not enjoying parliamentary immunity and some industrialists. Following a bitter parliamentary confrontation, almost all the parliamentarians accused of corruption and violation of the law on public financing of political parties have been stripped of their immunity and are awaiting trial.

There are, of course, different roots and different patterns of corruption.

Here I will deal briefly with political corruption only, defined as the system created by Italian politicians belonging to governmental parties and, in several cases, occupying governmental office. Understandably, a certain amount of political corruption had always characterized Italian politics. It was, so to speak, physiological. A modest quantity of individual corruption was accompanied by a modest quantity of partisan corruption. Both could be absorbed, though not absolved, by the system at large. At the beginning of the 1980s, the five-party coalitions deliberately changed all this. On the one hand, the parties in power felt insecure enough in their competition with the communists to grab all the money they could take for their electoral campaigns and their political headquarters, and some for personal enrichment, in addition to the money they needed to reward some of their most helpful supporters. On the other hand, especially towards the end of the 1980s, the members of the *pentapartito* felt so secure in power that practically and blatantly they set out to blackmail all those firms, companies and entrepreneurs (and there were many) that one way or another were obliged to work for and together with the state, often on state and local government contracts, as well as state managers. After all, state managers owed their jobs to political patronage, to *lottizzazione*. Therefore, they knew perfectly well that they could lose them immediately if they did not behave.

Most private entrepreneurs had taken for granted the continued existence of the communist threat. All governing parties and politicians exploited the existence and survival of this alleged threat to oblige the entrepreneurs, even powerful ones such as Agnelli and De Benedetti, to pay sizeable kickbacks. On both sides, the assumption was that those governing politicians could not be replaced in the foreseeable future. This assumption was, of course, to a large extent a sort of self-fulfilling prophecy. The immense amount of money poured by the entrepreneurs into the coffers of governing parties, factions and individual politicians helped them to win votes and to reproduce their governing power.

The nature of political corruption and its adduced motivation – anticommunism – spell out a major difference between the Italian case of corruption and all the other cases in democratic regimes, with the outstanding exception of Japan, so similar in several respects to Italy (a dominant, highly factionalized party, lack of turnover, a fascist past, a communist threat, an almost symbiotic relationship between entrepreneurs and politicians). Several Italian politicians took advantage of the political climate and the political opportunities offered by the *pentapartito* and happily and arrogantly enriched themselves. By so doing, they also enhanced their chances of successful political careers. For many Italian politicians, a successful political career also meant a major advancement in social status. Economic success bred political success.

Now these same politicians will go on trial and will, it is hoped, be removed permanently from the political scene. The corruption problem is, however, not just personal. It is structural. It is not just the problem of how to finance political parties and electoral campaigns and how to sanction violations to the existing laws. It involves shaping a politico-administrative system less exposed to corruption and more capable of preventing all types of corrupt practices. The Italian case can neatly be characterized as a major instance of systemic corruption. The political system as a whole – its political, economic and social protagonists and its rules, procedures and institutions – were corrupt in a technical sense.

Systemic corruption requires systemic correction. The problem derives from the very nature of the Italian political system. This explains why corruption is systemic from two points of view. Corruption is the product of the political system, and corruption has affected the entire system. Let me try to offer an explanation that goes to the very roots of the First Republic. Italian parties first wrote a constitution and created the institutions deriving from it. Then they manipulated the functioning of those institutions, parliament and government especially, but also the centre-periphery circuit, that is, the institutions providing for a limited and controlled dose of political decentralization. Inter-party and party-institution relationships were shaped and made to function according to what Italian jurists and scholars appropriately defined as the 'material' constitution. This material constitution was obviously quite different from the formal constitution. It was not, and it is not, merely the ever-present gap between formal rules and procedures and their practical application and implementation. It was the conscious manipulation of these rules and procedures that gave birth to the material constitution.

For more than a decade after the approval of the constitution, it was the opposition that repeatedly asked for its full implementation and the governmental majority that postponed it. It took seven years to inaugurate the Constitutional Court and twenty-two years to elect the regional governments. In so far as the constitutional and institutional systems worked, it was only because there was a dominant party located at the centre of the political alignment. The Christian Democrats were that dominant party, flexible and factionalized, capable and willing to accommodate many of the demands made by their governmental partners and even by the communist opposition. The constitution was never fully implemented, for instance in regard to citizens' rights, the recognition of trade unions and their representativeness, and the regulation of the role of the parties.

However, the constitution was frequently, though informally, violated. For instance, it was circumvented in the extremely important procedure concerning the formation of the government. It was never true that, as article 92 states, 'the President of the Republic appoints the President of the Council of Ministers and, on his proposal, the Ministers'. Up to the late 1970s, when as popular and maverick a president as Sandro Pertini decided to set aside the material constitution, the implemented procedure was quite different. The secretaries of the parties making up the prospective coalition would agree on the name of a Christian Democrat or, when the Christian Democrats themselves were divided, on a roster of DC names, and would submit it to the President of the Republic. He would then appoint the specified candidate or choose one from the roster. Then he would sign the list of ministers not chosen by the President of the Council of Ministers, but by the leaders of the factions of the parties making up the governmental coalition.

Obviously, there were many negative consequences. The President of the Council of Ministers chosen according to the material constitution could be replaced by party secretaries, as he often was, and did not really have the power to dismiss his own ministers without creating (the preconditions for) a governmental crisis. Neither individual party secretaries nor faction leaders could tolerate such an attack on their power and prestige. No governmental crisis was ever discussed in parliament, nor was a vote taken on it. All the governmental crises were provoked by partisan differences concerning persons, programmes and strategies, and solved outside parliament, usually by those same party secretaries.

The violations of the constitutional procedure were not a minor problem in a parliamentary form of government. No early dissolution of parliament, and there were five of them from 1972 on, was announced, in conformity with the constitution, by the President of the Republic, having received the advice of the Speakers of the two Houses. All the dissolutions were decided by the party secretaries making up the governmental majority, or by the most influential among them, i.e. those indispensable to the continuation of governmental collaboration. Having reached this point of constitutional manipulation, not even the full implementation of the constitution could represent a solution. The communists and several sectors of progressive public opinion pleaded for a long time for a return to the constitution, but to no avail, and with many unforeseen risks. A constitution based on the role and strength of political parties cannot be bent to function against their will. Italian institutions and institutional office-holders could not be pitted against Italian political parties and their leaders and sub-leaders. Strong party leaders against strong institutional leaders may be the best recipe for an institutional and constitutional crisis.

SISYPHUS' TASK: REFORMING THE CONSTITUTION

The battle for institutional and constitutional reforms started for real when in 1979 the issue was raised, though in a manipulatory manner, by the secretary-general of the Italian Socialist Party. The Great Reform became the name of the thing, though the perspective bestowed upon it by Craxi was as grandiose as it was vague. In any case, it was never followed by serious attempts to introduce concrete, significant reforms. The Socialist secretary became prime minister in August 1983. From then on, all he wanted was to strengthen the role of the government and the power of his office and to compress the role of parliament and the (limited) power of individual parliamentarians. The very nature of the DC, a confederation of competing oligarchies called factions, was opposed to this type of transformation. The governing ability of the Christian Democrats was based precisely on not deciding among competing interests, but in allowing a careful process of filtering, in not excluding any of those interests, in producing a slow, long-term, incessant intermediation. The political culture of the communists opposed any concentration of powers in any one single office, in one person, in the government at the expense of parliament. The organized and disciplined communist presence in parliament would have lost weight, their ability to bargain would have been sharply curtailed, their political indispensability would have been seriously questioned.

As was to be expected, exactly because he did not really desire any incisive reform, Craxi played the DC against the PCI. In so doing he unveiled the unwillingness and the inability of the two major parties to agree on some highly overdue institutional and constitutional reforms. For his part, Craxi adamantly opposed electoral reform since only proportional representation would allow his party to continue to enjoy a pivotal role in the fragmented party alignment. Most Christian Democrats did not want to abandon PR, fearful of destroying their traditional, faithful and subordinate political and governmental allies. Most communists went as far as to identify PR with Italian democracy, or democracy *tout court*. It was an uphill battle for the minority within the parties who truly desired the reform of the Italian form of government, the restoration and enhancement of the powers of the voters, the streamlining of the relationship between parliament and government, limitations on the powers of the parties and the possibility of alternation between competing coalitions. In order to pursue all these objectives, what was needed was a systemic reform.

To make a very long, complex and bitter story short, it quickly became crystal-clear that a parliament blackmailed by Craxi and by the majority of the Christian Democrats would never pass a reform of the electoral law. At that point, the reformers undertook an innovative strategy. According to the Italian constitution, 500,000 voters and/or five regional councils enjoy the right to request a referendum on existing laws. Italian referendums, however, can only repeal entire laws or sections of them. Constitutional articles are excluded from this procedure as well as some specific laws: fiscal and budget laws, amnesty measures, international treaties.

It is important to recall that the law regulating the referendum was passed by the Italian parliament only in 1970. It was the by-product of the explicit condition posed by the Christian Democrats not to filibuster against the law allowing divorce. It implicitly delivered the message that the referendum would be used as soon as possible against that law. Indeed, the Catholics easily collected the signatures and the first Italian popular referendum took place in 1974 on the divorce law. For the first time the Christian Democrats and the Catholics found themselves on the losing side of a major national consultation. Throughout the 1970s, the referendum instrument was utilized by the Radicals to challenge *partitocrazia* and to enhance and protect citizens' rights (e.g. abortion).

As to the electoral referendums, following an intense and acrimonious legal battle, the Constitutional Court decided that only one of them was admissible: the least important and supposedly the least damaging for the DC and the PSI. Those declared inadmissible were a referendum transforming the electoral law of the Senate into a mix of majoritarian (75 per cent) and proportional seats (25 per cent), and a referendum providing for a majority law to elect all Italian mayors. In any case, the remaining electoral referendum was not thought important enough to inflame the political debate and to enliven the electoral campaign. Admittedly, to ask the voters whether they were in favour of decreasing the number of preference votes from four and three, depending on the number of seats available in each constituency, to one, was not to rely on a highly mobilizing issue. Nevertheless, the promoters of the referendum, a handful of not very prominent parliamentarians and a few representatives of some cultural associations, succeeded in making it a pronouncement on the electoral law itself. The voters were invited to go to the polls not just to reduce the preference votes to one in order to prevent the creation of corrupt ties between clans of candidates and local and national interest groups. They were asked to cast a vote in favour of a closer relationship between voters and candidates and to express their preference for a non-proportional (plurality or majority) electoral system.

Leading Christian Democratic politicians, Craxi himself, monolithically supported by almost all the Socialist politicians, and the leader of the Lega Lombarda Umberto Bossi all campaigned in favour of abstention, hoping to render the referendum void. Italian referendums are void if the turnout is less than 50 per cent of the registered voters. The abstention campaign failed miserably. Much to the surprise of these powerful politicians, 62.5 per cent of the voters went to the polls and more than 90 per cent of them voted to reduce the number of preference votes. The overall message was correctly interpreted as a demand for a thorough reform of the proportional system (Pasquino, 1993) – so much so that the promoters of the referendum and their leader, the moderate Christian Democrat Mario Segni, almost immediately launched a new campaign. Having reworded the questions to be submitted to the voters, the promoters of the electoral referendums collected more than 1,200,000 signatures to repeal the relevant sections of the electoral law of the Senate to make it almost a plurality law and to transform the electoral law of city governments as indicated above. The cracks in what had appeared up to that moment an unassailable coalition dominated by the DC and the PSI became evident. The difficult politico-institutional transformation of Italian democracy had slowly begun. Some elements of systemic correction have already made their appearance. They all require serious analytical consideration.

THE COLLAPSE OF THE OLD SYSTEM

The results of the national elections of 1992 made it clear that the alliance known as CAF, Craxi–Andreotti–Forlani, was rejected by the voters. Their pre-electoral pact to divide the political spoils in advance (Andreotti or Forlani to become President of the Republic, Craxi to be appointed prime minister), came to nothing (on these developments see Pasquino and McCarthy, 1993). In the meantime, the investigation dubbed 'Clean Hands' had reached several of Craxi's close collaborators. When Oscar Luigi Scalfaro was elected to the Presidency of the Republic by a majority including the Democratic Party of the Left (PDS), it became clear that the entire strategy followed by the CAF had been defeated. Since they did not succeed in controlling the office of President of the Republic, they could not appoint a prime minister of their liking, not least Craxi himself. The task of forming the new government, made up by the same parties, was given to the Socialist, Giuliano Amato (June 1992–April 1993), a very close collaborator of Craxi who had been spared by the judges. The judicial investigation in Milan, later in Rome, and in Palermo produced the request that parliament authorize trials for Craxi, Forlani, Andreotti, and several of their close collaborators, most of whom were former ministers as well. The charges were different: Forlani, Craxi and many former Christian Democratic and Socialist ministers were accused of violating the law on public financing of political parties and of corruption. Andreotti was accused, among other things, of collusion with the mafia and of having ordered the killing of a journalist who was investigating Aldo Moro's assassination.

It is impossible and, at this point probably not very useful, to follow all the details of the collapse of a governing political class in a sea of corruption, crimes and misdemeanour. Much more interesting and more important is to analyse the dynamics of political and institutional change. The incrimination of Forlani, Andreotti and several other powerful DC faction leaders seriously wounded and weakened the DC. The referendum leader, Mario Segni, and his Popolari per la Riforma abandoned the party in October 1992. At the same time, in response, a new secretary was elected, the mildly reformist Mino Martinazzoli. But the renewal of the Christian Democratic party is slow and the strategy still confused.

A different story must be told about the PSI. Craxi's strenuous resistance in the office of party secretary produced a sharp political decline, almost the explosion, and then the quasi-disappearance of the Socialist Party. The socialists experimented with two new secretaries, both of them from the trade union movement. The first of them, Giorgio Benvenuto, lasted for a few months and was soon ousted after a power struggle. The second, Ottaviano Del Turco, must face the existence of two rump socialist groups. Of the old parties, only the Democratic Party of the Left, which is to be considered either partially old, as the heir to the PCI, or partially new, since it was founded in February 1991, appears to be in relatively good shape. It may be the only party capable of confronting the Lega Nord, which may have already become the largest party in the north of Italy.

A political system dominated by political parties will have to find a different political foundation when its parties decline or disappear if it is to preserve and enhance its democracy. Two developments are at work in the Italian political system. On the one hand, some important institutional changes are in the making. On the other hand, significant political efforts have already been made to adjust to these institutional changes, to take advantage of them, and to counteract them. Though, or perhaps really because, they have been punctuated by political incriminations and arrests, Italian political dynamics have experienced an acceleration. The political system itself has finally been subjected to the wind of institutional changes. The most important of these changes have again been fostered directly and indirectly by the referendums.

Precisely and only because it was spurred by a referendum request, in March 1993 parliament succeeded in approving two new electoral laws for city governments. In all towns with less than 15,000 inhabitants, the leader of the party, coalition or list having polled a plurality of the votes will automatically become mayor. His/her party, coalition or list will obtain 60 per cent of the seats, effectively a sort of governability bonus. The remaining seats will be allocated proportionally to the other parties, coalitions and lists. In all the other cities, the candidate who gets more than 50 per cent of the votes will immediately be elected mayor. Otherwise, there will be a run-off between the two best-placed candidates. The winner's party, coalition or list will get 60 per cent of the seats in the city council, the remaining seats again to be distributed proportionally to the other parties, coalitions and lists.

Administrative elections have already been held in almost all the important cities ravaged by governability crises: that is, coalitional instability, decision-making inefficacy, political corruption. These elections have all produced good results, both institutionally and politically. Institutionally, the mayor has indeed taken office immediately after his election. Politically, the mayor's election has created incentives for the formation of competing coalitions and for a realignment of the party system. Incidentally, unable to find good mayoral candidates and to participate in viable coalitions, the Christian Democrats and the Socialists have almost disappeared from the political scene at the local level, even in major cities such as Turin, Milan, Rome, Naples and Palermo, where they had governed for long periods of time.

Where parliament had finally succeeded, a special bicameral committee on institutional reforms failed. That is, because of multiple and irreconcilable internal divisions, the committee did not succeed in approving on time a new electoral law for the Senate (nor for the House). Therefore, on 18 April 1993 a series of referendums was held, paramount among them being one on the electoral law for the Senate. More than 80 per cent of the voters decided to repeal several portions of the electoral law for the Senate and, in fact, transformed it into a single-member plurality system with a proportional correction. With varying though high percentages of 'yes' votes, the Italian electorate also repealed the law on public financing of political parties and abolished several ministries (Agriculture, State Participations, Tourism), as requested by several regional councils. A smaller percentage also repealed the most repressive clause of a law on drug use.

The interpretation of these results was clear and unequivocal. Italian voters wanted a true electoral reform away from proportional representation and toward a plurality or majority system. They desired a reduction in the power of political parties and a true decentralization of functions and resources from the state to the regional governments. The foundations of a different politico-institutional system have been laid. More specifically, the space for parties has been reduced and the space for institutions and institutional office-holders has been potentially enlarged. A different balance of powers between the central state and local governments will have to be created by trimming the powers of the central state. Even more importantly, perhaps, a powerful challenge has been presented to the parties and the party system. They must transform themselves and realign because the new electoral laws offer significant new potential for competition and collaboration.

FROM ELECTORAL POLITICS TOWARDS POLITICAL ALTERNATION

The overall Italian problem is now very clear. The outcome remains uncertain. The problem consists in transferring power from (declining and corrupt) political parties to voters and institutions (and office-holders). This transfer requires a total restructuring of the Italian form of parliamentary government. By the end of 1993, only a few partial solutions had been attempted and only one had been implemented. In particular, following the results of the referendum, the House and the Senate had succeeded in drafting and approving their respective electoral laws. 4 August 1993 is a date to be remembered. The First Italian Republic practically buried the electoral proportional system that shaped its life and the nature of its protagonists. Though the product does not seem extraordinarily good, the new electoral laws promise to facilitate many further changes.

The foundation of the new electoral laws is the combination of 75 per cent of the seats being allocated in single-member constituencies through a plurality formula and 25 per cent of the seats being allocated proportionally by two slightly different methods. Specifically, for the Senate the proportional seats will be allocated in regional constituencies. For the House, the voters have two ballots: one is to be used to elect candidates in single-member constituencies through a plurality formula; the other to choose between party lists. The House proportional seats will be allotted in regional constituencies, as for the Senate, but only to those parties having polled at least 4 per cent of the national vote. There are several other technicalities that are as difficult to explain as they are easy to criticize. They all amount to a desperate attempt to retain some power for declining parties and their leaders. Not a single one of these technicalities pushes in the direction of encouraging coalitions. Therefore, the problem of how to elect a government and/or to designate a prime minister remains unsolved. The solution found for the election of big-city mayors has been rejected, though the issue of the direct popular election of the prime minister remains very much alive. Also, no attention has been paid to a further decentralization of political power to the regional governments, while the Lega Nord is still making the case for the creation of macro-regions, or even three confederated republics.

As to the consequences of the new electoral laws, it is important to take into account that all single-member constituencies must be designed from scratch. This factor alone will create a lot of uncertainty among parties and candidates. Certainly, there will be safe seats for the Lega in the north and for the PDS in several central regions, the famous 'Red Belt'. On the whole, most constituencies will have no assured winner, particularly in the south. The feared tripartite division of Italy therefore may not materialize, for two reasons. In the first place, the south will have a large share of constituencies that cannot be monopolized by a single party. In the second place, there will be an attempt to create broad coalitions including several participants with relatively different, though compatible, positions. If a risk has to be identified, it will be the formation of a national parliament without any cohesive majority, hence exposed to the classic Italian solution: *trasformismo*. Having independently won their own election, several deputies may be willing either to support or to oppose a government on the basis of the resources, favours or patronage that government will give them. And, conversely, a government will last only so long as it is capable of selectively providing these resources.

For several reasons, not least in order to prevent *trasformismo*, two political developments are to be expected. The first is that several parties will try to reach agreements to support individual candidates in single-member constituencies. In the process, they may even create something resembling a national coalition. This outcome remains difficult for the Lega because it is too strong in the north to be willing to look for allies, and too weak in the south to be appealing for potential allies. This outcome appears more likely for the PDS, especially in the light of its success in creating and participating in winning coalitions to elect mayors. The creation of coalitions is imperative for the Christian Democrats if they want to survive as a viable party. Whether or not constituency, regional, or national coalitions are created, the election of many candidates in single-member constituencies will depend on their personal qualities, political biography, vote-winning ability and local representativeness. In many cases, party organizers will be obliged to choose between putting up loyal candidates of their own with a slim chance of winning, or independent candidates representing a coalition and more likely to win. The second development then is that, gradually and inexorably, Italian electoral politics will move away from *partitocrazia*, from absolute party domination and move toward candidate-centred politics.

Public opinion seems finally inclined to get rid of the entire political class. Though still imperfect, the new electoral mechanisms will facilitate some circulation of the political class. However, it remains a moot question where the new political class will come from. Probably, a couple of national elections will be necessary to produce such a new political class. Perhaps it will then be possible to break the hold on Italian politics of too many individuals who have not lived for politics, but, as Max Weber feared, off politics. In sum, what is taking place in Italy is not a revolution. What is at stake is not democracy as such. It is not a revolution, though it may become a significant transformation of politicians, parties and institutions. Italian democracy itself is not threatened, but its quality may be considerably improved. The test of success for an accomplished political transformation and the precondition for an improvement in the quality of democracy will be the implementation of alternation among competing coalitions. Alternation has always eluded the Italian political system. Though the initial steps are promising, the path towards alternation still appears long, difficult and painful. Until then, one must suspend a definitive judgement.

October 1993

NOTE

Portions of this chapter have appeared in the *Journal of Democracy*, 5: 1994

REFERENCES

della Porta, D. (1992), *Lo scambio occulto. Casi di corruzione politica in Italia*, Bologna: Il Mulino.

della Porta, D. (1993), 'The Immoral Capital: the Kickbacks of Milan', in S. Hellman and G. Pasquino (eds), *Italian Politics. A Review, Volume 8*, London: Pinter, 98–115.

Hine, D. (1993), *Governing Italy. The Politics of Bargained Pluralism*, Oxford: Clarendon Press.

Katz, R.S. (1987), 'Party Government and Its Alternatives', in R.S. Katz (ed), *Party Governments: European and American Experiences*, Berlin: de Gruyter, 1–26.

Kirchheimer, O. (1965), 'Confining Conditions and Revolutionary Breakthroughs', *American Political Science Review*, 69: 964–74.

La Palombara, J. (1987), *Democracy Italian Style*, New Haven–London: Yale University Press.

March, J.G. and Olsen, J.P. (1989), *Rediscovering Institutions. The Organizational Basis of Politics*, New York: The Free Press.

Pasquino, G. (1987), 'Party Government in Italy: Achievements and Prospects', in R.S. Katz (ed.), *Party Governments: European and American Experiences*, Berlin: de Gruyter, 202–42.

Pasquino, G. (ed), (1993), *Votare un solo candidato. Le conseguenze politiche della preferenza unica*, Bologna: Il Mulino.

Pasquino, G. and McCarthy, P. (1993), *The End of Postwar Politics in Italy*, Boulder, Co: Westview Press.

Rokkan, S. (1970), *Citizens Elections Parties*, Oslo: Universitetsforlaget.

Scoppola, P. (1992), *La Repubblica dei partiti*, Bologna: Il Mulino.

10

A Victory Against all the Odds: the Declining Fortunes of the Spanish Socialist Party

José Amodia

As is well known, 1992 was Spain's *annus mirabilis*. The enormous success of the Barcelona Olympics, the gigantic and colourful Seville *Expo*, commemorating the fifth centenary of Christopher Columbus's discovery of America, and, on a lower level, Madrid's turn as the European capital of culture, all helped to create an aura of prestige and modernity. During those twelve months Spain was the focus of world attention. Only seventeen years after Franco's demise Spain was a totally different country.

In the midst of the festivities, another more politically relevant anniversary fell – on 28 October 1982 the Spanish Socialist Party (PSOE) had won a landslide victory, and ten years later it was still in power. The Socialists, naturally, commemorated the occasion as part of the great national *fiesta*, and had, they claimed, good reasons to celebrate. They had made Spain wealthier, had undertaken a profound programme of modernization, had consolidated the democratic system, and had placed the country back in the international arena. Undeniably, all these were considerable achievements. But behind the glittering facade of 1992, all was not well. As in a masked ball the colourful disguises were hiding a different reality; when the dancing stopped, the country and the ruling party had to face some very serious problems: a profound economic recession; a growing public mistrust of democratic institutions, in particular political parties; the disappearance of ideological goals and utopian horizons; an alarming proliferation of cases of public corruption; and, last but not least, factional divisions and clashes – growing bitterer and more frequent by the day – in the Socialist family, between right and left, between government and unions, between PSOE and government.

The early calling of elections, several months before parliament had completed its life cycle, took place against a background of crisis in both the PSOE and the Socialist government. The prime minister was appealing to the electorate in an attempt to renew his mandate for another four years before economic and political deterioration placed such an outcome beyond his reach. The pollsters had been worrying Felipe González and his party with ominous predictions for some time. They might just cling on to power, but if the decline continued a victory for the conservative People's Party (PP) was a distinct possibility. Going to the polls early was a very risky move for the prime minister to make, but inevitable given the worsening circumstances. An early election was a bid for survival. By the time González announced his decision to dissolve parliament, on 12 April 1993, all the celebrations of the previous year must have seemed like a very unreal and distant dream to him.

ECONOMIC GLOOM

The electoral triumph of the Socialist Party in 1982 can be seen as the final stage in the transition to democracy in post-Franco Spain. Until then public attention had centred on the need to set up a new and stable institutional framework. Spain had undergone a long constituent process that had given the early electoral confrontations – those of 1977 and 1979 and, to some extent, 1982 – a systemic nature. Voters had been called to the polls to choose the architects of the new democratic system. By the autumn of 1982 that operation, at least in its most formal aspects, had been completed, and the Socialist victory was interpreted as the final proof of democratic change – for the first time power was in the hands of non-Francoists. As if to prove the arrival of normality, the centre of gravity shifted from political to economic issues.

Seen in profile, the Spanish economy during the decade of Socialist rule peaks in the middle years with a clear depression at both ends. The Socialists took over an economy in crisis. As one of them wrote recently: 'In 1982 we found ourselves in the worst economic moment since the beginning of the transition' (Fernández Marugán, 1992: 140). The crisis was not limited to Spain and its roots went back to the mid-1970s, if not earlier, but the poor economic indicators were doubly worrying, coinciding as they did with the Socialist victory. The GDP had only achieved a meagre 1.2 per cent increase in the previous year; inflation was at 14.4 per cent and rising; unemployment had reached 2.2 million, more than 16 per cent of the labour force (*Anuario El País 1993*: 260–1). The recession continued for another three years, but then the economic upturn in the Western world, the reduction in oil prices and Spain's accession to the EC in 1986, which brought with it an avalanche of foreign investment, were to provide the necessary impetus for growth and development, at a rhythm well above the Community's average, and lasting to the end of the decade. However, the recession was to return.

The general lines of the Socialist government's economic policies during the 1980s are as follows: First, they applied what has sometimes been termed 'Spanish Socialist monetarism' (Rodríguez Braun, 1992: 53). Neither of the two finance ministers that Felipe González had in his cabinet during those years – Miguel Boyer and Carlos Solchaga – fitted comfortably into a socialist mould. Their main priority from the beginning was to reduce inflation by a tight control over the money supply, which in turn required the maintenance of high interest rates and a strong currency. A policy, in fact, not dissimilar from that of many right-wing governments elsewhere in Europe.

Second, they struggled to maintain some kind of balance between, on the one hand, the neo-liberal nature of many of their economic measures, and on the other the moral imperative to pay some heed to the two qualifiers – 'Socialist' and 'Working Class' – adorning the party's name. Felipe González's governments have been lauded for completing a belated bourgeois revolution, for bringing about the socio-economic modernization of Spain, and for narrowing the gap between Spain and other Western countries. The full integration into the EC/EU has been, and continues to be, the guiding light of their economic policy. This explains their process of industrial restructuring, their pandering to the needs of the market, their support for the private sector, and so on. Even the Madrid daily *El País*, never too harsh in its assessment of Felipe González and his government, had to recognize that, during the first ten years of Socialist rule, economic policy had been more in line with the ideas of the IMF and OECD than the party's programmes – *El País* even attributes the following words to an anonymous minister: 'The liberal thinking of the Bank of Spain has been far more important than any of the party's congresses' (*El País*, 28 October 1992).

It is equally true that during the 'red decade' – so termed ironically by the left (Umbral, 1993) – the Socialists tried to check some of the more damaging effects of their neo-liberal policies by broadening the boundaries of the welfare state. This required some increase in taxation – in the last ten years the tax burden has gone up from 31.4 per cent to 39 per cent of GDP to pay for higher pensions, wider unemployment benefits, and extra expenditure on education and health. However, and in spite of strong denunciations from the right (Jiménez Losantos, 1993: 124–7), the weight of the public sector in the Spanish economy is still 5 points below the average for the European Union. And it is not partisan to say that the creation of wealth and the requirements of the market have taken precedence over social services or the reduction of inequalities.

Finally, a third feature has been the acceptance of a permanently high level of unemployment. This has been the blackest spot on the government's record – especially black for a socialist party that came into office in 1982 with the firm commitment to generate employment. In fact, both employment and unemployment increased during the 1980s. Some 1.5 million jobs were created, though mostly in the non-productive sectors of the economy— regional administration, for instance – or in the form of temporary contracts (Guerra, 1992: 233–5). On the reverse side, the number of people out of work – especially young people – continued to escalate: towards the end of 1992 the figure was 2.75 million, 18.5 per cent of the labour force, more than twice the EC average, and still rising (*Anuario El País 1993*: 425).

Unemployment was, and still is, the main concern of most Spaniards, but it was by no means the only negative indicator in the economic charts at the time of the 1993 election. Gloom and despondency had replaced the optim- ism of the late 1980s. Spain was a more modern and a more prosperous country, but economic recession was obliterating the memory of past achieve- ments. Not even the hope of a united Europe, shared by most political forces in the country, seemed to offer a way forward. Spain was finding it difficult to meet the requirements of convergence. By the beginning of 1993 it only satisfied one of the five criteria – the level of public debt (*Anuario El Mundo 1993*: 219) – and the Maastricht Treaty, which Felipe González had adhered to with great enthusiasm, was beginning to fall apart. On the economic front the electoral battle promised to be a difficult one for the Socialists.

THE DEBASEMENT OF DEMOCRATIC INSTITUTIONS

Spain acquired democratic institutions at a time when the adequacy of those institutions was already being severely tested by the speed of change in post-industrial societies. Many have wondered whether the 1978 con- stitution, even though it has so far served the country well, provides a suitable political framework for the future, solid enough to sustain stable governance, yet with sufficient flexibility to allow democracy to grow and prosper. The years of Socialist government have, according to some, raised serious doubts about it (Otero Novas, 1987; Jiménez de Parga, 1993). Socialist power has been based not just upon overall majorities in parliament; they have had control, too, over more than half of the 17 'autonomous communities' (or regions) and over many of the larger municipal councils. This prepotency – to echo a term, *prepotencia*, often used by Spanish pundits in this context – has been reinforced by the lack of a convincing alternative to Socialist rule. Unchallenged power over a long period has led to the erosion of many democratic controls. The debasement of some public institutions is now perceived by many as unacceptable.

The word *rodillo* (steamrollering action) has often been used to describe the government's attitude towards the Cortes in general, and towards parlia- mentary minorities in particular. With an overall Socialist majority in both chambers, parliament has had a rather languid and politically irrelevant existence, its activities largely limited to endorsing proposals presented by the executive. Even the annual debates on the state of the nation, introduced by the Socialists soon after taking power, and shown live on television, have only served to spread the impression that little of importance is being decided. To this one could add the stubborn refusal on the part of the government to set up parliamentary committees to investigate cases of suspected deviation or abuse of institutional power; or, worse still, the tendency of ministers, and especially the prime minister himself, not to attend parliamentary sessions, even when matters as important as the budget are being discussed! (*ABC*, 28 October 1992).

This attitude of disregard for parliamentary practices may be partly motivated by the presidentialist nature of the Spanish political system. Parliament is dominated by the executive, and this in turn by the powerful figure of the premier. Personal qualities take precedence over institutional strengths, objective factors yield to subjective ones. The electoral system pushes in the same direction, providing party caucuses with total control over electoral lists, and encouraging them to organize their campaign around their candidate for the premiership. In the case of the PSOE, Felipe González, after twenty years as party leader and over ten as prime minister, largely unchallenged in both roles, has come to epitomize the personalization of power. Vote-catching in the end becomes more dependent on personal charisma than on party programmes or institutional processes.

Intentionally or otherwise, the process of degradation has filtered through to other areas of public life. In an attempt to remove all Francoist traces from the judiciary, the Socialist government has more than once curtailed the autonomy of its ruling council, imposing political controls and endangering in the process the sacred principle of judicial independence. The decision taken in 1985 to place in parliamentary hands the election of all the twenty members who sit on the Judiciary's General Council – the majority of them had previously been selected by their peers – was not only bordering on the unconstitutional, but was practically subjecting judicial power to any unscrupulous government with an overall majority in Congress (Esteban, 1992: 303–6). Of course, a Socialist government whose deputy prime minister, Alfonso Guerra, was, in the summer of 1990, announcing that Montesquieu's doctrine on the separation of powers was now dead, could not be unduly concerned with matters as trivial as judicial independence.

Relations between the government and the media have deteriorated noticeably. The PSOE victory in 1982 had been received with great enthusiasm by the press, radio and television, but the honeymoon did not last long. Party and government soon started to object to media criticism, and to express, publicly and in no uncertain terms, their displeasure. The sharpness of some ministers' attacks on certain publications went far beyond what would be considered acceptable in most Western democracies (Cavero, 1991; Sinova and Tusell, 1990: 195–219). Political and financial pressure was brought to bear upon the most outspoken newspapers, such as *El Independiente* and *Diario 16*. Conversely, the Socialists have not resisted the formation of large multimedia corporations with less unfavourable attitudes towards those in power – the best-known example being that of PRISA, a conglomerate of press, radio and television, with the daily *El País* as its flagship, recently described in a British newspaper as 'the sort of empire that would raise alarm bells among anti-trust authorities in other parts of the world' (*Financial Times*, 2 April 1993). As for television, they have been more than happy to emulate all their predecessors in exploiting a publicly financed service to disseminate government and party messages.

As early as 1983, the Socialists had announced their intention to introduce legal provisions for the setting up of private TV stations. The project was only given the go-ahead six years later. Since then, and after a great deal of public controversy over the granting of franchises, three independent channels have started to operate nationally. Their new presence has undoubtedly been felt – particularly in the 1993 general election – but in audience appeal and in financial and technical resources, they are still no challenge for the public network, which the government continues to manipulate to its own advantage. The content of news bulletins or *telediarios* is, at times, incredibly biased. The four directors general of TVE since 1982 have all been political appointees. At moments of heightened political tension – the NATO referendum in 1986 or the general strike of December 1988 – the messages on the screens of both public channels were unequivocally pro-government.

Bad practices tend to spread. The story repeats itself with the regional TV stations operating in certain autonomous communities, and not necessarily under Socialist control. Frequent accusations of interference and bias have been levelled against the nationalist party of Jordi Pujol in Catalonia, and even more frequently against Manuel Fraga Iribarne and his right-wing government in Galicia. Independence and objectivity are not easily associated with public television in Spain.

The general deterioration of public institutions could not fail to affect the main protagonists in the political arena – the parties. Party crises have been almost endemic from the inception of democracy in Spain (Claudín, 1980). The party system has undergone a number of mutations, and its lack of definition can, to a considerable extent, be explained by party instability (Amodia, 1990a). The PSOE had been the main exception to this rule. The Socialists had been able to follow an even course under the firm and unquestioned leadership of Felipe González and his *alter ego*, Alfonso Guerra, second in command both in the government, as deputy prime minister, and in the party, as vice-secretary general. But the long period in office would eventually take its toll. By the late 1980s profound internal divisions had begun to appear. A number of scandals concerning party finances and reaching the highest levels in the party did the rest. The internal cohesion that the party had enjoyed since 1979 started to break up.

POLITICAL AND FINANCIAL CORRUPTION

During the last few years the spectre of political corruption has reared its ugly head in many European countries, raising serious public morality issues even in some of the older and well established democracies. Political parties have become gigantic electoral machines whose voracious appetite can never be satisfied by legal means. The Spanish case, though only one among many, is paradigmatic.

Recent studies have shown that corrupt practices in the running of parties started well before the first Socialist victory in 1982 (Díaz Herrera and Tijeras, 1991; Cierva, 1992; Torres, 1993). It is known that the UCD, the ruling party during the early days of the transition, partly financed its activities in various irregular ways (Cierva, 1992: 307–30; Torres, 1993: 14–15). The truth is that none of the major parties is exempt from guilt. They have all been involved in financial scandals or have been accused of receiving undisclosed funds. The Socialists, however, had promised something different and better. They wanted to be seen as the heirs of a decent and caring tradition going back a century. In the 1979 election, which coincided·with the PSOE's first centenary, their propaganda boasted of *cien años de honradez* – one hundred years of honesty. And at the next election, three years later, when all the polls were predicting a massive Socialist victory, Felipe González promised Spaniards to bring about a profound ethical change so as to transform public morality in Spain. It was the only way, he claimed, to make the country work properly (*El País*, 8 October 1982).

All this made disenchantment all the greater when, towards the end of the 1980s, an increasing number of cases of corruption began to surface. Parliamentary majorities and wide powers and influence in other spheres of public life were being used by the Socialists to set up clientelist networks, to reward loyalty and services rendered to the party and its leaders, to amass fortunes by the less scrupulous among them, and, above all, to finance the astronomical expenditure incurred in running and maintaining the party in power. In short, the Socialists in office were neither different from, nor ethically better than other political forces. They all had their dirty linen to launder, but the Socialist basket appeared to be the largest by far.

Lack of space precludes any description of the numerous cases of corruption that have been uncovered in the last few years, usually as the result of investigative journalism. Their names – Ibercorp, Guerra, Renfe, Naseiro,

Burgos, Filesa, etc. – are now familiar to most Spaniards. It will suffice
here to offer a general outline of the background to such cases.

Political parties in Spain are financed with public money. The amounts
assigned to each of them fall into two categories: an electoral entitlement
determined by the number of seats and votes obtained by each party, and a
running costs allowance dependent on the size of each parliamentary group.
Private contributions are also permitted under certain conditions. All these
matters are regulated in a political parties finance law passed in July 1987.
But legal hopes and reality are separated by an abyss of malpractices, abuses
and secretive activities.

The proliferation and the escalating costs of elections make unlimited
demands on party funds. Since Franco's death, Spaniards have been called
to vote in six general, four municipal and eighteen regional elections (in
this calculation the elections held simultaneously in thirteen of the seventeen
autonomous communities are counted as one). They have also had European
elections and several referenda – among these the one held in March 1986
to decide Spain's membership of NATO, on which the Socialists spent
some 5,000 million pesetas – £26 million – (Torres, 1993: 22) . The high
expenditure incurred in so many elections is compounded by the excessive
length and nature of the campaigns, which are run on the American principle of saturation marketing, generating costs far in excess of the sums
they are likely to recoup from the public purse. According to official figures
issued by the Ministry of the Interior, the total amounts paid out to parliamentary parties in the period 1987–89 reached 30,399 million pesetas –
£160 million; and yet the main parties were still deeply in the red: the
PSOE's official debts reached 8,500 million pesetas – £44.3 million – and
the PP's 5,500 million – £30 million – (*Cambio 16*, 14 May 1990).

Confronted with such enormous deficits, party treasurers and their teams
are forced to take advantage of any opportunity to raise money. For those in
power, the temptations to act fraudulently are legion: double accounting,
tax evasion, insider dealings, slush funds – a whole range of illegal activities
which, in those instances when they are forced into the open, create an
impression in the public's mind of widespread corruption in the political
system. The Socialist Party and government – often supported by the guilty
silence of the main opposition party, involved in similar, if smaller, scandals
– have predictably tended to dismiss such accusations as unfounded, or at
least unproven, refusing to set up committees of investigation, deflecting
possible culpability from the institutional to the personal level, and at-
tempting to bury any immediate political responsibility in the slow and
complex processes of the judicial system.

TENSION AND CONFLICTS INSIDE THE PSOE

As mentioned earlier, lack of internal cohesion was a feature present in all the major Spanish parties throughout the 1980s. Factional infighting, frequent changes in leadership and party names, and even a willingness to cohabit with strange bedfellows were common to all of them; save for the Socialists who, having discarded much of their ideological ballast in two dramatic party congresses of 1979, were to unite behind Felipe González and enter the most stable and successful period in their long history. Among the reasons accounting for such stability and success one must include: the charisma and popularity of the party leader, González; his partnership with Alfonso Guerra, based upon a long-standing friendship and a symbiotic compatibility of temperament and roles, which allowed them to impose control and harmony over party and government; continued electoral success at national, regional and local levels, which provided endorsement of official party policy and allowed the generous distribution of rewards and sinecures among the faithful; and, last but not least, the strong discipline – sometimes described as Leninist – imposed on the party by Guerra and his acolytes, which left little room for dissident factions, and turned the party congresses held since 1979 into occasions for unanimity and enthusiastic applause.

A large party like the PSOE was bound to carry in its midst the seeds of divergence and conflict. For a number of years, confrontations, when they did occur, tended to be limited in scope, affecting only small sectional interests. The referendum on Spain's membership of NATO in 1986 did lead to divisions and acrimonious clashes in the Socialist ranks, but order and unity were soon restored with the electoral victory that followed a few months later. However, as the 1980s progressed the maintenance of unity became more and more difficult (Gillespie, 1994). Major cracks appeared as a result of irreconcilable differences between government and unions. The government's economic and social policies, leaning heavily towards neoliberal solutions, were perceived by many on the left of the party as 'getting weaker with the strong and stronger with the weak' (García Santesmases, 1993: 13). They were on a collision course with the main trade unions, and in December 1988, Felipe González and his Socialist cabinet had to suffer the humiliating experience of a widely supported general strike (Gillespie, 1990; Juliá, 1989). To add to the bitter aftertaste, the following year Nicolás Redondo, leader of the UGT, a union closely linked to the PSOE for over a century, told union members that his conscience did not allow him to recommend support for the Socialists at the forthcoming election (Amodia, 1990b: 297) – his personal view was massively confirmed soon after by the UGT's Confederal Committee (*El País*, 16 September 1989). The rift between union and government, and between their respective leaders, has continued to the present. Overcoming their profound differences was, in fact, one of the central aspirations in the PSOE's 1993 electoral programme.

Another very profound, and politically more significant, split appeared when, as a result of a financial scandal, Alfonso Guerra was forced to resign as deputy prime minister, thus bringing to an end his partnership with Felipe González, which until then had been one of the main pillars of Socialist unity.

Alfonso Guerra had never enjoyed great popularity. His surly manner, his caustic pronouncements, often accompanied by a certain air of intellectual superiority, his almost incestuous proximity to Felipe González, and his iron-fisted control over the party machinery had all served to project a political image devoid of warmth and attraction. From the opposition side, he had always been depicted as the Socialist bogeyman. Inside party and government, his often populist claim to be the guardian of ideological purity had brought him into conflict with other ministers – the so called renovators and neo-liberals. When the Guerra scandal broke out in December 1989, the support he received from some of his government colleagues was less than enthusiastic. It concerned one of his brothers, who had used the government's offices in Seville to conduct some dubious business which had brought him considerable wealth and, probably, the party coffers some badly needed funds. Alfonso Guerra refused to accept demands for his resignation, arguing in parliament that he had not been aware of his brother's financial activities. Initially, Felipe González lent him his support to the point of threatening to resign 'if the honour of his deputy was put into question' (*El País*, 10 November 1991). However, claims of innocence were not sufficient to blow away the political storm and, eventually, Guerra left the government at the beginning of 1991.

His departure had serious political consequences for the Socialists. Soon after his resignation, González carried out a cabinet reshuffle, reducing considerably the number of *guerristas* (*El País*, 12 February 1991). As for Alfonso Guerra, he has continued as deputy secretary-general in the party – where he still has a strong power base – and from that position he has felt freer to criticize the government: and not just the work of those ministers with whom he had disagreements before his downfall; his criticism has also extended to the prime minister for having forced his resignation (*El País*, 1 November 1991).

Thus by the early 1990s the carefully maintained unity was shattered. In the forthcoming election the PSOE would not just have to fight against other parties. Felipe González's main problem now was how to hide the internal divisions from the electorate.

EARLY ELECTIONS: AN EXERCISE IN DAMAGE LIMITATION

When on 12 April 1993, at a press conference, Felipe González announced that he had decided to dissolve parliament and hold a general election nearly five months before it was due, nobody was surprised. It was a gamble forced upon him by the rapidly deteriorating image of his government. Public opinion polls had been predicting at best the disappearance of the comfortable majority the Socialists have been sitting on for a decade, and, as time went on, a victory by the conservative PP was gaining in probability. In the 1989 election the gap between the PSOE and the PP had been 14 per cent (Amodia, 1990b: 296). By November 1992 it had been reduced to 5 per cent (*El Mundo*, 3 January 1993), and in March 1993 both parties were neck and neck – PSOE, 33.9 per cent and PP, 33.3 per cent (*El País, Edición Internacional*, 22 March 1993). All news had been bad for the government from the beginning of the year. Recession was deepening and unemployment reached 3 million – more than 20 per cent of the labour force (Banco Central Hispano, 1993: 50). Little by little the size and ramifications of the Filesa scandal were coming to light through the searching work of Marino Barbero, the judge entrusted with the investigation by the Supreme Court of Justice. In March a report produced by a team of tax inspectors fleshed out the suspicions with facts and figures. The report asserted that Filesa, under various commercial and financial guises, had chanelled some 1,000 million pesetas – £5.2 million – into the PSOE's coffers, without any taxes having been paid on the said amount (*El País, Edición Internacional*, 22 March 1993). The PSOE, which had wanted to be seen as representing honesty and ethical change, was fast becoming the symbol of corruption. Accusations from opponents were to be expected and could always be dismissed as adversarial politics, but voices from inside the party started to be heard demanding a cleaning out operation. Even Felipe González's charisma began to be tarnished by rumour and innuendo.

González has always denied knowledge of any financial irregularities in his party. He claimed to have heard about Filesa through the press. But on 25 March, when he visited the Autonomous University of Madrid to address a large student audience, it must have dawned on him that his own reputation was at stake. He was confronted with noisy barracking and strong insults – *chorizo* (thief) and *golfo* (rogue) – and, under the pressure of questioning, he had to state his determination to demand political responsibilities inside the party, and his willingness to resign as prime minister and party leader if it became necessary. A few days later, he made the same promises to the press: 'We will accept our responsibilities in the Filesa affair' (*El Mundo*, 4 April 1993). Behind the scenes pressure was also being applied by some ministers and ex-ministers – Serra, Solana, Barrionuevo,

Almunia, etc. – who wanted a thorough cleansing of the party's image, whatever the cost in personal responsibilities (*El Mundo*, 31 March 1993).

In the end, nothing was done because nothing could be done. To carry out his promises, González would have had to get rid of the men who controlled the party apparatus: namely, Alfonso Guerra, vice secretary-general, and Txiki Benegas, in charge of party organization. Anticipating any such move on González's part, Benegas had already sent him a confidential letter offering his resignation and denouncing, in no uncertain terms, those who pointed accusing fingers at him. The letter had been sent privately on 1 April, but was released to the press by Benegas himself a few days later (*El País*, 6 April 1993). It was a cunning move. Benegas and Guerra realized that their dismissal would cause a real earthquake inside the party and would represent too great a risk before an election. Their gamble paid off. In spite of the many rumours about resignations and even the possible calling of an extraordinary party congress, Felipe González had to accept a temporary compromise: an early election which would impose a truce on party infighting and would hopefully divert attention away from the Filesa affair.

The PSOE executive met at the party headquarters in Madrid on 10 April and took a number of decisions along the lines indicated. To show that something was being done about Filesa, they accepted the resignations of the party treasurer, Guillermo Galeote, and one of his collaborators, the Catalan deputy Carlos Navarro. Otherwise, the executive committee made their collective responsibility in the affair dependent on the future ruling of the courts. Benegas's resignation was not accepted, nor were the sensitive contents of his letter discussed. Up to this point the party apparatus seemed to have the upper hand. In exchange for all these concessions, González was given control of two important committees: one that would approve electoral lists and one in charge of electoral strategy.

Two days later González announced the dissolution of the Cortes. An early election had become inevitable, he claimed, because the opposition had infused so much tension and irrationality into public life that only the verdict of the people could calm things down. In his long monologue, he made no direct reference to the main reasons behind his decision. The state of the nation debate, due later in the month, and in which the prime minister was likely to come under considerable pressure, would obviously be postponed; and the Filesa investigation which the high court judge Marino Barbero was carrying out would, for the time being, be shelved in order not to interfere with the electoral process. The conservative newspaper *ABC* would sum up the situation with a sharply ironic headline: 'It is Barbero who is dissolving the Cortes' (*ABC*, 13 April 1993).

A LONG AND DIFFICULT CAMPAIGN

Even though the length of the campaign was officially reduced to two weeks, it was to be one of the longest. When the dissolution of parliament was announced there were nearly two months left to polling day. Both Felipe González and his main challenger, José María Aznar, started campaigning almost immediately. In fact, all the main political parties had been tuning up their electoral machines from at least the middle of 1992.

It was also a difficult and demanding campaign, especially for the PSOE. González and his party were confronted with the toughest electoral contest since the return of democracy to Spain. The defeats of 1977 and 1979 could, with hindsight, be interpreted as relative successes for the Socialists. They had been able to establish themselves as the major force on the left, well ahead of their main rivals, the Spanish Communist Party; and by not being in power during those difficult years, they did not have to bear the responsibility of steering Spain through the stormy waters of the transition, an undertaking that weakened and eventually destroyed the UCD, the ruling party at the time. After that, and with the democratic system already launched, the PSOE won three consecutive elections with overall, though diminishing, majorities. But now and for the reasons discussed above, they were facing possible defeat or, if able to stem the tide, a modest victory leading to minority government, with all the wheeling and dealing involved in pacts and coalitions.

The weeks leading to the official opening of the campaign brought little cheer to the Socialist camp. The other parties, especially the communist-based United Left (IU), would not allow them to forget the Filesa affair, and when the PSOE decided to include in some of its lists a number of independent candidates – Baltasar Garzón, a young judge who had distinguished himself in the fight against drugs and terrorism, was placed second in the Madrid list, immediately after González – in order to offer voters new and more trustworthy faces, the intention was too obvious to be credible. On 1 May the leaders of the two main trades unions, UGT and CCOO, made public their refusal to support the PSOE (*El Periódico*, 2 May 1993). To compound the party's troubles, in the middle of the month, just before the official campaign began, the economy was shaken to its roots. On 13 May, 'Black Thursday' as *El País* labelled it, the Spanish peseta was devalued by 8 per cent within the ERM – the third devaluation in nine months. Meanwhile, inflation turned upwards and unemployment seemed to be getting out of hand with 3.3 million (22 per cent of the labour force) out of work (*El País*, 14 May 1993).

And yet, notwithstanding all the bad omens, González organized a campaign that would bring him victory against what appeared to be overwhelming odds. It was achieved by concentrating the whole operation around the leader's image. The electoral programme counted for little. Its messages were neither new nor distinctive. Over the last decade, the party had drifted so much towards the centre and had reduced ideological differences with its main rivals to such an extent that both the PP and the CDS accused the PSOE of plagiarizing their programmes (*El Periódico*, 2 May 1993 and *El Mundo*, 5 May 1993). The platitudinous verbosity of electoral programmes was, if anything, accentuated on this occasion, with the contents reduced as usual to simplistic and catchy formulae in order to reach the voters (Brooksbank Jones and O'Shaughnessy, 1993). As in 1989, it was a campaign based on slogans, television shows and personalities.

The PSOE mounted the most highly personalized campaign since 1977. The old electoral banners could no longer be used. Socialism had been watered down beyond recognition by government policies, and, in any case, since 1989 events in the East had totally devalued most socialist symbols. The party's image had been degraded by financial scandals and by the ostentatious lives of some of its members. Even the many achievements of the last ten years were overshadowed by the spectre of recession. The only trump card for the PSOE to play was that of its leader, whose popularity, although somewhat diminished, was still greater than any of his rivals'(*El País, Edición Internacional*, 22 February 1993). Hence the presidentialist tone of Socialist strategy, a one-man campaign, an election turned into a plebiscite about Felipe González. In some ways the situation resembled the 1979 crisis over the Marxist definition of the party, or the struggle to gain a narrow victory in the 1986 referendum to remain in NATO. On both occasions González's personal appeal had been decisive.

The contrast with the previous election was remarkable. In 1989 González had been a reluctant campaigner, trying instead to project the image of a statesman more concerned with international politics than with the daily grind of domestic affairs. He seemed to be tired, made very few public appearances at election rallies, and hinted more than once that he was probably fighting his last election as party leader. But three and a half years later all this had changed. He campaigned intensively all over Spain, taking part in more rallies, press conferences and television debates than ever before. Whilst in the 1989 campaign he had only spoken at nine electoral rallies, in 1993 he addressed twenty-two (*El País*, 6 June 1993). In contrast with the apathy and weariness of 1989, he was now determined to go on, boasting towards the end of the campaign in Barcelona: 'I still have the energy to continue fighting for another four years, and another four, and another four ...' (*El País*, 5 June 1993).

A careful reading of González's electoral speeches, interviews and debates shows the constant reiteration of certain lines of argument:

a) The deep economic recession was primarily caused by external factors – the parallel recession in the rest of the Western world – and getting out of it would be a long and painful process which would require a 'social pact' between government, employers and unions.
b) There are hardly any references to ideological and party matters – the emphasis continued to fall on the idea of modernization, the great achievement of the 1980s, though subtly transformed into progress and solidarity.
c) Public corruption merited few mentions, and they were followed always by promises of new legislation to impose greater controls on party finances, but without addressing the question of why this had not been done before.
d) He was understandably reluctant to accept the possibility of a minority government or to indulge in conjecture about future coalitions, although, towards the end, he did intimate his preference for some kind of pact with the Basque and Catalan nationalists.
e) Given the gloomy economic climate, there were few references to his government's achievements during the previous parliament. The best, he promised, was still to come – a message encapsulated in the party's slogan, *Vota futuro* – Vote for the Future.
f) The general tone of his discourse was predominantly negative, concentrating primarily on discrediting his main rivals in the PP. Its leaders, he stated, lacked experience and had little to offer to overcome the problems facing the country. At the end of the campaign, when a PP victory was becoming a distinct possibility, González did not hesitate to frighten the electorate with the claim that such an outcome would represent a step back towards the Francoist period. He was appealing to what Spaniards called *el voto del miedo* – the vote of fear – (*El Mundo*, 5 June 1993).

The imputation of Francoist proclivities to the PP was far from the truth, though understandable in the heat of the electoral battle – after all, González and his party had been on the receiving end of comparable accusations when in 1979, with the polls predicting a Socialist victory, Adolfo Suárez, then leader of the governing Union of the Democratic Centre (UCD), was able to turn the tide in his final television appearance, by warning voters that the PSOE would legalize abortion, impose a collectivist economy, forbid religious education, etc. However, the PP, under Aznar's leadership since 1989, had undergone a considerable transformation. It had moved ideologically towards right of centre positions; it had reorganized its structure, bringing in new and younger faces at all levels – in the last three years more than half of the party's provincial and regional leaders had been replaced (*El País*, 3 June 1993); and it had, in the process, acquired an internal cohesion that had been missing during the 1980s.

Like the Socialists, the PP ran a rather negative campaign, and its programme suffered too from a lack of concrete and convincing proposals to get the country out of recession. Apart from a promise to reduce public spending and a greater emphasis on private enterprise, what they proposed was just the continuation and improvement of the modernization process of the last ten years. In fact, their basic electoral offer was a new team with an alternative leader. This was to prove their main weakness. In a highly personalized campaign Aznar was no real match for González. He had considerably improved his electioneering technique since 1989, and he did surprisingly well in the first of two confrontations he had with the Socialist leader in front of the television cameras, but in the end González's experience, powers of communication, and populist appeal carried the day.

The other parties could only aspire to a supporting role and hope that, if the voters' verdict were not decisive, they might be needed by a minority government. The United Left (IU), with the Communist Party as its driving force, had the most distinctive message. As in 1989, it presented itself as the only real alternative to the two main parties which, IU claimed, were hardly different from each other, and were trying to reduce the election to a two-horse race. IU's attractive and radical electoral offer – which included some rather controversial proposals, such as work sharing to reduce unemployment – was badly affected in the eyes of the voters by constant infighting over issues as fundamental as their Communist inheritance, the Maastricht Treaty, or the advisability of entering into a post-electoral coalition with the Socialists. Internal divisions, latent in IU since its foundation in 1986, exploded into the open just before the electoral campaign got underway, leading to the exclusion of some of their best-known names from the electoral lists. Matters seemed to get worse when, one week into the campaign, IU's leader, Julio Anguita, suffered a heart attack which left him out of the fray. The impact on IU's performance is difficult to assess. IU's campaign managers did their best to turn adversity in their favour by using the image of the 'wounded warrior' and appealing to voters' tenderer feelings with the improvised slogan: *Anguita no puede votar, vota tú por él* – 'Anguita can't vote, you vote on his behalf'.

The CDS, a party founded by Adolfo Suárez after his resignation as prime minister in 1981, was struggling to survive. Suárez, its main attraction, had abandoned politics, and the party itself was being squeezed out of the ideological centre by the centripetal tendencies of both the PP and the PSOE. The chances of their holding on to any of the fourteen seats they had won in 1989 were very remote indeed. In sharp contrast, the expectations of nationalist parties in Catalonia and the Basque Country were suffused with optimism. Whoever won the elections, they realized, would be unable to govern without their support. Convergència i Unió (CiU), the dominant force in Catalan politics, expressed such a mood in the unmistakable terms of its slogan: *Ara decidirem* – 'Now we shall decide'.

AN ELECTORAL VICTORY FULL OF UNCERTAINTIES

Spaniards did not vote as the final opinion polls had predicted. Not only did the Socialists win their fourth consecutive election, but the margin of their victory was larger than had been expected. The uncertainty surrounding the outcome until the very end must have served as an encouragement to vote. The level of participation – 77.28 per cent of the electorate – was the highest since 1982. Many of those undecided till the last moment in the end must have cast their vote for the PSOE. The result goes against the European trend which for some years had shown a decline in the Socialist vote. Within Spain, however, it cannot be interpreted as a great Socialist success. The figures show a slight loss in the PSOE's share of the vote, a considerable reduction in the gap separating them from their main opponents, and, of course, the loss of their overall majority. It was nevertheless a victory, but a victory for Felipe González rather than his party – a personal triumph against considerable odds. Against many predictions and fears, defeat was avoided and in the process González's position was considerably strengthened.

The Socialists are now in power with the smallest parliamentary majority of any government since the restoration of democracy in Spain. The UCD's minority governments during the transition were not so precariously placed. Of course, it can be argued that what has happened represents a return to normality. The proportional system under which Spanish elections are held was from the beginning expected to produce minority governments. The parliamentary majorities enjoyed by the PSOE during the 1980s were probably the exception to the rule.

The fact that the PSOE has lost its hegemonic position is bound to have important repercussions inasmuch as it will affect institutional balances and inter-party relations. The Socialists will not be able to rule with the same arrogant superiority of the last decade. In the Cortes dialogue and negotiations will take the place of the *rodillo*. The government can no longer govern alone. So far the attempts at forming a permanent coalition have proved unsuccessful. In any case, González has clearly expressed his preference for a more flexible formula based on partial and/or temporary agreements and pacts with other parliamentary groups. He is unlikely to receive much support from the left, as IU's leader, Julio Anguita, is adamantly opposed to the government's running of the economy. Everything seems to suggest that the life of this parliament will depend almost entirely on the understanding between González's new government and the Basque and Catalan nationalist parties, PNV and CiU. For some, such an understanding could represent the most positive outcome of the recent election. The direct participation of nationalist parties in the running of the state would be an ideal way to check the centrifugal and secessionist tendencies in Catalonia

Table 10.1 Results of the Spanish general elections of 1989 and 1993

| | 1989 | | 1993 | |
	Votes (%)	Seats	Votes(%)	Seats
PSOE	39.56	175	38.68	159
PP	25.84	107	34.82	141
IU	9.05	17	9.57	18
CDS	7.91	14	1.76	0
CiU	5.04	18	4.95	17
PNV	1.24	5	1.24	5
CC	–	–	0.88	4
HB	1.06	4	0.88	2
Others	10.30	10	7.22	4

Sources: For 1989 *Anuario El País 1990*: 60–61, and for 1993 *El País* and *El Mundo*, 8 June 1993.

Key:

PSOE   Spanish Socialist Party
PP   People's Party (main conservative party)
IU   United Left (left-wing coalition centred around the Spanish Communist Party)
CDS   Social and Democratic Centre (centre party founded by Adolfo Suárez in 1982)
CiU   Convergence and Union (a Catalan centre-right coalition)
PNV   Basque Nationalist Party
CC   Canary Islands Coalition
HB   Herri Batasuna (Popular Unity, a Basque nationalist movement closely associated with the terrorist organization ETA)

and the Basque country; the cohesion of Spain would be all the stronger for it. On the contrary, others argue, the government, negotiating from a position of weakness, will, in order to survive, have to yield to the pressures of Catalan and Basque nationalists who will be looking to widen their region's autonomous powers and obtain concessions and privileges not available to other Spanish regions.

Although the position of the Socialist government has obviously become more precarious, that of González in relation to his own party looks better than it did before the election. Tensions and internal strife have not abated, but a personal victory at the polls has reinvigorated his leadership and possibly given him the opportunity to impose his authority. It will not be an easy task and it may eventually endanger party unity. Since the election, González has sided unequivocally with the so-called 'renovators' and against the faction headed by Alfonso Guerra inside his party. The composition of the new government reflects his desire to make it as independent as possible from the party apparatus. The most important figures from the renovator faction continue to hold seats in the cabinet, among them the deputy prime minister, Narcis Serra, whose position and powers have been reinforced; six of the seventeen ministers are not party members; and, for the first time, there is no representative of the *guerrista* faction in the government.

Since the election, confrontations between González and Guerra have become more open and acrimonious. Recently, at a large gathering of party members in Granada, González did not hesitate to denounce his old ally's call for a turn to the left in party and government as utopian and escapist demagogy, inviting those present to adopt a more realistic and responsible attitude instead (*El País*, 25 October 1993). The enthusiastic reaction of his audience seems to suggest that the *guerristas* are losing ground even in their Andalusian stronghold. The PSOE's federal congress, due to take place in the spring of 1994, could be the occasion for González to regain control of his party, doing to it what he has already done to his cabinet. However, the risks involved in such an operation could be considerable. Ironically, the search for cohesion between party and government could produce a major split in the Socialist ranks.

Stability continues to evade the Spanish party system. Ten years of Socialist hegemony had given credit to the theory of the 'predominant' party model – not so much for the size of the PSOE vote as for the absence of a credible alternative – but the 1993 election has altered that perception. The party system now stands somewhere between an imperfect two-party and a moderate multi-party model (Sartori, 1978). There is a large concentration of the vote on the two leading parties. Only in 1982 was their share greater, but so was the difference between them. Now the PSOE and the PP together account for 73.5 per cent of the vote and, with the built-in bonus granted by the electoral system to large parties, 80 per cent of the seats. Neither party can run the country for long without the assistance of other parliamentary groups, and the relation between government and opposition is now on a far more sensitive and finely balanced footing. Ideological differences have been reduced, thus making the possible transference of power from the PSOE to the PP, at some future election, less traumatic than it would have been only a few years ago when the conservative forces still carried the stigma of their Francoist roots. The PP, with 3 million votes more than in 1989 and less than 3 points behind the PSOE at the polls, has, for the first time, become a possible alternative government. Aznar has now to prove himself as an effective opposition leader if he is to convince the electorate of his potential as a future prime minister. As for Felipe González, after adding another trophy to his large collection of political successes, he is confronted by the same complex issues that pushed him into an early election. His personal standing may be stronger, that of his government less so. In order to survive during this parliament, he will have to demonstrate, yet again, his ability to win against the odds.

REFERENCES

Amodia, J. (1990a), 'Taxonomía e inestabilidad del sistema de partidos en España', *Journal of the Association for Contemporary Iberian Studies*, 3, 1: 39–49.

Amodia, J. (1990b), 'Personalities and slogans: The Spanish elections of October 1989', *West European Politics*, 13, 2: 293–8.

Anuario El País 1993, Madrid.

Anuario El Mundo 1993, Madrid.

Banco Central Hispano (1993), *Spain: Economic Outlook (August–September)*, Madrid.

Brooksbank Jones, A. and O'Shaughnessy, M. (1993), 'Policy, rhetoric and the 1993 Spanish election campaign', *Journal of the Association for Contemporary Iberian Studies*, 6, 2: 4–14.

Cavero, J. (1991), *El PSOE contra la prensa. Historia de un divorcio*, Madrid: Temas de Hoy.

Cierva, R. de la (1992), *Historias de la corrupción*, Barcelona: Planeta.

Claudín, F. (1980), *Crisis de los partidos políticos*, Madrid: Dédalo.

Díaz Herrera, J. and Tijeras, R. (1991), *El dinero del poder*, Madrid: Cambio 16.

Esteban, J. de (1992), *El estado de la constitución*, Madrid: Prodhufi.

Fernández Marugán, F. (1992), 'La década de los ochenta: Impulso y reforma económica', in A. Guerra and J.F. Tezanos, *La década del cambio*, Madrid: Sistema.

García Santesmases, A. (1993), *Repensar la izquierda*, Madrid: Anthropos.

Gillespie, R. (1990), 'The break-up of the socialist family. Party–Union relations in Spain, 1982–89', *West European Politics*, 13, 1: 47–62.

Gillespie, R.(1994), 'The resurgence of factionalism in the Spanish Socialist Party', in D.S. Bell and E. Shaw (eds), *Conflict and Cohesion in West European Social Democratic Parties*, London: Pinter.

Guerra, A. (1992), *Las Filípicas*, Barcelona: Planeta.

Jiménez de Parga, M. (1993), *La ilusión política. ¿Hay que reinventar la democracia en España?*, Madrid: Alianza Editorial.

Jiménez Losantos, F. (1993), *La dictadura silenciosa*, Madrid: Temas de Hoy.

Juliá, S. (1988), *La desavenencia. Partidos, sindicatos y huelga general*, Madrid: El País/ Aguilar.

Otero Novas, J.M. (1987), *Nuestra democracia puede morir*, Barcelona: Plaza & Janés.

Rodríguez Braun, C. (1992), 'De la agonía a la agonía', in J. Tusell and J. Sinova, *La década socialista*, Madrid: Espasa-Calpe.

Sartori, G. (1978), *Parties and Party Systems. A Framework for Analysis*, Cambridge: Cambridge University Press.

Sinova, J. and Tusell, J. (1990), *El secuestro de la democracia*, Barcelona: Plaza & Janés.

Torres, A. (1993), *La financiación irregular del PSOE*, Barcelona: Ediciones de la Tempestad.

Umbral, F. (1993), *La década roja*, Barcelona: Planeta.

Much of the source material has been extracted from the Spanish daily and weekly press, especially from *El País, El Mundo, El Periódico, ABC,* and *Cambio 16.*

11
Crisis in Algeria

Martha Crenshaw

Violence in Algeria reached crisis proportions in 1993. Militant Islamic factions expanded their range of targets, adding assassinations of civilian government officials, secular intellectuals and foreigners to a regular pattern of attacks on the security forces. Violence spread through the country. Although typically attributed to the outlawed Front islamique du salut (Islamic Salvation Front, FIS), most actions were unclaimed, and it was unlikely that a centralized organization directed or controlled them. In the last months of 1993, the Armed Islamic Group emerged as the most aggressive and intransigent known radical faction. It appeared, however, to be independent of the FIS. The extent of popular support for violence was impossible to gauge. The Algerian military maintained its hold on the country and continued to follow the repressive security policies adopted in January 1992, despite the formation of a new government in mid-year and regular if unanswered appeals for a 'national dialogue' to unite all political groups. In November, after three French consular officials were kidnapped, the French government cracked down on FIS sympathizers in France, a step the Algerian government had sought for some time. This measure, however, primarily served to heighten French vulnerability. Attacks on foreigners in Algeria increased; by 29 December a total of twenty-four people of different nationalities – including French, Spanish, Russian, Croatian, Belgian and British – had been killed.

To understand the situation in 1993, one must look back to the conditions in Algeria that precipitated the riots of 1988, which mark the beginning of the rise to power of the FIS; since then the country has experienced the movement toward democratic government, the suppression of the FIS by the government when it proved capable of winning in free elections, and the abandonment of the process of democratization. This analysis will focus first on the period 1988–92 for the background to the current intensification of violence, and then turn to developments in 1993.

THE BACKGROUND

The riots of 1988 were a result of the profound failure of the post-revolutionary Algerian state. From the acquisition of independence in 1962 to the 1990s, Algeria was under the control of the Front de Libération Nationale (FLN), whose rule was characterized by rigid authoritarianism, economic mismanagement and political corruption. The FLN neither tolerated opposition parties nor created channels of communication from society to the state within the single party. Inheriting a country rich in petroleum resources, the FLN took a rigorously socialist view of the path to economic development, establishing large state enterprises, including agricultural collectives, and focusing investment on heavy industry. State domination of economic and political spheres left 'a public sector characterized by low productivity and bureaucratic redundancy' (Vandewalle, 1992: 708). Although Chadli Benjedid, who was elected president in 1980, tried to implement some measures of liberalization, the drop in oil prices in the 1980s undermined his efforts. By 1988 Algeria's population was suffering from severe housing shortages, an agricultural system that had declined dramatically (although close to self-sufficiency in the 1960s, Algeria could supply only a quarter of its food needs by the 1980s), a shortage of consumer goods, numbing bureaucratic inefficiency, high levels of unemployment and rising inflation. In 1986 the government introduced an austerity plan to reduce the country's $23 billion external debt. Adding to these problems, Algeria faced a sharp population increase, from nine million in 1962 to at least 25 million in 1988, making it a country with a majority of citizens under 18.

The FLN was thus unable to rely on performance standards as a basis of political legitimacy. Two alternative principles were offered to justify the FLN's monopoly of power and to sustain popular loyalty, although neither proved adequate to the task. One was the heritage of the revolution. The FLN, as the party that led the country to independence, claimed to incarnate the values behind the heroic struggle against French colonialism. This claim was tarnished in part by the fact that a number of revolutionary heroes had deserted the party and sought asylum outside the country, including 'chef historique' Mohamed Boudiaf, who would be called back to rescue the government from its difficulties in 1992. Furthermore, revolutionary memory and mythology were increasingly irrelevant for Algeria's youthful population.

The second related base of legitimacy was Islamic and Arab nationalism, expressed in official adherence to Islam as the state religion from the time of independence and in a policy of 'Arabization' begun in the 1970s. Reliance on Islam was linked not just to the reality of the demographic situation – that the majority of Algerians were Muslim - but also to the FLN's resolute anti-colonialism. FLN leaders were individually ambivalent and divided on the issue of promoting Islam versus promoting the socialist republic, but they agreed that religion, like all other facets of society, was to be dominated by the state. The policy of 'Arabization' was a means of asserting an anti-Western position as well as preserving the regime's dominance by undercutting the position of Algeria's secular, French-speaking intellectuals. Arabic was to be taught in schools and used in government service and all pro-Western orientations were to be opposed. It was predictable that Algeria's Berber minority, which is Muslim but culturally distinct from the majority of Algerians, would resist Arabization. Furthermore, students who did not learn French found themselves without skilled jobs, a situation caused by the deficiencies of the Algerian economy as well as their lack of technical training. According to Tahi (1992: 412),

> The Arabisation programme of the last decades has made Algeria a refuge for thousands of ill-equipped Iraqi, Egyptian, and Palestinian educators, thereby steadily replacing the teaching in French which had given the country its highly qualified cadres. The classical Arabic of the Middle East has meshed poorly with Algerian dialects, producing a confused generation that is illiterate in both Arabic and French, and hence unable to face the deepening economic crisis.

It is also worth noting that among these teachers were members of the Egyptian Muslim Brotherhood. Furthermore, the FLN found it problematic to deny the right of Islamic associations to issue public appeals to the same values the regime ostensibly espoused. When Islamic organizations began to move from criticism based on religious and cultural beliefs to political opposition, the regime was divided on how to respond. Last, the endemic corruption of some FLN cadres – who, for example, publicly vaunted Algeria's system of socialized medicine but flew to Paris for their own medical treatment, or who manoeuvred their luxurious Mercedes through the narrow streets of the Algiers Casbah, past markets where no food was available for the ordinary Algerian – stood in sharp contrast both to their stated Islamic principles and to the moral piety of religious leaders.

The democratic opening of 1988

Although President Chadli Benjedid had begun attempts to reform the economy and to promote some political liberalization, the results were meagre. Poverty and unemployment persisted, as did opposition to reforms within the FLN. What distinguished the riots of October 1988, which followed two years of strikes and unrest related to the government's economic austerity programme, and which included incidents of semi-organized violence from the Islamic opposition, from earlier demonstrations was the fact that the army fired on protesters in Algiers, killing several hundred

people. Public outrage spurred Chadli to separate the FLN from the state
and to allow representative elections. 'By its own standards as well as those
of other Arab states, Algeria's democratic opening was radical, even historic'
(Entelis, 1992: 75). Referendums in November 1988 and February 1989
overwhelmingly approved fundamental changes to the Algerian constitution
that promised respect for civil rights and permitted the formation of independent political associations.

Among these was the FIS, founded on 18 February 1989 at the Al-
Sunna mosque in the Bab el-Oued district of Algiers. The government
officially recognized the FIS in September: apparently the prime minister,
Mouloud Hamrouche, pressed for its legalization despite the opposition of
some army leaders (Lamchichi, 1992: 101). Under the leadership of Abassi
Madani and Ali Belhadj, the FIS became a true mass organization, reputed
to have three million adherents. Belhadj was the more radical and outspoken
of the two leaders, while Madani was more pragmatic and moderate. Led
by a forty-member council, the Majlis al-Shura, the FIS pursued a flexible
and multifaceted strategy. FIS propaganda, disseminated through sermons,
tape-recordings, and publications, concentrated on criticism of the state,
the bureaucracy, the western secular elite, corruption, and moral dissolution,
while appealing for the creation of an Islamic state based on Islamic law.
The FIS was also adept at popular mass mobilization, using two basic
methods: organizing social services on a neighbourhood basis (thus showing
up the deficiencies of the regime) and mounting large street demonstrations,
which both excited enthusiasm among Algeria's dispossessed and angry
younger generation and demonstrated the movement's power. The FIS
showed great expertise in public relations and the use of the media, as well
as in the techniques of popular mobilization (see Lamchichi, 1992, especially
100ff.). Each Friday, nearly 20,000 people assembled to hear Belhadj preach.
In April an FIS demonstration calling for legislative elections attracted
50,000 people.

When the National Assembly approved a system of proportional representation for Algeria's first democratic elections, the move was criticized as
favouring the FLN. However, in local elections in June 1990, which eleven
political parties contested, the FLN was defeated decisively. To the government's dismay, the FIS captured a majority of seats at the municipal and
departmental levels and gained control of almost all of Algeria's major cities.
However, two significant political organizations boycotted the elections: the
secular Berberist party, the Front des forces socialistes (FFS) led by Hocine
Ait Ahmed, a revolutionary leader who returned in 1989 from twenty-three
years of exile, and the Mouvement pour la démocratie en Algérie (MDA)
led by former president Ahmed Ben Bella, who also returned from exile in
September 1990. Nevertheless, it was difficult to ignore the extent of the
FIS victory or of the FLN's collapse. Many observers had thought that the

large demonstrations in Algiers in May 1990, which assembled a million Algerians to protest against the intransigence of the radical Islamic programme, was a sign that secular, tolerant, democratic parties would win the elections. But after June, the widespread appeal of the FIS as a populist, militant, millenarian force and the unpopularity of the FLN were undeniable (see Lamchichi, 1992: 76–7). The question that became increasingly urgent was whether the FIS would observe democratic norms and procedures if it came to power, or whether it would establish an Iranian-style religious totalitarianism.

The first round of legislative elections was scheduled for a year later, in June 1991. The FLN, however, aimed to prevent another FIS victory by gerrymandering the electoral districts. The National Assembly in April passed a new electoral law that allowed disproportionate representation from the districts that had voted for the FLN in the local elections. According to Lamchichi (1992: 78–9), this law gave the FIS a fortuitous pretext for rebellion, since the party's ability to govern the constituencies they had won was not outstanding. Other observers thought that the FIS governed reasonably well under the circumstances. Still other sources (e.g. Tahi, 1992: 403) suggest that the government's military security forces had infiltrated the FIS, provoking factionalism and encouraging violence, in order to have an excuse to outlaw the party. At any rate, in late May Abassi Madani, apparently against the advice of the majority of the Majlis al-Shura (Lamchichi 1992: 103), called for a general strike, the abrogation of the electoral law, and the adoption of an Islamic state through jihad and civil disobedience. Violent street demonstrations spread through Algiers. The army intervened to restore order, and the government declared a state of siege. Then in rapid sequence the government collapsed, the elections were postponed, a new government was formed after consultation with different political groupings, and President Chadli Benjedid resigned as head of the FLN. Through the summer, relations between the government and the FLN, which controlled the National Assembly, deteriorated as they quarrelled over the management of the economy and especially electoral reform. Finally, in October President Chadli announced that the first round of legislative elections would be held in December, and the second in January 1992.

Despite Chadli's willingness to move ahead with the elections, the army, having assumed responsibility for security upon the declaration of the state of siege, was less tolerant of the Islamic movement, which became the target of a vigorous campaign of repression. The army was undoubtedly less concerned about the anti-democratic leanings of the FIS than with the threat to its own power. As a corollary to repression, the political strategy was to identify the Islamic movement with disorder and opposition to democracy, and thus to discredit it before the December elections, which would be the first free elections for the National Assembly in Algeria's history. Consequently on 30 June, Madani, Belhadj and six other leaders of the FIS were arrested. Abdelkader Hachani, reportedly a moderate who favoured an electoral strategy, became the provisional president. Despite persecution and internal divisions, the FIS managed to maintain its popular support, largely because the despair that had prepared the ground for the emergence of a militant Islamic opposition movement still persisted and because the FIS had now effectively seized the banner of nationalism from the FLN. Furthermore, the secular opposition parties, who professed a commitment to democracy, failed to secure a popular base. They appeared elitist, concerned more with internal squabbles than with mobilizing support. The political spectrum remained polarized between the FLN and the FIS.

In December the FIS was victorious again. They won 25 per cent of the vote, against 13 per cent for the FLN, which meant that they would probably hold 188 of the 231 legislative seats that were contested. However, the abstention rate was 41 per cent and nearly 12 per cent of votes were spoiled, so only 47 per cent of the population could be said to have participated in the election. Only three parties remained eligible for the second round of elections in January: the FIS, FLN and FFS. It was certain that the FIS would win a majority.

In early January, the FFS called a protest march in Algiers to 'Save Algeria and Democracy,' to reject both the 'intégrist' state and the police state. Several hundred thousand people joined the march. Certainly many Algerians were profoundly alarmed by the prospect of an Islamic majority in the National Assembly, which might alter the constitution to restrict women's rights and halt the processes of modernization. While some parties wanted to call off the elections, others such as the FFS wanted to continue the democratic process.

The interruption of the democratic process

Power in Algeria resided, as it always had, in the hands of the military, not the visibly active political groupings, and the army leadership decided to respond to the imminent victory of the FIS with a 'legal coup d'état.' On 11 January President Chadli Benjedid was forced to dissolve the National Assembly and then to resign, and the elections, then five days off, were annulled. Since Chadli had from the beginning favoured compromise and cohabitation with the FIS, his continued leadership of the country was now unacceptable to those elements of the military and the FLN who refused any power sharing that might diminish their status. A new institutional arrangement, a Haut comité d'état (HCE), was introduced to act as a collective head of state until the expiration of the president's term in

December 1993. Mohamed Boudiaf, one of the most prestigious and long-time opponents of the FLN, a great historical figure of the war for national liberation, was called back from exile in Morocco to preside.

The FIS, cheated out of electoral victory in free elections, immediately rejected the 'legal coup' as illegitimate but instructed its militants to avoid violence. The FFS and the FLN formally denounced the takeover as well. The army, evidently unimpressed, proceeded to arrest religious leaders, Islamic journalists and thirty of the FIS representatives elected in the first round of the elections. On 22 January Abdelkader Hachani was arrested, probably due to his repeated appeals to the military to revolt and join the side of the people. The arrests and the ban on both public gatherings near mosques and political sermons produced a predictable response: violent clashes between police and Islamic militants became a familiar happening from 29 January onwards. Two days of violence in February left forty dead and 300 wounded. An ambush of police in the Algiers Casbah killed six.

As violence escalated, the HCE declared a state of emergency throughout Algeria. Its provisions were harsh: the Minister of the Interior could intern anyone whose activity he considered dangerous for public order, restrict or ban the movements of individuals, deport or place under house arrest people whose actions were deemed harmful, close public meeting places, order searches both day and night, and ban demonstrations. Five detention centres were opened in the Sahara to hold the thousands of Islamists who had been arrested (5000 according to the government, more according to the FIS; Lamchichi, 1992: 86). In early March, as violence continued, the FIS was outlawed. This was merely a juridical confirmation of fact, since the FIS headquarters in Algiers had been closed, its publications banned, the 250 city halls under its control occupied, its principal leaders imprisoned, and its militants interned or silenced by threat.

Thus after spring 1992 the FIS had no legal means of expression or visible structure in Algeria. Any followers who were not arrested went underground or fled the country. It was no longer possible to judge its influence on the Algerian public. There were no mass protest movements in its favour, but public demonstrations were forbidden if not approved by the government.

Clashes between armed militants (whether FIS or not) and the security forces became endemic. Among the most active Islamic militants were the 'Afghans,' veterans of the combat against the Soviet Union. Some of these groups were not affiliated with the FIS, while others were former adherents who broke away in summer 1991. Burgat (1993: 289–90) argues that their guerrilla experience against the Soviets conferred a prestige that was disproportionate to their actual training; rather than being an arm of the FIS, 'they regularly placed it in difficulty by their activist excesses, which the media usually attributed to the FIS.' In February 1992 an attack on the headquarters of the navy in Algiers had left seven soldiers and one policeman dead, and in May three more death sentences were handed down. The group's leader, Mourad al-Afghani, alias Mourad Hanni, was killed in the attack. A disturbing note for the regime, however, was that among those condemned to death were soldiers, revealing a pattern of infiltration of the military that has continued. At least two 'Afghan' leaders were former army officers. In early March, a court in Tlemcen also handed down three death sentences for militants who were members of the 'Hezbollah' group, which was founded in March 1990 under Jamaleddine Bardi. In May 1992 a military court condemned to death thirteen Islamists suspected of being affiliated with another non-FIS militant group, who were accused of attacking a military post in November 1991.

The question of how to deal with the radical fringe divided the FIS leadership from the time of the state of siege on. There was no concrete evidence that the FIS as an entity was trying to organize an armed insurrection. As Lamchichi (1992: 189) noted, 'the disorganization of the movement, the movement underground of all its cadres who were still free, provokes confusion and impossibility to distinguish between those holding the "legalist" and "pragmatic" line and the most radical "dissidents".' On 28 March, when two soldiers from the Republican Guard were killed in Algiers, a FIS communiqué explained that although the FIS had attempted a dialogue, the government had responded with official violence, which led the 'children of the people,' without receiving orders from anyone, to resort to means other than dialogue to promote their religion (Lamchichi, 1992: 242).

The severity of the repression against the Islamist movement also drew criticism from journalists and human rights groups. The government responded with censorship and in May the expulsion of the correspondent from *Le Monde*. This hardline response naturally did little to alleviate dissatisfaction, which grew as the repression tightened. Many critics of the Algerian government noted the cruel irony of the similarity between the French response to the FLN in the war for independence and the FLN response to the Islamist challenge - arbitrary arrests, detention without trial, lack of due process in judicial procedures, torture of suspects, and executions (both judicial and non-judicial).

Militant groups, however decentralized and fragmented, began to switch from military and police to civilian targets with a bomb at the University of Constantine on 6 May, which killed several people. On the same day, buses were burned in Algiers and two people were killed in a demonstration. Three days later two bombs exploded at newspaper offices in Algiers.

However, the most shocking incident of terrorism in 1992 was unlikely to have been the work of the FIS or other militant Islamic groups. On 29

June, Mohamed Boudiaf was assassinated by one of his own security guards while he was inaugurating a cultural centre in Annaba, 350 kilometres to the east of Algiers. Some Algerians suspected that FLN leaders associated with Chadli Benjedid, who were being investigated as part of an anti-corruption drive, instigated the assassination. According to Burgat (1993: 305), 'The act was attributed to the FIS but most probably [was] executed by those who had brought the old militant back to power.' Tahi (1992: 419) agrees that

> The cold-blooded and professionally prepared attack on Boudiaf suggests that this was an inside job,'ordered' by what is widely known in Algeria as the 'political mafia.' No HCE members were present when he was gunned down while addressing a public meeting in Annaba, soon after announcing his 'determination' to tackle corruption in a country where it has been officially declared that the FLN régime had allowed the Treasury to be embezzled by as much as $26,000 million. (See also Callies de Salies, 1993: 114.)

Boudiaf was replaced by Ali Kafi, already a member of the HCE, a former colonel in the Armée de Libération Nationale (ALN), and a member of the central committee of the FLN, thus a person with impeccable credentials of the old school. Tahi (1992: 419) describes him as a stooge of the FLN, someone whom Ait Ahmed called a representative of 'nationalist fundamentalism.' Redha Malek then joined the HCE from the presidency of the Conseil Consultatif National (CCN), appointed by the HCE in April as a sixty-member consulting body to act in place of the unelected National Assembly. Within the week, Prime Minister Sid Ahmed Ghozali was replaced by Belaid Abdesslam, who had been minister of industry and oil under the Boumedienne government from 1965 to 1977. A proponent of socialism and the command economy, he had promoted the development of heavy industry based on the profits from oil and gas resources, and was often blamed for the economic difficulties of the 1980s. Mortimer (1993: 41) notes that although the military may have seen Abdesslam as resolute and secular, in the eyes of most Algerians he was a throwback to the past. However, he continued the liberalization of the economy begun by his predecessor and pursued the austerity programme required by the IMF. The situation he confronted was dire: an inflation rate of 32 per cent; 25 per cent unemployment; and 55 per cent of the population aged 19 or less, to satisfy whose needs the country would have to build 200,000 new housing units per year to the year 2000 and triple education and health budgets (Callies de Salies, 1993: 112). The external debt absorbed over half the GDP. Since 1986, export revenues had fallen by half. Abdesslam thought to ameliorate the financial situation by attracting foreign investment, but the political situation was scarcely propitious. The spectacular progression of terrorism undermined the process of economic reform (ibid: 113). On the day he announced his cabinet, militant groups organized attacks in three cities.

In July, Abassi Madani and Ali Belhadj were sentenced to twelve years in prison. Although to most people this verdict did not seem excessively punitive, Islamic militants surely felt differently. On 26 August, a bomb at Algiers airport left nine dead and 128 wounded. Again, no organization claimed responsibility. The government responded with a new anti-terrorism law that strengthened the regime's repressive powers, but also with offers of leniency. In September, an official decree broadened the definition of terrorism and made it a criminal act. Special courts were established to try those accused of terrorism. However, terrorists who had not caused deaths or injuries were amnestied, and others could receive a prison term rather than the death penalty if they surrendered before December. In addition, the government tried again (building on a hesitant and futile attempt in May) to open a 'national dialogue' to decide on constitutional reforms and the timing of new presidential and legislative elections. Several political groups responded favourably, including the FFS, the FLN, and moderate Islamic groups such as Hamas. Simultaneously Algeria began to try to break out of the diplomatic isolation occasioned by the crackdown on Islamists and by Algeria's support for Saddam Hussein during the Gulf War. However, Algerian officials continued to criticize France for giving asylum to FIS leaders, although French Foreign Minister Roland Dumas did attend Boudiaf's funeral and President Mitterrand seemed more sympathetic to Algeria's plight after the shock of the assassination.

THE ESCALATION OF TERRORISM IN 1993

With few exceptions, some of which could not be attributed directly to the FIS or to other militant Islamic groups, violence before spring 1993 was restricted to armed attacks on the police, gendarmes and the military. Such attacks continued – in late March, an attack on an army post 100 kilometres south of Algiers left eighteen soldiers dead – as did government efforts to maintain security. After the attack, the government announced that since the passage of the anti-terrorism law the preceding December, 211 Islamists had been killed, 3,800 arrested, and more than a thousand others were being actively sought *(Le Monde,* 1 April 1993). In the campaign against terrorism, the army was careful to use only the professional army and to keep conscripts in the barracks. However, the strategy was not working. Not only was the loss in military personnel in the March attack one of the heaviest since the violence began, but four members of the army unit helped the attackers surprise their comrades.

In February an attempt was made to assassinate General Khaled Nezaar, Minister of Defence and key member of the five-person HCE. What shocked

Algerian society more, however, was a series of assassinations of members of the CCN, civilians who had no connection to the military. Three of its number were assassinated in a two-day period in March. In reaction, labour and pro-democracy movements organized a demonstration against terrorism, the first demonstration to be authorized since the imposition of the state of emergency, even though these organizations were not thought to be sympathetic to the regime. *Le Monde* reported, however, that few young people were among the crowds (1 April 1993). Shortly thereafter, Hamas also condemned terrorism. But these negative reactions to the killings did not discourage violence.

At the end of May, the trial of the Islamists accused of the August 1992 airport bombing concluded with thirty-eight death sentences (twenty-six in absentia), a penalty that exceeded what the prosecution had asked for. Since little is known of the decision-making behind terrorism or even who the most influential actors are, it is impossible to decide whether subsequent violence was connected to this verdict. In any case, attacks on secular intellectuals began in May and June. On 26 May, prominent author and journalist Tahar Djaout was assassinated. He edited a weekly newspaper and had written three novels, published in Paris, critical of both the FLN and Islamic militancy and intolerance. On 15 June, psychiatrist Mahfoud Boucebei was assassinated. He, too, was a major figure in the Algerian intellectual community, one of the 'laico-assimilationistes' who had been criticized not just by Islamists but by Prime Minister Abdesslam. He had helped to establish a committee to investigate the assassination of Tahar Djaout. A week later terrorists killed sociologist Mohamed Boukhobza as he was leaving his home in the centre of Algiers. Boukhobza had replaced Djilali Liabes (who was assassinated in March) as director of the Institut national des études de stratégie globale, Algeria's prestigious think-tank. *Le Monde* (24 June 1993) reported a reaction of 'immense stupor' and anguish in Algiers.

Although the prevailing assumption was that militant Islamists were responsible, no specific claims of responsibility appeared, although leaders of the FIS in France sometimes praised the assassinations. Some observers noted pointedly that the government had criticized secular intellectuals and was trying actively to win over FIS supporters. At his funeral, friends of Tahar Djaout implicitly accused the regime of laxity, if not complicity, in his death (*Le Monde*, 24 June 1993).

Governmental reorganization

The regime could not remain passive in the face of this deterioration in the security situation. In June, Foreign Minister Redha Malek went to Paris to ask for French assistance in combating terrorism and received promises of help from the new conservative government of Edouard Balladur, elected in March. In July, General Lamine Zéroual was installed as the new minister of defence, replacing Khaled Nezzar, who remained a member of the HCE. Mohamed Lamari became the new army chief of staff. This change at the highest level of authority in Algeria, the military, was soon followed by political adjustment. In August, Abdesslam was replaced by Foreign Minister Redha Malek. Malek was said to be more receptive to the positions of the new army chief of staff (*Le Monde*, 24 August 1993). Malek is a cosmopolitan Algerian politician, a proponent of dialogue between Islam and the Western world. He had recently written a book on the relationship between modernity and Islam in Algeria. During the revolution, he edited the FLN's primary journal in French, *El Moudjahid*. After independence, he pursued a distinguished diplomatic career, becoming Algeria's ambassador to Yugoslavia, France, the Soviet Union, the United States, and Great Britain. While ambassador to Washington, Malek played an important role in the negotiations that led to the release of the American hostages in Iran, and formed an amicable relationship with American Secretary of State Warren Christopher.

Only a few hours after the announcement of these governmental changes, Algerian society was shaken by another major assassination. Kasdi Merbah, a former government minister and head of military security for seventeen years, from 1962 to 1979, fell victim to an ambush that also led to the deaths of his son, brother, chauffeur and bodyguard. Influential in bringing both Boumedienne and Chadli Benjedid to power, Merbah had become prime minister after the riots of October 1988, but had lost his post in September 1989, which provoked a crisis within the FLN. In 1990 he had broken completely with the FLN and founded an independent political party. From this position, he was severely critical of the FLN's performance, arguing that without economic improvement, security could not be restored (see *Le Monde*, 24 August 1993). He was certain, then, to have had enemies on many sides of the political spectrum. The attack, like so many others, was unclaimed, but seemed to be professionally carried out by five gunmen who fled without being apprehended.

The announcement of the composition of Redha Malek's cabinet, as well as the execution in late August of seven Islamists convicted of responsibility for the August 1992 airport bombing, indicated that the government intended to harden its position on terrorism. The post of minister of the interior was allocated to a retired colonel, Sélim Saadi. This appointment was supposedly connected to a projected unification of police and military units in the fight against terrorism, under the Minister of the Interior. The selection of Malek as prime minister was also thought to point in the direction of tougher measures against violence. The government was thus tacitly admitting that the massive security measures taken in the previous year and a half had not succeeded. Official sources were now talking of 2,000 deaths since the beginning of the year (*Le Monde*, 7 September 1993).

Attacks on foreigners

Scarcely three weeks after the installation of the new government, with its hardline mandate, terrorism took a new turn with attacks on foreigners, beginning with the most important of symbols, French citizens. On 21 September, the bodies of two French surveyors, employed by a French firm to help install electricity lines in the region south of Oran, were found. They had been kidnapped the previous day by an unidentified armed group near Sidi-bel-Abbès. The Algerian government was sufficiently alarmed to send the minister of the interior himself to the scene.

In early October, Islamic militants kidnapped a German family and released them with a warning to foreigners to leave the country. A week later, two senior Russian military officers who were teaching in an aviation school at Laghouat, 400 kilometres south of Algiers, were assassinated. A group previously unknown to the public, the 'United Company of Holy War', claimed responsibility for the killings (*New York Times*, 20 October 1993). Furthermore, attacks on Algerian intellectuals started again: a television newscaster and a former head of the national network were assassinated in the first weeks of October.

Almost simultaneously, the government indicated another policy shift, a 'last-chance' measure according to some, which appeared both to involve the army more directly in politics and to offer some possibility of a compromise. The authorities announced the formation of a 'commission of national dialogue', composed of five civilians and three generals, and headed by Hassan Khatib, a physician. Although the government had been promising a 'dialogue' for more than a year, all the efforts of the HCE to promote one had been in vain. Their hope had apparently been to hold a 'national conference' of various political interests in order to prepare a two-year transition period leading up to national elections. The new commission would have the same objective but greater influence. The engagement of the military in the process was thought to be especially significant. Possibly the formation of the commission indicated that military leaders were dissatisfied with the HCE, on which only General Nezzar represented their interests. On the other hand, the commission could have been a response to the long-standing complaint of the FFS that no solution was possible without the participation of the military, who had to guarantee any political accord. A compromise that did not have the backing of the military could not be implemented. The FFS had publicly refused to participate in any 'dialogue' and remained reserved (see *Le Monde*, 18 October 1993). However, on 29 October *Le Monde* reported that a member of the new commission had been in touch with Abdelkader Hachani of the FIS, who had been detained since January 1992.

This conciliatory gesture did not reduce the violence. Almost immediately, three foreign employees of an Italian firm were kidnapped and killed in the area south-west of Algiers. An attempt to seize two Japanese businessmen near Blida was thwarted by a police patrol. Then on 24 October three French diplomats – consular officials – were kidnapped on a major street in the heart of Algiers. The policeman guarding their building was killed. The kidnapping spread fear among the French community of Algeria, which officially numbers about 25,000. Already alarmed by the killing of the French surveyors, the French were hardly reassured by the French government's appeal to them to remain calm, prudent and careful. The vacation of the Toussaint gave them the opportunity to send their children back to France (ten official French schools operated in Algeria). At least 3,000 people returned to France for the holiday, and it is likely that few returned.

The Algerian government also took this kidnapping seriously. The minister of the interior appeared on national television to denounce the attack and to warn the kidnappers not to harm their hostages. The minister of defence called for a consensual solution but warned with ominous ambiguity that the army could not remain indifferent to events that would determine the future of the country. But it was difficult to see what measures the government could take. An army of 40,000 career professionals was engaged in a combat against a campaign of terrorism led not by a unified leadership with a clear strategy but by small, clandestine groups with no centralized control. French commentators recalled that during the Algerian war, 500,000 French soldiers were deployed in Algeria, with a population then of 9 million, whereas in 1993 the population was at least 27 million (*Le Monde*, 21 October 1993). *Le Monde* reporters frequently referred disparagingly to 'immobilism' at the top and chaos at the bottom.

A week later the Algerian government won a brief reprieve when the three hostages were released unharmed. The Algerian authorities had mounted an intensive search and claimed to have located the hostages and secured their freedom. This version of events was of course self-serving, and the other side of the story was that the kidnappers had managed to hold their hostages for a week without being discovered. Apparently the kidnappers abandoned their hostages under pressure from the search. After their release, the Algerian security forces continued intensive searches of the Islamist quarters of Algeria's largest cities, using armoured personnel carriers, helicopters and all-terrain vehicles.

More alarming than the circumstances of the release of the hostages was the threat they brought with them. One of the hostages, Michèle Thevenot, brought with her a message warning foreigners to leave the country within the month: 'Leave the country, we give you a month's time. Persons exceeding this limit will be held responsible for their own sudden deaths. There will be no more kidnappings and this will be more violent than in Egypt' (translated from *Le Monde*, 5 November 1993).

The kidnappers (one of whom was arrested in late November, and another killed in early December) were apparently members of the Armed Islamic Group, said to be under the direction of Si Ahmed Mourad, also known as 'Djaafar el Afghani.' In a communiqué to news agencies, dated 16 November and from Algiers, the group represented itself as independent of the FIS and hostile to all dialogue, negotiation, or reconciliation with the government (*Le Monde*, 23 November 1993). However, the FIS managed to implicate itself when one of its leaders in exile suggested that the French officials might be spies and thus justifiable targets.

The French government reacted swiftly to the new threat. Foreign Minister Alain Juppé announced immediately that the size of the diplomatic mission (around 1,500 people) would be reduced. At home the government went on the offensive. Apparently during the kidnapping the Minister of the Interior, Charles Pasqua, had promptly warned known representatives of Islamic militancy that retribution would follow any tragic end to the kidnapping. When the hostages were released, a large-scale operation was launched against Islamic radicals living in France. Three million Muslims live in France, among whom 900,000 are Algerian immigrants. The FIS was not thought to have a wide following, but the police conducted sweeps in Paris, Marseilles, Lyons, Lille, Bordeaux and Toulouse. Among the eighty-eight people arrested were Moussa Kraouche and Djaffar El Houari, leaders of the Algerian Brotherhood in France, an organization founded in 1990 to act as an adjunct to the FIS, which was then legal. All were subsequently released. The highly publicized crackdown seemed to be a warning to radical Islamic circles in France – not just Algerian but Iranian as well – that France would not tolerate the importation of violence onto French territory.

The FIS responded to the hardening of the French position (and perhaps to the extremism of rival groups in Algeria) with intransigence. On 15 November, Paris news agencies received a FIS communiqué issued in Algiers and signed by Abderrazak Redjem, the former head of the audio-visual department of the FIS who went underground in March 1992. It warned explicitly that: 'Those who cooperate with a regime that has no other objective than to stay in power will be considered as associated with the crime against the Algerian people' (translated from *Le Monde*, 17 November 1993). It also rejected any dialogue, reconciliation or peace with the Algerian government and warned that France was reponsible for the death of its representatives and the danger posed to its interests. Similarly on 14 November, from the United States, Anwar Haddam, claiming to be a member of the executive of the FIS abroad, announced that French policy would have grave effects on 'ideological minorities' in Algeria, who were the heirs of French colonialism.

As the year closed, these warnings were borne out. At the end of November the unofficial estimate was 3,000 deaths in the past two years (*The Economist*, 27 November 1993). In the period from 16 May to 16 December, eight judges were assassinated, three of them in the first two weeks of December. A high-ranking official in the foreign affairs ministry, Salah Fellah, head of the Asia Department, was shot in early December. Nine policemen were killed in an ambush in the Algiers suburbs on 24 November, and eight were killed in early December. Attacks on foreigners also escalated. The deadline for foreigners to leave the country was 30 November. In the first week of December, the victims were French, Spanish, Russian, British, and Italian. On 14 December, near Blida, south of Algiers, an armed group attacked a group of Croatian construction workers and stabbed to death twelve Christians, sparing the Muslims. In a statement to a London newspaper, the Armed Islamic Group claimed responsibility and announced that the killings were a response to the violence against Muslims in Bosnia (*New York Times*, 17 December 1993). The group also promised more attacks on foreigners.

The government responded with an announcement of its determination to eliminate terrorism, but seemed to have no plan other than a continuation of military repression combined with unanswered appeals for 'dialogue': in November the HCE issued another futile offer of compromise with any political groups who respected the law. No political faction had solid popular support and the army appeared to be divided and uncertain. The government still lacked an official economic policy and seemed unable to decide how to deal with the growing economic crisis. At the end of November, *Le Monde* (30 November; see also *Le Monde Diplomatique*, December 1993: 8) reported that Abdesslam's tenure as prime minister from July 1992 to August 1993 had been disastrous. Algerian industry was working at only 50 per cent capacity. The construction industry, dependent on imports, was practially shut down. Repayment of the foreign debt was costing Algeria 75 per cent of its earnings from petroleum exports. Officially 20 per cent of the active population was unemployed. The IMF was reported to be seeking at least a 50 per cent devaluation of the Algerian dinar, a move the government resisted not only because of the social consequences – imports, especially food, would become exorbitantly expensive – but because it would constrain private investment. However, the foreign investment that the government sought in order to reduce its external debt was unlikely to materialize so long as terrorism against foreign interests continued. Despite the government's security measures, foreigners, many of whom worked in the petroleum industry, were leaving. Most countries had evacuated diplomatic dependents and reduced the size of their embassy staffs by late

December. Algerians, especially intellectuals and the professional classes, were desperately seeking visas to leave the country.

Further evidence of the regime's irresolution came in mid-December when, barely two weeks before the expiration of its mandate, Prime Minister Redha Malek announced that the term of the HCE would be extended to 31 January 1994. A 'national conference' was scheduled for 25 and 26 January to discuss a three-year transition period leading up to legislative elections. During that time, the HCE would cede its powers to a collective executive composed of a president and two vice-presidents. A 180-member National Transition Council would function as the legislature. The programme promised a continuation of the struggle against terrorism and structural reform of the economy, but the details of the implementation of these policies remained obscure.

The announcement of the delay predictably elicited more violence. On 28 December prominent poet and writer Youssef Sebti was assassinated, and on 29 December a Belgian woman and her Algerian husband were killed. The government's policy of combining tough measures against violence with offers of negotiation had not paid off, and economic and social conditions had only worsened. At the end of the year, 780 Islamists remained in detention in two internment centres in the Sahara (*Le Monde*, 4 January 1994). The FIS had hardened its stance during the year, a result of the government's repression of Islamic militancy as well as the intransigence of the Armed Islamic Group. Even if the regime had succeeded in opening a 'dialogue' with the imprisoned leaders of the FIS (a policy said to be favoured by military leader Khaled Nezzar but not Prime Minister Redha Malek), it was not certain that the FIS had sufficient control of the Islamist movement to be able to uphold its side of a bargain. No alternative political organizations had emerged with whom the government could form an alliance, even one of convenience. Decentralized terrorism proved impossible to control. However dispersed its sources, the pattern of terrorism was alarming. It seemed intended to eradicate Western influence by driving foreigners out and intimidating secular intellectuals; equally, it sought to destroy the state's ability to govern and to exact retribution by attacking officials such as judges, to keep the security forces off-guard, and to disrupt the regime's economic development strategy. Certainly its effects were corrosive, and the regime's response did nothing to reduce tensions. Nevertheless, it seemed unlikely that terrorism would succeed in separating state from society or mobilizing active mass opposition to the regime so long as the military remained united and hostile to an Islamic takeover.

CHRONOLOGY: POLITICAL VIOLENCE IN ALGERIA
SINCE 1988

1988

6 October State of siege declared in Algiers after riots cause the deaths of several hundred people.

10 October President Chadli Benjedid promises political reforms.

3 November Referendum approves constitutional revisions.

5 November Kasdi Merbah named prime minister, to replace Abdelhamid Brahimi.

22 December President Chadli Benjedid re-elected for a third term of five years.

1989

23 February New liberal constitution, permitting a multi-party system to replace the one-party system dominated by the FLN, approved by referendum.

10 September Mouloud Hamrouche replaces Kasdi Merbah as prime minister.

14 September Government recognizes legal existence of the FIS (Front islamique du salut, or Islamic Salvation Front).

1990

12 June The FIS makes significant gains in local/municipal elections.

27 July General Khaled Nezzar named minister of defence.

1991

5 June Sid Ahmed Ghozali replaces Mouloud Hamrouche as prime minister.

30 June Leaders of the FIS, Abassi Madani and Ali Belhadj, are arrested.

26 December In the first round of legislative elections, the FIS wins 188 seats.

1992

2 January Approximately 500,000 people demonstrate in Algiers in support of the Front des forces socialistes (FFS) to 'save democracy'.

11 January President Chadli resigns under duress.

12 January Legislative elections are cancelled.

14 January A Haut Comité d'Etat (HCE), headed by Mohamed Boudiaf, is established to complete the term of the president; amnesty announced for around 6,000 people who had not committed crimes against the security and authority of the state.

9 February The HCE declares a state of emergency throughout Algeria, to last one year.

4 March The FIS is dissolved.

22 April President Boudiaf announces the creation of the Conseil Consultatif National (CCN), with sixty members chosen by the HCE.

30 May The HCE announces a programme of 'Rassemblement patriotique' to unite the country around a constructive national dialogue; the next day more than 150 Islamists are released.

29 June President Boudiaf is assassinated at Annaba.

2 July Ali Kafi becomes head of the HCE.

8 July Sid Ahmed Ghozali resigns as Prime Minister; replaced by Belaid Abdesslam.

15 July A military court sentences FIS leaders Madani and Belhadj to twelve years in prison.

26 August A bomb at Algiers airport leaves nine dead and 128 wounded; bombs at Air France and Swissair offices fail to cause casualties.

12 September HCE announces opening of discussions with other political organizations in a 'national dialogue' to discuss constitutional revisions and a transition period leading up to presidential and legislative elections.

30 September Announcement of a stringent new anti-terrorism law.

October Prefects specially charged with security duties and provided with extra resources are sent to certain departments.

December Curfew declared in Algiers and surrounding districts.

1993

January Executions of two Islamists; government announces that censorship of information concerning security will be reinforced; French Foreign Minister Roland Dumas makes an official visit to Algiers.

18 February Belaid Abdesslam visits Paris.

13 February Attempted assassination of General Khaled Nezzar, Minister of Defence.

22 February Redha Malek, member of HCE and minister of foreign affairs since 5 February is sent to Morocco to repair relations damaged when Hassan II in January said that it would be interesting for the region to see the Islamists in power.

27 March Algeria breaks diplomatic relations with Iran and recalls ambassador from Sudan.

16–17 March Djilali Liabes, Laadi Flici and Hafid Senhadri, members of the CCN, are assassinated.

22 March Demonstration in Algiers against terrorism organized by the General Union of Algerian Workers (Union générale des travailleurs algériens, UGTA) and the Rassemblement pour la culture et la démocratie.

22 March Islamic militant 'commando' raid in Boughezoul (100 km. south of Algiers) leaves forty-one dead, including eighteen military personnel.

1 April The Mouvement de la société islamique, Hamas, condemns terrorism.

26 May Author and journalist Tahar Djaout is assassinated.

15 June Psychiatrist Mahfoud Boucebei is assassinated.

17–18 June Redha Malek visits Paris and obtains French aid for the struggle against terrorism.

22 June Sociologist Mohamed Boukhobza assassinated.

10 July General Lamine Zéroual replaces Khaled Nezzar as minister of defence.

3 August Television journalist Rabah Zenati is assassinated.

21 August Redha Malek replaces Belaid Abdesslam as prime minister.

21 August Kasdi Merbah (prime minister from November 1988 to September 1989, who entered the opposition in November 1990) is assassinated.

31 August Execution of seven Islamists found guilty of Algiers bombing in August 1992 (bringing to thirteen the number of executions since 1992).

4 September HCE names new government, including Mourad Benachenou as minister of the economy, a post up to then held by the prime minister, and Sélim Saadi, former minister of agriculture, as interior minister.

21 September Two French surveyors are kidnapped and assassinated near Sidi-Bel-Abbés near Oran in the west of Algeria (the first foreigners to be killed since the violence began in 1992); responsibility claimed by Armed Islamic Group.

11 October Execution of twenty Islamic militants condemned for terrorism.

14 October Mustapha Abada, former head of Algerian national television, is assassinated.

16 October Two Russian military officers are assassinated at Laghouat (400 kilometres south of Algiers).

18 October Smail Yefsah, television news editor, is assassinated (the seventh journalist assassinated in the past five months).

19 October Killing of three foreign oil technicians (employees of the Italian firm Sadelmi), at Tiaret; responsibility claimed by the Armed Islamic Group.

23 October Minister of Defence Lamine Zéroual invites all political groups, without exception, to find a consensual solution before the end of the year.

24 October A police officer is killed and three French diplomatic employees are kidnapped in central Algiers by the Islamic Armed Group.

31 October French hostages are released with a warning that all French citizens should leave the country by 30 November.

4 November French Minister of Foreign Affairs, Alain Juppé, announces that French diplomatic, consular, and cultural services in Algeria will be reduced.

5 November French Interior Minister Charles Pasqua in a televised interview warns members of the FIS not to carry out political activities on

French territory that run counter to the interests of the French government.

9 November French police arrest eighty-eight suspected members of the FIS living in France; all eventually are released.

15 November The 'provisional executive bureau' of the FIS in Algiers issues a communiqué rejecting all dialogue with the government.

24 November Nine policemen are killed in an ambush at El Harrach, east of Algiers (among forty-three people killed in the week before 30 November).

2 December A Spanish businessman is assassinated 85 kilometres south of Algiers, while driving from Oran to Annaba.

5 December A Russian woman (wife of an Algerian citizen) is assassinated in Algiers.

7 December Salah Fellah, head of the Foreign Ministry's Asia department, is assassinated in Algiers.

7 December A British technician and a retired French citizen are assassinated.

9 December An attack on the police claims the lives of eight officers and two civilians in Sidi Moussa, south of Algiers.

14 December Twelve Christian Croatian and Bosnian construction workers on a dam project near Tamesguida are stabbed to death; responsibility claimed by the Armed Islamic Group.

16 December Judge Seddik Guentri of the Tizi Ouzou court is assassinated (the eighth judge killed since May).

19 December Prime Minister Redha Malek announces that the term of the HCE will be extended to 31 January 1994.

28 December Poet and writer Youssef Sebti is assassinated.

29 December A Belgian woman and her Algerian husband are assassinated.

REFERENCES

Burgat, F. (1993), *The Islamic Movement in North Africa* (trans. W. Dowell), Texas: Center for Middle Eastern Studies at the University of Texas.

Callies de Salies, B. (1993), 'L'Algérie dans la tourmente', *Défense nationale*, 49: 109–19.

Entelis, J.P. (1992), 'The crisis of authoritarianism in North Africa: the case of Algeria', *Problems of Communism*, 41: 71–81.

Lamchichi, A. (1992), *L'Islamisme en Algérie*, Paris: L'Harmattan.

Mortimer, R.A. (1993), 'Algeria: the clash between Islam, democracy, and the military', *Current History*, January: 37–41.

Tahi, M.S. (1992), 'The arduous democratisation process in Algeria', *Journal of Modern African Studies*, 30: 397–419.

Vandewalle, D. (1992), 'At the brink: chaos in Algeria', *World Policy Journal*, 9: 705–17.

12

Elections and Reform in Morocco

George Joffé

On 17 September 1993 Morocco completed its complex legislative electoral process which had begun on 25 June that year. In June, Moroccan voters – Morocco operates a system of universal suffrage – went to the polls to elect 222 members of the country's national assembly, the Chamber of Deputies (Majlis an-Nawab), by direct election. In September, the remaining one third of the Chamber – 111 deputies – was elected in an indirect election from among the country's municipal councillors, members of professional bodies and the professions. The indirect elections brought to an end the first national electoral experience for nearly nine years.

In theory, legislative elections must be held every six years, according to the Moroccan constitution. However, in 1989, King Hassan proposed that the elections should be delayed by two years (a proposal that was approved by referendum) in order to try to complete the resolution of the Western Sahara issue. This was not achieved, with the result that, during 1992, municipal elections went ahead throughout the whole country including the disputed Western Sahara. The experience was repeated in the legislative elections of 1993 on the same basis. The Moroccan government has, in short, thereby treated the Western Sahara as if it were *de jure* an integral part of Morocco. In the interim, between the end of the extended eight-year term of the previous Chamber of Deputies and the latest legislative elections, Morocco was ruled by a caretaker government of national unity under the authority of the king, Mawlay Hassan II and led by the veteran politician and former head of the Office Chérifienne des Phosphates, Karim Lamrani. A new government was due to take office towards the end of 1993 under the terms of the constitutional amendments passed by referendum in 1992.

The constitutional changes, which were approved by a 99.96 per cent majority on 4 September 1992, provided for future governments to reflect the political composition of the Chamber of Deputies, with the majority party being able to select its own cabinet for royal approval. Previously this had been part of the royal prerogative. The Chamber also acquired the right to pass a vote of confidence on the programme proposed by a new

Table 12.1 Morocco: legislative electoral results – 1984 and 1993 (seats in Chamber of Deputies)

Movement	Direct		Indirect		Total	
	1984	1993	1984	1993	1984	1993
USFP	35	48 (49)	1	4	36	52 (53)
PI	24	43	17	7	41	50
MP	31	33	16	18	47	51
RNI	39	28 (26)	22	13	61	41 (39)
UC	56	27	27	27	83	54
PND	15	14	9	10	24	24
MNP	–	14	–	11	–	25
PPS	2	6	0	4	2	10
OADP	1	2	0	0	1	2
PDI	–	3 (4)	–	6	–	9 (10)
PA	–	2	–	0	–	2
SAP	0	2	0	2	0	4
CDT	0	0	3	4	3	4
UMT	0	0	5	3	5	3
UGTM	2	0	0	2	2	2
PCS	1	0	0	0	1	0
TOTAL	206	222	100	111	306	333

Sources: Europa, 1994; *Maghreb Quarterly Report*, 11 (August 1993); *Cedies Informations*, 1899 (25 September 1993); *Keesing's Record of World Events 1993*, p. 39, 665.

Notes: See Table 12.3 for names of parties and movements. In thirteen bye-elections held on 26 April because of invalidation by the Constitutional Council, the RNI lost two seats, while the PDI and the USFP each gained a seat. In the fourteenth bye-election casued by the death of the incumbent, the USFP candidate was returned. The corrected totals are shown thus ( ).

government on coming into office. The Chamber will also remain in session during a state of emergency, rather than being prorogued as was the case in the past. There were also provisions safeguarding human rights. King Hassan, however, on the grounds that his Islamic duties prevented him from instituting a constitutional monarchy, retained the right to prorogue the Chamber at will (Europa, 1994: 709). In April 1992 the king had also promised that the anticipated elections would be 'free and honest' and, as a result, the following month had set up two commissions to review the electoral law and to monitor the electoral process.

The new electoral law, passed by the Chamber of Deputies on 4 June 1992 despite a boycott by the opposition parties, had been a source of considerable political friction before the elections. It provided for a continuation of an electoral process split between direct and indirect elections, although it reduced the minimum voting age to 20 years and the minimum

Table 12.2 Morocco: municipal elections – 1983 and 1992 (% of seats won)

Party	Percentage	
	1983	1992
Independents	22.2	13.9
UC	17.6	13.5
PI	16.8	12.5
RNI	14.1	21.7
MP	2.9	12.0
PND	11.7	7.6
USFP	3.5	7.0
PPS	0.1	0.8
MNP	–	10.2
Others	11.1	0.8

Source: EIU, 1985 (London); *Cedies Informations*, 1852: 24 October 1992.
Note: See Table 12.3 for names of parties and organizations.

candidate age from 25 to 23 years. It also provided for equal state funding and media exposure for all political parties. The opposition's objections – by now the USFP and Istiqlal had fused together to form the Bloc Démocratique or Koutlah and were soon to be joined by the PPS and the OADP – were that they sought a minimum age of 18 years for voting and of 21 years for candidates and, more importantly, a two-tier voting process under an independent supervisory body. Despite their objections, however, and in the wake of the successful vote in the Chamber, although the anticipated legislative elections were delayed beyond the expected September deadline, the government was dismissed in August and replaced by an interim government in which no ministers with formal party affiliations participated (Europa, 1994: 710).

THE AFTERMATH OF THE ELECTIONS

In fact, after the delayed legislative elections, the new constitutional provisions for the selection of a new government did not operate as expected. Although the Koutlah formed the largest political grouping after the elections were over, it rejected the opportunity to form a government. It also refused to participate in a government nominated by King Hassan, even though he offered it thirty-one of the thirty-five portfolios available, retaining only the premiership, interior, foreign affairs and justice in his own gift. The reason for this was, ostensibly, that the leadership of the USFP, the largest party within the coalition, wished to protest against electoral abuses and, together with Istiqlal, wanted the king to annul the elections on these

Table 12.3 Morocco: political parties and movements*

Party name	Tendency
Koutlah (Bloc Démocratique)	opposition
1. Union Socialiste des Forces Populaires (USFP)	socialist
2. Parti Istiqlal (PI)	nationalist
3. Organisation de l'Action démocratique et populaire (OADP)	extreme left**
4. Parti du Progrès et du Socialisme (PPS)	communist
Parti du Centre Social (PCS)	centre socialist
Union Nationale des Forces Populaires (UNFP)	socialist
Parti de l'Action (PA)	linked to Koutlah
Conservative (Entente Nationale)	
Mouvement populaire (MP)	Berberist
Union Constitutionelle (UC)	former UNFP
Mouvement national populaire (MNP)	former MP
Parti national démocrate (PND)	former RNI
Independent	
Rassemblement nationale des Indépendents (RNI)	pro-Palace
Parti démocratique pour l'indépendence (PDI)	democratic
Trades Unions	
Confédération démocratique du Travail (CDT)	affiliated to USFP
Union Générale des Travailleurs marocains (UGTM)	affiliated to PI
Union marocaine du Travail (UMT)	affiliated to UNFP
Sans Appartenance Politique (SAP)	independents

Note: * With seats in the Chamber or the municipalities. ** Formerly part of the clandestine 'Front Progressiste' and on the extreme left of UNFP/USFP.

grounds and hold fresh elections. Indeed, the USFP leader, Abderrahman Youssoufi, had threatened to resign in protest against irregularities in the direct electoral process.

There were undoubtedly abuses of the electoral process during the direct elections in June. Several of the monitors supplied by the US-based International Foundation for Electoral Systems reported significant irregularities which benefited established politicians. The Foundation had acted as the official observer of the direct elections, at the request of the Moroccan government. Seasoned observers of the Moroccan political scene commented that such abuses were probably not the result of interference by the Ministry of the Interior – as had undoubtedly been the case in the past – but of actions by the local administration in the constituencies concerned, wishing to curry favour with political representatives, much to the embarrassment of central government, in view of the king's promises that the elections would be 'free and honest'.

The indirect elections, in which Morocco's professional organizations, chambers of commerce and local government organs elect members to the Chamber, were another matter entirely. The surprising surge in support for the centre-right led to the Union Constitutionelle, led by former UNFP leader Maati Bouabid, obtaining more seats than any other party in the Chamber. Yet Bouabid's election in a Casablanca constituency had been marred by serious irregularities. This caused a storm of protest. Suspicions centred on the role played by the veteran interior minister, Driss Basri, who was popularly believed to have rigged the results in favour of the centre-right, in order to counter the success of the left-wing coalition, the Koutlah, in the direct elections. It was this development, more than any other, that led the Koutlah to refuse to participate in a new government and to demand that the elections be declared null and void.

Despite protracted discussions between the king and the opposition coalition, the crisis over Morocco's new government in the wake of the elections persisted into November. On 6 November, the official anniversary of the famous 'Green March' – in which 350,000 Moroccans massed on the borders of the Western Sahara in 1975 to underline Morocco's determination to annex the then Spanish colony, at a time when Spain was in the throes of a succession crisis caused by the death of Franco – the king finally made clear his views on Morocco's political future. In a speech to the Moroccan people that evening, he rejected the demand for the elections to be re-run, claiming that no authority existed to do this within the constitution. He went on to explain what he had offered the opposition coalition, stating that he had only reserved the premiership and the portfolios of the interior, foreign affairs and justice within his own prerogative.

The premiership, he maintained, could not be offered to the Koutlah because, although it commanded the largest number of seats as a coalition, the Union Constitutionelle was the largest single party in the new Chamber. The Union Constitutionelle, however, had declined to exert its rights. In any case, neither of the major parties in the Koutlah had held power for many years. Istiqlal had not led a government for nine years, while the USFP last provided the prime minister thirty-three years ago. Neither, therefore, had people with the experience to occupy the post at this delicate juncture. Foreign affairs had to be reserved because of the opposition's pro-Iraqi attitudes during the conflict in the Gulf in 1991 – Morocco's official position had been to support the UN-authorized and US-led Multinational Coalition. Furthermore, Morocco was commencing delicate negotiations over the Western Sahara issue as the UN-sponsored referendum approached, and the king had an obligation to supervise this process. Justice had to remain a royal prerogative because the king's sacred duty as an Islamic ruler and caliph did not permit him to hand over control of the shariah – Islamic religious law which is, in theory, the basis of political legitimacy within Muslim states. Interior affairs, too, touched on vital royal interests, namely ensuring social and political order, and could not be handed over to politicians who might have different agendas.

King Hassan noted, however, that despite his disappointment at the behaviour of the opposition, Morocco's political life was increasingly being expressed as a form of 'bipolarization', between the Koutlah, or Bloc Démocratique as an opposition and what he called the 'Entente nationale' formed by the centre-right. He approved this bipolarization, which he saw as being similar to the situation in Britain or the United States, and hoped that the political landscape would soon restructure itself formally along such lines. The implication was that then there would be no need for royal intervention in the process of government formation, for this could then occur as provided for in the constitution. On 10 November, just four days after the speech, a technocratic non-party government, headed once again by the veteran prime minister, Karim Lamrani, was installed in power.

THE BACKGROUND TO POWER

The evolution of the political situation in Morocco over the election issue in fact reveals the basic reality of power in the country. It demonstrates the way in which a traditionalist political system has adapted to the modern world and how that system has exploited an indigenous political culture to ensure its continued dominance. It emphasizes the personalised nature of power there but also, paradoxically, indicates the limits of this *ancien régime* and the degree to which it is being challenged by the institutions that it has itself created. Indeed, Morocco's immediate future is likely to be dominated by the way in which this political crisis is resolved, and its resolution will have profound significance for the political and diplomatic choices that will determine the path ahead into the twenty-first century. There is also a second agenda: the role played within the Moroccan political scene by the fundamental economic reforms that have been undertaken throughout the past decade.

There has been a long tradition of cohesive political culture in Morocco, stretching back to the Idrissid dynasty in the tenth century. Furthermore, the colonial period did not mark a rupture with the past, as was the case in Algeria and Tunisia. Instead, it was one of evolution of a political system, albeit under extreme pressure, rather than its destruction by the colonial experience. The Moroccan monarchy emerged in charge of independent Morocco in 1956 with its prestige enhanced – largely because of its association with the national independence movement, Istiqlal (Joffé, 1985: 306). Its political control was also universalized – by the colonial administrative legacy – in ways that had never existed in the pre-colonial Moroccan state.

At the same time, the state itself had begun a process of modernization and economic development and the tensions that ensued were to do much to damage the post-colonial legacy. Under King Hassan II, Morocco has experienced two attempted *coup d'états*, one rural rebellion, a major war in the Western Sahara and several significant constitutional changes. Under his father, King Mohammed V, there were also two major rural rebellions. Yet all this occurred within the context of a fundamental assumption that the Moroccan political system is one that involves strong elements of limited and democratic constitutional monarchy (Joffé, 1988: 201–9). This contradiction between violent attempts to alter governmental behaviour and the normative assumptions of controlled political change illustrates the degree to which practical politics in Morocco have differed from the democratic ideal.

In fact, the underlying nature of the Moroccan political scene is far more complex than this. In reality, the informal but fundamental political dynamic in Morocco is to preserve political stasis and balance. Thus, the political system has traditionally been based on the process of balancing patron–client groups off against each other in a situation of political metastability. The essential component in this process has been the sultanate, traditionally weak and thereby obliged to arbitrate (Ayache, 1978: 5–21) between such groups, particularly in the *bilad as-siba* – the 'lands of dissidence' where the sultan lacked the military power to enforce his writ, although his position as a spiritual suzerain was fully recognised. In those areas in which the sultanate was fully in control – the *bilad al-makhzan* – sultanic power was usually repressive and absolute. Indeed, the sultanate's very weakness, particularly in the *bilad as-siba*, has to a large extent been its guarantee of a political role, for, although it could not threaten an established patron–client group there, it offered each and any of them the opportunity to profit from its vital function of diffusing tensions between them through mediation or arbitration.

At a normative level, however, the sultanate was legitimized by the status of its occupant as *amir al-muminin* (commander of the faithful) – one of the traditional titles of the caliphate, the political institution in the Muslim world that embodied the legitimate succession of the power, duties and prestige of the Prophet Muhammad after his death. Indeed, the Moroccan sultanate considers itself to be sharifian (genealogically descended from the Prophet) and caliphal and is so considered by the Moroccan population at large. Traditionally, this element ensured its survival as an essential component of the political structure of the *bilad as-siba*. The result is that, in addition to its instrumental role, it has sufficient prestige not only to ensure its survival but to displace any other claimants to the same position.

Furthermore, although the caliphate was originally an elective position amongst the Prophet's descendants, in which the occupant had to fulfil certain specific functions, including ordering the Muslim world for the correct practice of Islam – typified by the Moroccan tradition of the *bay'a* (Cherifi, 1988: 28) – the growth of religious orthodoxy during the first 700 years of Islam established the contrary principle that the caliph – indeed, any ruler – should not and could not legally be displaced from his position (Kedourie, 1992: 3–9). This was particularly important in those regions where direct sultanic rule applied – the *bilad al-makhzan* – and where the sultan's power was traditionally absolute. Thus the Moroccan sultan's role as arbiter was bolstered by religious status and legal precedent (Waterbury, 1970: 144–58).

In the post-colonial world, however, the vital assumption that the sultan-ate was weak could not apply. After all, the major legacy bequeathed to an independent Moroccan state by France and Spain in 1956 was the assurance that the forces of law and order operated equally effectively over the whole territorial extent of the modern state. Yet, at the same time, the political culture of the weak sultanate, rendered vital to political stability by its mediating role, survived. It was for this reason that a system of limited democracy, with a superficially constitutional monarch, became an essential part of the post-colonial political dispensation. In effect, however, behind this political culture Morocco developed into a clientalist state in which the sultan–monarch became the supreme patron (Waterbury, 1970: 267–74).

The key, then, to political survival in modern Morocco is to create structures that diffuse localized power and yet permit the local elites to be associated with the monarchist core of the political system. The formal parliamentary system is part of this process and, in reality, its members tend to represent interest groups and elites that either have or seek to acquire a vested interest in the regime. However, it is buttressed by other components. Morocco's municipal system, for example, is decentralized through the system of the *collectivités locales*, in which municipalities and communes have autonomy over local expenditure and receive a subvention from the state which they may supplement in order to provide local services. The government has proposed that, once the Western Sahara question is finally resolved – presumably in Morocco's favour – a similar system of administrative and legislative decentralization should apply at provincial level, with Morocco's fifty provinces gathered into eight regions, each in charge of its own internal affairs.

The system of the *collectivités locales* thus provides local, largely rural or non-metropolitan urban elites with a vested interest in the system under a superficially democratic guise – for the individuals involved are chosen by popular suffrage. Of course, the culture of patronage–clientage and cultural consensus ensures that elite members are actually selected by the democratic process. None the less, formally at least, the process is democratic.

It is bolstered by a further participatory system, that of the *associations culturelles*. These bodies, funded by the Royal Palace, control vast areas of cultural and communal life. They, again, tend to be dominated by elites. These elites are largely urban in nature and are thus tied into the formal structure of the administration which, however decentralized it is formally, is also closely scrutinized by both Royal Palace and the government.

A system of this kind, formally democratic at several levels but permeated with a consensual patron–client political culture, is extremely effective at neutralizing political threats and at preserving a basically conservative social order. In so far as it is dominated by the Royal Palace, given its monopoly of the instruments of legitimate state violence and its status as the religiously sanctioned ultimate legal authority (because it is the embodiment of the caliphate), it also has the monopoly of arbitrary power under the cloak of legality. Thus, those who are not integrated into the system can be effectively repressed by it and, indeed, implicit violence of this kind is traditionally an intrinsic element of the political culture as well. It has been persuasively argued recently that the counterpart to the concept of an elective caliphate as the origin of Morocco's political system (Lahbabi, 1962) is the fact that the sultanate has always depended on its arbitrary repressive power in the last resort, based on the duty due to the caliph as the 'shadow of God upon earth' (Kedourie, 1992: 8). This has meant that repression has always played an important role in the exercise of power by the modern sultanate, for monarchy in Morocco is quintessentially 'hierocratic' (Munson, 1993: 35–9).

The very complexity of the system also means that many of the threats that face its neighbours in North Africa do not threaten the Moroccan political system in the same way. Islamic fundamentalism, although it certainly exists in Morocco, cannot compete effectively against the power, religious prestige and status of the monarchy (Munson, 1993: 176). Thus, no Islamist movement has been really effective in threatening the *status quo*. Similarly, violent protest has occurred in Morocco – in January 1984 and in December 1990. However, it has no political focus because the political parties and their associated organizations, such as the trade unions, are also integrated into the complex political game and have a vested interest in its survival. Attempts to form a new political focus outside the formal party structure are simply repressed, as the Front Progressiste discovered in the 1970s.

After all, the democratic system now in force, which is based on the 1972 constitution, was introduced in 1976 as a specific response to formal political party support over the Western Sahara issue. The parties know the limits of their power and the Palace encourages their participation. Indeed, the king frequently goes above the party political scene to achieve consensus amongst party leaders if some major step is contemplated, in a process that is redolent of the principle of *shura*: consultation and consensus. Conversely, however, this relationship can give the political parties some leverage over the Palace. For example, in the recent crisis over government formation, the Koutlah warned King Hassan of the danger of foisting a party-based government on the country, a warning that appears to have persuaded the king to choose a non-partisan governmental team instead. Indeed, misjudgement by the Palace, as occurred during the Gulf crisis in 1990–91, when King Hassan initially enthusiastically supported the American initiative against Iraq, can also provide the political parties with leverage.

In fact, this crisis very neatly underlined the way in which the monarchy's control of power had personalized the political process in Morocco, despite its formal democratic nature. Indeed, the king's very dominance in the Moroccan political process is a major danger for the survival of the dynasty, and King Hassan must be aware that a genuine constitutional monarchy will eventually have to be created if it is to survive. This implies a voluntary restriction of the monarch's arbitrary powers in order to legitimize the system of government that he has created. It also implies the primacy of the legal process and the legislature over the executive and the abandonment by the monarchy of its legislative function as sanctioned by Islamic constitutional tradition. Yet, by doing this, the monarchy will also lose its major source of current legitimization, even though, in theory, it will be replaced by constitutionalism. Not surprisingly, this is a risk that King Hassan is loath to take too speedily and many observers believe that it will be delayed until his son, Crown Prince Sidi Mohamed, replaces him on the throne. Until then, Moroccans will have to be satisfied with the limited options offered by the 'procedural democracy' that King Hassan has created, rather than by the 'substantive democracy' they seek (Zartman, 1963: 12).

THE IMPLICATIONS OF ECONOMIC REFORM

Just over a decade ago, in September 1983, Morocco began a process of economic restructuring and reform which is only now approaching its end. The process was initiated when Morocco could not meet its repayment schedule on some $13 billion-worth of foreign debt and had to turn to the International Monetary Fund (IMF) for help. This was not the first time that Morocco had benefited from IMF support. Growing imbalances in the external account and over the budget deficit had led, in 1980, to Morocco seeking a $1 billion loan from the IMF's Extended Fund Facility and a parallel $500 million Structural Adjustment Loan from the World Bank. Both arrangements collapsed in 1981–82 and, after a foreign exchange crisis starting in March 1983, Morocco had to reschedule its debts, despite an IMF standby arrangement in 1982 (Horton, 1990: 1–13).

As a result, a new IMF standby loan, worth SDR300 million, was provided in September 1983, to be followed by others in 1985 and 1986 totalling $718 million, as well as by two World Bank industrial and trade structural adjustment loans and two similar loans for the agricultural sector, plus education and privatization loans, all totalling over $1 billion (Horton, 1990: 109–10). This support from these multilateral institutions enabled Morocco to arrange vital debt rescheduling operations with its official creditors in the Paris Club and, albeit with greater difficulty, with its commercial creditors in the London Committee. Two major rescheduling operations occurred with the London Committee and six with the Paris Club – in October 1983 ($1.152 billion); in September 1985 ($1.124 billion); in March 1987 ($1.008 billion); in October 1988 ($969 million); in September 1990 ($3.200 billion); and in February 1992 ($1.500 billion) – for a total of $8.953 billion-worth of debt principle (Kuhn and Guzman, 1990: 4). Morocco also benefited from two further IMF standby operations: a new standby credit for SDR220 million in 1988 which was renewed for a further eight months in July 1990, and a final standby credit of SDR92 million in January 1992 (Europa, 1994: 717).

Morocco anticipated that, once this standby had expired in March 1993, it would require no further IMF help, as it would be able then to return to the international capital markets for all necessary funding, and so far this has proved to be the case. However, despite the fact that the country had rescheduled $8.9 billion-worth of official debt and up to $3 billion-worth of private debt, the outstanding debt burden was still $21.2 billion at the end of 1991. Of this total, $10.6 billion was owed to Paris Club official creditors, $1.6 billion to the USA, $3.6 billion to London Committee commercial creditors, $3.3 billion to the World Bank and $0.6 billion to the IMF. All that could be said was that total external debt was at least on a declining trend, having peaked the previous year at $23.6 billion, and that Morocco could at least cover repayments from foreign exchange earnings, having seen its debt service ratio fall from an estimated 60 per cent in 1983 to around 29 per cent eight years later.

Table 12.4 Morocco: external debt 1984–91 ($ billion)

	1984	1985	1986	1987	1988	1989	1990	1991
Total	14.3	16.5	17.9	20.8	21.1	21.7	23.6	21.2
Long-term	13.1	15.3	17.1	19.9	20.7	21.4	23.2	20.9
Short-term	1.2	1.2	0.8	0.9	0.4	0.3	0.4	0.3

Sources: World Bank, 1993; International Bank for Reconstruction and Development (Washington)

The help Morocco received from the IMF in resolving its foreign debt problem did not come free, however. In return for the standby credits Morocco was required to restructure its economy extensively through a combination of stabilization and structural adjustment programmes. Government subsidies were removed from consumer commodities and government expenditure was generally cut back in order to eliminate the budget deficit as part of the stabilization programme, while the World Bank supported economic restructuring. This involved liberalization of the trade regime, moves towards currency convertibility and measures to stimulate growth in export revenues. Eventually the structural role of the public sector was transformed by a wide-ranging programme of privatization of public sector assets (see Bourguignon and Morrisson, 1992: 21–8).

The importance of this experience of economic restructuring lies in the degree to which it affected the social situation in Morocco. It has to be borne in mind that the Moroccan government was well aware of the need to cut public sector deficits before the advent of the rescheduling crisis. Indeed, in June 1981 it attempted to reduce consumer subsidies only to be confronted with very serious riots in Casablanca which resulted in around 630 deaths, according to opposition sources. Official sources claimed that only 66 people died (Europa, 1994: 701). Not surprisingly, therefore, the government's attempts to comply with the 1983 IMF-approved stabilization programme met with considerable resistance when, in January 1984, cuts of 50 per cent in consumer subsidies on flour, sugar and cooking oil were announced. The subsequent riots which spread throughout the country resulted in at least 110 deaths and considerable damage. Around 1,800 people were arrested and many were sentenced later to long terms of imprisonment.

Although the government later rescheduled the consumer cuts over a longer period, they went ahead none the less and, despite the fact that the situation was eased by excellent harvests in the mid-to-late 1980s, poverty continued to increase. In December 1990 fierce riots broke out in Fes, in a final burst of popular anger over the effects of the reforms. Indeed, observers have pointed out that poverty increased significantly in urban areas, with income losses reaching as much as 30 per cent in Fes. In rural areas the effects were much less marked and in some cases poverty declined. Although in part this could be put down to increases in official purchase prices for agricultural goods, the real reason was the dramatic improvement in agricultural output, particularly of cereals and legumes, as a result of a series of years of good rainfall, and it had nothing to do with the stabilization or structural adjustment programmes (Bourguignon and Morrisson, 1992: 49).

Other observers have argued that urban poverty would have been far more severe had Morocco not developed a significant informal sector to its economy, estimated to comprise as much as 40 per cent of the overall national economy. There can be little doubt, however, that resentment at the widespread price rises which formed part of 'la politique de la vérité des prix', as the IMF-style price reforms became known in Morocco, added significantly to popular estrangement from government and to the growth in extra-parliamentary forms of protest, whether through riots or through growing support for Islamic fundamentalist movements. Indeed, the increasing gap between rich and poor provided a powerful stimulus to popular anger and it has been seized upon by Islamic fundamentalist leaders to increase their audience (Munson, 1993: 155–7). The most surprising aspect of this crisis of popular confidence, however, has been how relatively little popular support Islamic fundamentalists have received in the current situation.

CONCLUSION

There can be little doubt that the major social effect of economic reform in Morocco has been to create disillusion with the political process amongst much of the population . They see the Chamber of Deputies as part of a power structure from which they are excluded and generally do not believe the claims of the political parties to be committed to public welfare. The turnout for the June legislative elections was only 62.75 per cent, well down on the turnouts usually reported for national referenda, for example (Keesings, 1993: 39,535). It is also clear that this sense of disillusion has been stimulated by the long drawn-out economic crisis that Morocco has faced and the fact that improvements at the macro-economic level are not reflected throughout society as a whole. Indeed, although a minority has certainly benefited from the economic restructuring programme, the majority has not and this has led to great resentment and alienation from the political process.

Yet, quite apart from these generalized consequences of Morocco's economic crisis, there are other profound problems that will affect the future of democracy in the country. The most important of these is the innate political culture of Morocco, which is traditionally directed towards consensus and stasis. It sees patron–clientage and arbitration as the major techniques of the political process in which radical change is the least desired outcome. The parliamentary and electoral processes are therefore viewed from this standpoint, rather than as opportunities to achieve social and political change.

These attitudes are reinforced by the role of the Royal Palace within the political system. King Hassan's dominance of the political process and his ability to subvert it or abandon it, if he chooses, gives the practice of parliamentary democracy a conditionality that seriously damages its credibility. Nor is this situation likely to change, for the king's determination to reject the constitutional monarchy option means that all modifications of the political system will be merely cosmetic in effect.

At the same time, however, it is also the case that there is a growing number of Moroccans who now form a significant group within the population at large and who have become socially mobile during the past two decades, as a result of mass education and the social consequences of economic development and reform. They are now transferring into the politically conscious elite which seeks a genuine transformation of political culture and behaviour. For them, the potential of a democratic process is not confined to the 'retour eternel' to the political culture of the past. They seek genuine democratic participation and inform the growing civil society inside the country. There are, after all, now four human rights monitoring organizations (Joffé 1992: 214) in the country – one of them official – and other political pressure groups are beginning to emerge, often against considerable official hostility.

Criticism of the status quo, although still likely to attract official repression, is also becoming more outspoken. In November 1993, the French-language daily newspaper of Istiqlal, *L'Opinion*, published an article that complained that for twenty years Morocco was dominated by a 'single party', with 'hidden powers', known as the 'administration party' – the Ministry of the Interior. The author went on to argue that Morocco had never known real political plurality and that real democratization required ' ... a redefinition and the limitation of the powers and prerogatives of representatives of [state] authority.' Not surprisingly Driss Basri, the powerful minister of the interior who is renowned for having King Hassan's ear, reacted unfavourably but his criticisms were, in turn, denounced by the political opposition, in terms that suggested that they, at least, believe that real change is on the way.

Indeed, the 'bipolarization' of Moroccan politics that King Hassan now seeks does offer hope for the future. Such a system would provide a clearcut division within the political arena through which political choices could be made. It would also offer the politically conscious elite an opportunity to participate in the exercise of accountable power, if the amended constitution were put properly into effect. This would require, however, considerable restraint on the part of King Hassan. Furthermore, unless stability in the social and economic environment can be maintained, it is doubtful if the current democratic experiment in Morocco will evolve. Yet it must move beyond the 'scriptural' democracy that exists at present towards the 'substantive' democracy that will be ultimately essential for the survival, both of the monarchical regime and of Morocco's nascent democratic institutions themselves. Indeed, unless it does, that growing community of modernist and politically-aware Moroccans will become increasingly estranged from the current political process and, thereby, make its eventual conversion even more difficult to achieve.

REFERENCES

Ayache, G. (1978), 'La fonction d'arbitrage du Makhzen,' *Bulletin Economique et Social du Maroc*, Rabat: Actes de Durham: recherches récentes sur le Maroc moderne.
Bourguignon, F. and Morrisson, C. (1992), *Adjustment and equity in developing countries: a new approach*, Paris: Organisation for Economic Cooperation and Development.
Cedies Informations, Casablanca: Confédération Générale Economique Marocaine.
Cherifi, R. (1988), *Le Makhzen politique au Maroc: hier et aujourd'hui*, Rabat: Afrique Orient.
Economist Intelligence Unit (EIU) (1985), *Annual Regional Review: The Middle East and North Africa 1984*, London: Economist Publications.
Europa (1994), *The Middle East and North Africa 1993*, London: Europa Publications.
Horton, B. (1990), *Morocco:analysis and reform of economic policy*, Washington: Economic Development Institute of the World Bank.
Joffé, E.G.H. (1985), 'The Moroccan nationalist movement, Istiqlal, the sultan and the country,' *Journal of African History*, 26.
Joffé, E.G.H. (1988), 'Morocco: monarchy, legitimacy and succession', *Third World Quarterly*, 10, 1 (January).
Joffé, E.G.H. (1992), 'Human rights in the Western Arab world', in Nonneman, G. (ed.), *The Middle East and Europe: an integrated communities approach*, London: Federal Trust for Education and Research.
Kedourie, E. (1992), *Politics in the Middle East*, Oxford: Oxford University Press.
Keesings Record of World Events 1993 (formerly *Keesings Contemporary Archives*), Harlow: Longmans.
Kuhn, M.G. and Guzman, J.P. (1990), *Multilateral official debt rescheduling: recent experiences*, World Economic and Financial Series (November), Washington, DC: International Monetary Fund.
Lahbabi, M. (1962), *Le gouvernement marocain à l'aube du XXième siècle*, Casablanca: Editions Atlantides.
Maghreb Quarterly Report, London: Middle East Economic Digest (MEED).
Munson, Jr, J. (1993), *Religion and power in Morocco*, London: Yale University Press.
Waterbury, J. (1970), *The Commander of the Faithful: the Moroccan political elite – a study of segmented politics*, London: Weidenfeld & Nicolson.
World Bank (1993), *World Tables 1993*, Washington: International Bank for Reconstruction and Development.
Zartman, I.W. (1963), *Government and politics in Northern Africa*, London: Methuen.

13

Papandreou in Government Again: a New 'Change'?

George Doukas

Following the statement of independence by a relatively unknown MP on 9 September 1993, New Democracy (ND) lost its majority in the Greek Chamber of Deputies (*Vouli*). The government was forced to resign and to call early elections. On 10 October the ballots produced an almost expected result: the Panhellenic Socialist Movement (PASOK) obtained a sizeable majority: 46.88 per cent of the votes and 170 seats in parliament as opposed to ND's 39.30 per cent and 111 seats. After three and a half years in opposition, its septuagenarian leader would again become prime minister. The rivalry between Andreas Papandreou and Constantine Mitsotakis was brought to an end by the emphatic victory of the former.

Heralded by PASOK as 'a new victory of the people', and despite POLAN's (Political Spring) claim to have defeated bipolarization, the result was actually a victory for the latter. Once again, the two main parties obtained more than 85 per cent of the vote; while POLAN gained 4.88 per cent and ten deputies, and the left had its worst showing since the restoration of democracy: the orthodox Communist Party (KKE) won 4.54 per cent of the vote and nine seats, while the renewal left in the form of Synaspismos (Alliance of the Left) failed to pass the threshold for parliamentary representation with 2.94 per cent.

The elections took place in a gloomy atmosphere on all levels; economic, foreign policy and political. Emergency economic measures introduced in August 1992 just managed to prevent total economic collapse, but on the whole ND's 'neo-liberal' austerity measures had failed to produce any significant improvement of the main macro-economic indicators (inflation, unemployment, foreign debt, public deficit). At the same time, the real income of the low-paid economic strata (public and private sector workers, pensioners) had been significantly reduced.

The lack of a comprehensive long-term strategy as well as tactical mistakes had resulted in the country becoming a part of the Balkan puzzle. Foreign policy problems were at an impasse: the UN-sponsored negotiations

Table 13.1 Results of the October 1993 elections for the Greek parliament (Vouli)

	No. of votes	(%)	Seats
Panhellenic Socialist Movement (PASOK)	3,235,017	46.88	170
New Democracy (ND)	2,711,737	39.30	111
Political spring (POLAN)	336,460	4.88	10
Communist Party of Greece (KKE)	313,001	4.54	9
Synaspismos (Alliance of the Left)	202,887	2.94	–

Note: Registered: 8,861,833; Voted: 7,019,925; Valid votes: 6,900,311
Source: Ministry of the Interior, 19 Ocober 1993.

with the Former Yugoslav Republic of Macedonia (FYROM) had been stalled, not only due to the apparent intransigence of both sides, but also because of vociferous domestic nationalistic opposition to any 'dignified' settlement. Moreover, relations with Albania had been deteriorating markedly over the past two years. The Greek side had been accusing the Sali Berisa regime of mistreating ethnic Greeks in Northern Epirus (southern Albania) and of turning a blind eye to, if not encouraging, the massive flow of illegal economic refugees into Greek territory. Finally, relations with Turkey had reached a new freezing point, while the Cyprus issue looked as far from a 'viable and permanent' resolution as it had ever been.

The political climate was tense owing mainly to the timing of Yorgos Sympilidis' departure on 9 September 1993. His was the last, and apparently the most significant, in a series of defections from the governing party to the ex-foreign minister's POLAN. Antonis Samaras had resigned accusing the government of abandoning the programme upon which it had been elected in April 1990, and of mishandling the 'Macedonian issue'. In June 1993 he announced the formation of a party that purported the 'transcendence' of the political system, the renovation of political life and the establishment of a 'new morality' of political behaviour. The new party's message had only limited success in its aim of attracting support from all sides of the political spectrum. More significantly, however, it managed to gain support from among New Democracy ranks. The exodus of ND MPs was as much the result of the attraction of the new party as the culmination of a crisis that had been brewing inside ND for more than a year.

Criticism of the prime minister and his entourage had been coming from all sides of the party. The 'nationalists' were disputing the pragmatic handling of the Macedonian issue and were calling for tougher action against the FYROM; the 'neo-liberals' were demanding tougher austerity measures to combat inflation and reduce the deficits; the 'traditionalists' (such as party notables Miltiadis Evert and Athanasios Kanellopoulos) were voicing disagreement with the finance minister's running of the economy. In fact, these were thinly veiled attempts to discredit Mitsotakis's authority and challenge his hold over the party. In that sense, Sympilidis' defection was less a factor in the government's downfall than it appeared at the time.

All this time, PASOK was benefiting from its main rival's problems. At least it managed to present a united front. Papandreou's trial by the Special Court for the Koskotas affair, which involved allegations of corruption and had been presented by PASOK as a political prosecution, had rallied party members and cadres around the undisputed leader. Furthermore, throughout the three and a half years of ND government, PASOK had cleverly opted for a 'sit-and-wait' tactic. True, it criticized governmental policies in relation to both domestic and foreign policy issues, but it had failed to present viable alternatives. Rhetorical confrontation, which disguised essential convergence on some of the more significant issues (austerity measures, privatization, the Macedonian Question), was used to obtain political gains. PASOK accused ND of 'social insensitivity', but never questioned the aim of 'convergence' with the rest of the EU economies; and convergence demanded the continuation of unpopular measures and increased taxation. Regarding the contentious foreign policy issues, the differences between the two parties were of style rather than content. For example, the name of the FYROM was of pivotal importance for both; but naturally the government was more susceptible to accusations of compromise, defeatism and 'selling out'.

During the pre-electoral period, Papandreou's party followed a similar path. In his rare public appearances and interviews, PASOK's leader made confusing, and sometimes conflicting, pledges regarding the contentious issues. While he was careful to eliminate the word 'socialism' from his vocabulary, he was quick to promise economic growth, stabilization, the reduction of deficits, and social welfare measures. These would be achieved via the reform of the tax system, increased productivity, controlled privatization and improved competitiveness.

Bureaucratic planning in the traditional sense had failed during PASOK's previous administrations and, with the exception of the Communist Party, it is now regarded as outdated. Governmental management of the economy is restricted not only by the structural deficiencies of the domestic economic system, but also by the workings of the international environment which particularly affects small and problematic economies. In view of the fact that the Greek economy is becoming increasingly dependent upon capital inflow from the EU cohesion fund, any government is bound to take measures aimed at achieving the macro-economic targets set at Maastricht. Despite the rhetoric, these facts have been tacitly accepted by all parties bar the KKE.

In the absence of real differences, the electoral battle thus became a symbolic confrontation; and on that level PASOK was the clear winner.

One posssible explanation is that PASOK has enjoyed the support of social strata that have been fully incorporated into the capitalist system but have refused to accept its self-regulatory effects. Since New Democracy was the only party to openly advocate the 'advantages' (and consequently to appear to accept the adverse effects) of neo-liberalism, it was punished by the electorate.

The crisis of political discourse also became apparent as all sides focused on discrediting their opponents rather than on projecting a positive and credible message. In the case of New Democracy, the opponents were both PASOK and POLAN. In 1989, ND's main slogan had been 'katharsis' (cleansing of political life). In 1990, the party had called for a strong government majority that was needed for the adoption of radical measures to liberalize the economy and cure the ills caused by 'socialist mismanagement'. Then the message had managed to attract the crucial votes at the centre of the political spectrum and those of the 'undecided'. In 1993, the anti-PASOK rhetoric focused on that party's experience in government in an attempt to retain ND's electoral gains of the previous two elections. However, since 1990 ND had lost credibility as a result of continuing economic crisis, growing signs of corruption linked to the privatization programme, and some of the governmental habits for which PASOK had been criticized (prime ministerial control over major decision-making, unaccountability, lack of openness). As a result, the centrists either returned to the fold (PASOK) or opted for POLAN.

The latter party's populist and nationalistic message was aimed primarily at the disenchanted rightist and centrist voters, and secondly at those who did not identify with any party. To the extent that it had no clear programme to differentiate it from the rest, apart from vaguely advocating a 'rupture' with the established polity, POLAN attracted the votes of the apolitical. The party also benefited from the fact that, following the government's loss of its parliamentary majority, Samaras became the target of violent verbal and personal attacks on the part of both ND officials and hard-core ND supporters. In the end, it was the victor of the battle among the three smaller parties for the privileged position of 'third actor' in a political system dominated by the two rivals for power.

The KKE won the battle to retain the symbols of the left. It presented itself as the sole rightful heir to the left tradition by remaining religiously loyal to Marxist-Leninist roots, while it successfully utilized its organizational capabilities. The pre-electoral slogan 'five parties, two policies' was used cleverly to underline KKE distinctiveness and discredit its main rival, Synaspismos, which was thus presented as a party complementary to the establishment. For the KKE, the 1993 elections provided the battleground for the replay of the twenty five year old confrontation between orthodoxy and 'revisionism'.

Synaspismos, on the other hand, was fighting for its political survival and parliamentary representation rather than for the unity of the left, which was destroyed in 1991 when KKE left the alliance. According to its president, Maria Damanaki, the party's main opponent was polarization and populism rather than the KKE. However, the party failed to take any initiative over the main contentious issues (the Macedonian Question, the rise of nationalism and the economy) and therefore failed to challenge the two main rivals. Even its rapprochement with the ecological movement was perceived as too little too late.

Furthermore, despite claims to the opposite, Synaspismos did not follow an 'equal distance' policy: it openly adopted an anti-New Democracy stance, while only having 'reservations' towards PASOK in an effort to prevent the leftist vote from moving towards the latter. In the end it appeared as a force that was complementary to rather than an alternative to Papandreou's party, and it lost votes both to PASOK and to the KKE. Synaspismos underestimated the persistent anti-rightist syndrome of left-wing voters, and suffered due to its organizational weakness and the perceived ambiguity of its intentions.

The October 1993 vote was a functional one in as much as ideology tends to play a far less important role now than in 1977 and 1981. Disenchantment with politics and cynicism has replaced ideological divisions. The state is perceived as a mechanism for distributing incomes and securing privileges. In that sense, the choice for the vast majority is one between two 'managers' of the state machine. It was also a negative vote in the sense that the government was voted out of, rather than the opposition being voted into, office. In that respect, the 1993 result was a reversal of the 1990 contest, rather than a repeat of the 1981 election. Therefore it would be superficial, if not misleading, to interpret it as a victory for 'socialism'.

In the absence of radical initiatives aimed at the restructuring of the modus operandi of the established system of government, the political discourse and consequently the alternatives offered to the consumer/voter will be limited. This will continue to be determined by the confrontation between the two main rivals for power, despite the governmental change and the removal of one of the 'dinosaurs' from the political scene. The saying sounds banal and yet it applies here: in Greece, 'old habits die hard'.

14

Leadership Change in Turkey

İlter Turan

Within the last four years, three major Turkish political parties have elected new leaders. The Motherland Party, the party of government until the elections of October 1991, and currently leading the opposition, elected a new head in 1990 when its leader Turgut Özal was chosen as president of the Turkish Republic. Within months, the new party head was replaced by another at the ordinary convention of the party. More recently, the True Path Party also elected a new leader after its own leader, Süleyman Demirel, was elected president following the death of President Özal from a heart attack. Finally, Erdal İnönü, the leader of the Social Democratic People's Party, the junior partner in the current coalition government, decided that he would retire from that position, opening the way for the election of a new party leader. Murat Karayalçın was chosen to head the Social Democrats at the party convention held in mid-September 1993.

In some democratic societies, the change of political leadership is a matter of course. In Great Britain, for example, the ability of a party leader to retain his/her position is tied in general to his/her ability to sustain or improve the electoral fortunes of the party. It is also felt that the tenure of the leader of a political party ought to be limited. Therefore, party leaders, even if they personally want to continue to remain in their position, may find it difficult to convince the rank and file that their tenure should be prolonged time and again.

In France, a different tradition has prevailed. Parties have usually been built around the personalities of political leaders, and they have served as personal electoral machines. In such a context, we would not expect the parties to change their leaders since the fortunes of the latter and their own are closely tied to each other. This style of leadership change has affected even those French political parties in which ideology rather than personality has been perceived as the core around which the organization has formed. President Mitterrand served as leader of the Socialist Party for a long time while his party was in opposition. Until he finally decided to retire quite recently, Georges Marchais appeared to be the unchanging leader of the French Communists.

Turkish political parties, not unlike the French, do not change their leaders easily. Unlike some of the French parties, however, most are not personal electoral machines; rather, they are leader-dominated organizations. The tenure of party leaders tends to be long. This longevity would probably make many a French leader envious.

A TALE OF TWO LEADERS

Let us take a look at some of the major Turkish political leaders to appreciate the length of tenure of office that they have enjoyed. İsmet İnönü (the father of Erdal İnönü, mentioned in the preceding section), the head of the People's Republican Party (RPP, the founding party of the republic) assumed both the presidency of the republic and the leadership of his party in 1938 upon the death of Kemal Atatürk. He retained this position during the transition to multi-party politics in 1946–50. In 1950, his party lost an election to the newly founded Democratic Party. For the next ten years, İsmet İnönü led his party in opposition. During this time, his party lost two elections. In 1960, the competitive political process was interrupted by a military intervention.

The National Unity Committee, as the ruling junta was known, allowed a return to civilian politics in 1961. İsmet İnönü led his party into elections in which it received a plurality of the vote. During the next three years, the RPP was a partner in several coalition governments except the last one, which led the country into the 1965 elections. In the 1965 and 1969 elections, the RPP continued to lose votes.

In the meantime, an internal debate had begun in the party in an attempt to find it a new place in the political spectrum. Turkish society had undergone many social and economic changes since the founding of the republic, but the party had clung to its original goal of being first the exponent, and then, when in opposition, the defender of the Kemalist Revolution and the associated policies of cultural transformation and secularization. Now, many members felt, the party had to respond to the new circumstances if it were to survive as a credible political organization capable of offering a genuine alternative to the electorate. The debate culminated in the adoption of a policy orientation that was called 'the left of centre'. But soon fears were expressed that this ideological turn might lead the party onto a socialist path. İsmet İnönü's attempt to retreat to his party's former ideological position created significant resistance among the rank and file who were convinced that the old line would not take the party to electoral victory. The party convention in 1972 was a battle between İsmet İnönü and the secretary-general of the party, Bülent Ecevit, who had come to symbolize change. İsmet İnönü was defeated. He stepped down, left his party and resigned from his seat in the National Assembly in order to return to a seat in the Senate to which he was entitled as a former president. Many observers feel that İsmet İnönü would not have lost had he been younger, but that at the age of 88 he was no longer capable of putting up a vigorous fight against the tide of opposition that challenged his leadership. When he lost the leadership of his party, İnönü had been occupying that position for no less than thirty-four years.

Let us examine next the political past of Süleyman Demirel, the current president. He started his political career after the military intervention of 1960. At that time, he had been serving as director-general of the State Hydraulics Works. His agency had been established by the Democratic Party, which ruled the country from 1950 to 1960 as part of its efforts to develop major infrastructures in the country in order to promote economic development. An able administrator, Demirel soon earned himself the nickname 'the King of Dams'. When the military decided to intervene against the Democratic Party, Demirel, perceived by the military as being too close to the ruling party, lost his job.

The military stayed in power for almost a year and a half. During this time, they disbanded the Democratic Party and prohibited its re-establishment under its original or any other name. Parliamentarians and other leaders of the party were tried, and some were sentenced to prison terms of varying lengths for having violated provisions of the constitution and breaking other laws. All were banned from establishing political parties or assuming positions of responsibility in them.

If the Democratic Party movement wanted to continue in some form, it had to be done by people who had not been involved formally with the Democratic Party. The party established to claim the legacy of the Democratic Party was the Justice Party. Its first leader was a general who had been forced to retire after the military intervention in May 1960. He died within a short time of having taken office. In the search for a dynamic leader who would lead the party to electoral victory at the next elections, Süleyman Demirel was identified as the man with the right credentials. He had not been involved in active politics, so avoided the ban on members of the Democratic Party. He had served the Democratic Party governments loyally as a technician-bureaucrat. He was a member of the core of young, educated professionals whose star was on the rise; that is, they were identified as the generation who would shape the future. Despite his lack of experience Demirel won the leadership of his party in 1962, and stayed in that position until late spring 1993, when he was elected president. Off and on, he had served as leader of his party for no less than thirty years when he ascended to the presidency.

The tale of two leaders is but a sample of the prolonged life of Turkish political leaders. Many others are the subject of similar stories. They have been at the head of their party for a long time. On occasion, they may have encountered challenges to their leadership position, but usually their opponents were not crowned with success.

Why do Turkish political leaders have long life expectancies in office? How do they manage to retain their power? Several explanations may be offered. These, it should be noted, are not alternative but complementary in nature. Together they constitute a more comprehensive explanation than each would provide on its own.

THE TRADITION OF THE STRONG CENTRALIZED STATE

The Turkish state is a highly centralized political and administrative entity. This centralization emanates from two different deep-rooted traditions. First, the Ottoman dynasty, from the very beginning of its rule, worked to subdue social forces that could constitute the basis of a challenge to its absolute right to rule the empire. By the late sixteenth century, the Ottoman rulers had succeeded in consolidating their political domination of society and in freeing themselves from challenges against the legitimacy of their right to rule (Shaw and Shaw, 1976: 55–110).

Second, the modernization movement, which started in the eighteenth century, gained speed during the nineteenth, and succeeded in establishing a republican nation-state in the early twentieth century, relied on achieving control over and developing further the instruments of centralized political and administrative power (Lewis, 1961: 89–90; Shaw and Shaw, 1977: 36–40). These were then used to bring about technological, cultural and later political and economic transformations of society, eventually including changes even in the nature of the political system, and the basis on which political legitimacy was established (Frey, 1967: 29–43).

The two traditions were inherited by the republic. The first assured that there were hardly any autonomous groups in society that could challenge the doings of the state. The second provided the state with a sophisticated set of political and administrative instruments which it utilized in exercising centralized control over society. The debate that ensued after the Second World War regarding a possible transition to competitive politics was more about replacing the team in office than evidence of a yearning for pluralism. There was, for example, hardly sufficient discussion of the devolution of power, or of greater liberty for voluntary associations and individuals. The power of the centralized system has begun to erode only in recent years.

The tradition of the strong state has affected the structure of Turkish political parties and their leadership patterns. To begin with, parties themselves have been organized initially at the national level, and only gradually have they sought to establish roots in the provinces. This is one of the main reasons why the national organizations of Turkish political parties tend to dominate local organizations, at both the legal and the behavioural level.

At the legal level, the national organs of the party are empowered to abolish local branches and to annul the results of elections of local leaders. Further, they can dismiss the latter from office when they deem it necessary, and they can appoint local officers for prolonged temporary periods before opting for a convention of the local party in which new leaders are elected (Kabasakal, 1991, *passim*; Bektaş 1993: 21–38 and *passim*).

In recent years, as regards finances, the national party has become less dependent on the local organizations while the latter have become more dependent on the national party. This is because the government has begun to allocate financial support to political parties on an annual basis (Turan, 1988: 70). The intention of this act of generosity is to ensure that parties can live independently and can avoid becoming highly reliant on major contributors whose interests they would be obliged to represent. The money is given to the national bodies which then decide how it ought to be spent, and how much, if any, should be passed on to the local organizations.

At the level of behaviour, the national leadership of a party takes it for granted that it is above any local organization and that it has the right to exercise power over the latter, which is seen as not having much autonomy. It feels that it is not particularly accountable to any local organization but that local organizations are responsible to it. This stance is reinforced by the political reality that in a centralized system, those that are in the national capital are usually in a better position to deliver personal and/or community goods and services to constituents than are those located at the local level. In fact, on many occasions, the local branch of a political party is no more than a processing office for constituents and groups that demand something from the government which, after all, is located at the national centre.

Turning to internal party communications, it is not surprising that these tend to be vertical and not horizontal. Put differently, leaders and members of local party organizations communicate more regularly with the national bodies of their party than with their colleagues at local level. Such a communication pattern effectively prevents local organizations from constituting a force that could affect significantly the behaviour of the centre. Rather, each is vulnerable to the intrusions of the centre and has to be compliant in order to preserve its own existence and prosperity.

In summary then, the tradition of the strong central state has shaped the structure and mechanisms of Turkish political parties, making them centrally-dominated institutions. This means that anyone who manages to become the national leader of a political party has access to legal, material and even attitudinal resources that can be mobilized to ward off challenges to his/her leadership. The fact that local organizations are isolated from each other, are therefore divided and tend to interact mainly with the centre, renders it all the more easy for national leaders to put pressure on, manipulate and penalize those who want to challenge the incumbent leadership.

FRAGMENTATION OF POLITICAL FORCES

Political parties are coalitions of various political forces in a society. Although these forces may compete between themselves within the framework of a party, it is generally assumed that they share a sufficient amount of interest and outlook for them to remain a part of the same political organization. The ties that bind the various groups that have come under the umbrella of a political party may not be very strong, however.

In a society like Turkey, which is in the process of transformation from an agricultural–rural society (surviving until after the Second World War), to an urban–industrialized society, any political party is likely to contain a number of groups whose interests are inimical to each other, but who find themselves in the same political party for a variety of reasons. Almost all Turkish political parties contain widely divergent groups which stay in the party despite very fundamental differences between them (Sayarı, 1975: 123–6). They are all accorded some of what they want and therefore feel that they get a better deal by staying in the party than by leaving it.

The existence within the same political party of groups whose interests are sometimes diametrically opposed creates a situation in which factions flourish. These factions often expend a lot of energy struggling against each other, and they present many opportunities for the party leader to act as a broker between them. The way each group is tied to the party is through having good relations with the party leader and having access to him (Sayarı, 1975: 125). In bringing factions into a coalition, the catalytic role of the party leader is critical. Otherwise, the factions are incapable of coming together. This enables the party leader to build temporary coalitions against any faction that challenges him.

To cite an example, in the past (and in fact still today), the True Path Party under Süleyman Demirel contained farmers who were interested in low agricultural input prices and high agricultural support prices, and businessmen who were interested in non-subsidized market prices for agricultural inputs and low support prices for agricultural commodities. It contained groups that were wholly dedicated to the secularism of the republic and groups that argued for an increased role for religion in public life. It contained other rival groups as well. Since each group was linked to the party through Demirel, as head of the party, Demirel was in a unique position to know who wanted what and how badly. He was in a position, therefore, to manipulate factions so that serious challenges to his leadership would be minimized.

THE ABSENCE OF THE CONCERNED CITIZEN

The introduction of change from the centre, the allocation of a passive role for the citizen as the object of centrally devised and implemented policies and the proclivity of the central government to restrain the input of the citizen into the political process have all produced an attitude on the part of the citizenry according to which the individual is not expected to be an active participant in the political process. Rather, he/she often thinks that he/she cannot influence the government. The laws compound the reluctance to get involved in the political process since they harbour various rules that prevent large numbers of citizens including soldiers, public servants, university professors and students from becoming party members. This does not enhance the successful operation of the competitive party model.

In the absence of large numbers of citizens who join political parties and take part in their activities, the field is dominated by party regulars, relatively few in number, who do party work with the expectation that they will be rewarded in a concrete way by the national party organization. The end product is a patronage network in which the prosperity and political fortunes of local party regulars are tied closely to their willingness to cooperate with the national party bodies. Those who challenge the national leadership lose in two ways. First, they are deprived of the benefits that accrue from extending political support to national leaders. This, in turn, reduces their local power base. Second, as suggested earlier, they may be relieved of their responsibilities by the national leadership.

If there were extensive participation in party activity by the citizens, then the national leadership might find it more difficult to influence the behaviour of local party officials. To retain their positions, the latter would be more reliant on the local rank and file. As things have stood in the past, however, local leaders have relied on the national party leadership to keep them in their positions. They have usually failed to prevail in the formulation of policy.

The reliance of local party leaders on the national leadership is replicated at the national level. There, the party leader ensures his dominance by undermining the power base of others in the national leadership who oppose him. In this way, the party leader may perpetuate his rule so long as he is interested in retaining the job.

THE WEIGHT OF HISTORY

Until recently, leaders of many of the Turkish political parties could truthfully assert that they had played critical roles in the founding of their parties or in ensuring their survival. When challenges emerged to their rule, the indispensable services rendered to the party by the leader were always cited as a way of delegitimizing the opposition. The symbols utilized were powerful and emotional. They provided the incumbent national leaders with a significant resource which they could use to ward off challenges to their rule.

Evidence of this may already be found in the discussion of the political life story of the two political leaders, İsmet İnönü and Süleyman Demirel. The former had been a hero of the national war of independence, a founding father of the republic, one of the main architects of the transition to democratic politics, a political fox who had managed to manoeuvre his party safely through two military interventions without anyone getting hurt. Many members found it psychologically difficult, in the last analysis, to participate in a fight against a man of such stature, without feeling that they were somehow betraying him.

Similarly, Süleyman Demirel had pulled his party out of the despair it was experiencing under the watchful presence of the military during its founding stage and had led it to two major electoral victories during the 1960s. He had also held his party together and managed to stay in the government coalition during the indirect military intervention of 1971. He had been able to keep his team together after his party was banned in 1981 under adverse political circumstances. By 1991, he had been able to lead it back to being the largest party and the major partner in a coalition government. He was too closely identified with the history of his party to be removed easily from the position of leader. Many members would view voting against him as an act of betrayal.

Similar accounts could be given of other leaders. Alpaslan Türkeş, the aging head of the Nationalist Action Party, engaged in a long-lasting struggle which landed him in jail on several occasions before he managed to establish his party as a permanent feature of the Turkish political scene. Necmettin Erbakan, the head of the religiously conservative Welfare Party, not unlike Süleyman Demirel, kept his team together under difficult circumstances. His party, which had different names during its early years, had been banned both by the courts and by military administrators before becoming an accepted actor in Turkish politics.

THE RESULTING INSTABILITY

The inability of the rank and file of Turkish political parties to change the party leader promotes, with reasonable frequency, the formation of splinter parties. When important factions try to challenge the party leader and fail, arousing the wrath of the leader in the process, they are often left with no option other than to leave the party, usually to form a new party. These experiments rarely prove successful in the end, but they destabilize political life, sometimes by bringing down governments and always by rendering Turkish politics volatile and unpredictable.

The difficulty of changing party leaders also means that parties are deprived of one of the major means through which they can adjust to changing conditions. The failure of parties to adjust to change, on the other hand, causes them to lose voter support. The value citizens accord to the multi-party system is also undermined in the process. The loss of credibility of political parties as sources of solutions to the critical problems the country was facing was probably one of the major reasons why the public initially sighed with relief when the military took over in 1980, although regret quickly replaced relief as the more typical reaction.

THE ELECTORAL PROCESS AND THE NEW LEADERS

Electing a new party leader is the prerogative of the highest organ of a political party according to both Turkish law and Turkish political traditions. Thus, at the ordinary national conventions of Turkish parties, which are held at regular intervals, the election of the party leader is always on the agenda. On most occasions, however, as has been described above, it is no more than a ritual to re-elect the incumbent. If a leader dies, moves to another office like the presidency or resigns while in office, then an extra-ordinary national convention is held to elect a new leader.

The emergence of four opportunities for three major Turkish political parties to elect new leaders during the last four years was a unique develop-ment. The first occasion arose with the expiration of the term of Kenan Evren as president in 1990. The then prime minister Özal, who exhibited a keen interest in transforming the Turkish parliamentary system into a presidential one, ran for the presidency. His party, enjoying a parliamentary majority, supported him in his bid for this largely symbolic position.

Upon becoming president, Turgut Özal had to sever his ties with the Motherland Party. He made clear, however, that he would not cut his moral and emotional ties, a diplomatic way of saying that he would continue to be active in its internal affairs. He proceeded to designate his own successor. Wanting to be the head of government in addition to being head of state, he recommended that Yıldırım Akbulut, a mild mannered, non-assertive and obedient man of limited abilities, be elected to head the party. The party convention conceded the wishes of its former leader.

Heading the party and therefore the government by proxy did not prove to be a workable arrangement. The president could not openly run the government. The prime minister, on the other hand, lacked the ability even to follow instructions. The public found the formula by which Turkey was being ruled confusing and not matching their expectations of proper govern-ance. The Motherland Party began to lose electoral support, as was indicated by opinion polls. The close association of government with the president constituted a further liability as the flamboyant lifestyles of the president and his family proved unpopular with the public.

Challenges began to form against Akbulut's leadership. Gradually, Mesut Yılmaz emerged as the major challenger. Despite the opposition of President

Özal, Yılmaz won at the regular convention of the Motherland Party, taking over an organization whose electoral fortunes were on the decline. The defeat of Akbulut was atypical, but it reflected the fact that his election to the party presidency was not his own achievement in the first place.

Mesut Yılmaz, who succeeded Yıldırım Akbulut, is a young businessman who entered politics in 1983 at the time of the founding of the Motherland Party. Born and raised in Istanbul, a graduate of the prestigious Faculty of Political Science at Ankara University, he pursued graduate studies in Germany and Great Britain. Coming from a Black Sea family with a tradition of involvement in politics, he had the right credentials to immediately attract the attention of Turgut Özal . Yılmaz served in ministerial capacity in all the cabinets formed by the latter after the 1983 and 1987 elections. His candidacy for the top position of his party, unlike Akbulut's, did not lack credibility.

Yılmaz won his bid for the leadership of his party in a tough battle in which Turgut Özal and his family were also involved. Despite the bitterness of the competition, he was able to achieve full control over his party shortly after assuming the top position. He reversed the party's declining electoral fortunes, and led it into an early election. The Motherland Party lost the elections and is currently the leading opposition party in the Grand National Assembly. It is expected to do well in the next municipal and provincial elections. Mesut Yılmaz withstood a strong challenge to his leadership at an ordinary convention of the party. He appears to be firmly established in his leadership position and unlikely to be challenged in the near future.

The unexpected death of President Özal in spring 1993 and the election of Prime Minister Demirel to the presidency opened the way for a leadership battle in the True Path Party. There was no person whose succession to the post could be regarded as natural. As aspirants looked to see if the outgoing leader would indicate some preference, Tansu Çiller, the minister of state for economic affairs, announced her candidacy. Dr Çiller was a newcomer to politics. After having received a BA at the American-operated Robert College (now Boğaziçi University) and a PhD in Economics in the United States, she had joined the faculty at her *alma mater* in Istanbul. Her interest in going into politics coincided with the efforts of the True Path Party to recruit new members and develop a new image which was more in tune with the urban, sophisticated appearance Turkey had acquired during recent years.

Shortly before the elections of 1991, Dr Çiller left her academic position and joined the True Path Party. She was made a candidate in one of the multi-member districts in Istanbul and won a seat. Although she had no previous political experience, because of her professional background it was assumed that she would be made a cabinet minister when, as leader of the party that had won most seats, Süleyman Demirel was asked to form a government. She became minister of state for economic affairs. In office, she found it difficult to work with some other ministers who were also involved in the making of economic policy. It sometimes seemed that she had difficulties getting along with the prime minister himself.

When the party leadership became vacant, she moved before others to present her candidacy. Many party members wanted Hüsamettin Cindoruk, the president of the Grand National Assembly and a widely respected figure, to become a candidate. He declined, insinuating that he was not sure if Süleyman Demirel would be able to keep his hands off the party. Two other candidates, the ageing lifetime political colleague of Süleyman Demirel and the then minister of the interior, İsmet Sezgin; and a younger member of the pre-1980 Justice Party governments of Demirel and the then minister of national education, Köksal Toptan, waited to see if they would receive a clear indication of support from their former boss. When no clear signals were forthcoming, both belatedly joined the race. Many observers, pointing to the fact that Tansu Çiller was not acquainted with the provincial party organizations and rank-and-file members, and that she lacked experience, anticipated that she might make a good showing but she would not win the contest. Much to everyone's surprise, Çiller led her rivals by a wide margin in the first round of voting. Sezgin and Toptan announced their withdrawal before the second round started. In the next round, Çiller received almost unanimous support, and went on to become prime minister.

Rather than trying to build an intra-party coalition, based on senior figures from different wings of the party, Tansu Çiller appointed a cabinet comprised mainly of unknown deputies. There were constant complaints that she neglected to consult her party's deputies before she acted, and that she failed to pay attention to their constituency-related requests. Nevertheless, she managed to get re-elected without opposition in the ordinary convention of her party a few months later. Those interested in challenging her were discouraged by delegates to the convention who argued that she had not been in office long enough, and she should be given sufficient time to prove herself.

The change of leadership in the Social Democratic People's Party is unique in that Erdal İnönü, the head of the party, decided to step down of his own accord. He had been recruited into politics from his university post in 1983, when a suitable person was being sought to resuscitate the People's Republican Party of the pre-1980 period under a new name since the military junta would not allow it to resume its activities under its former name. İnönü resisted for a long time before he accepted the leadership of the party out of a sense of duty to the memory of his father who, as shall be recalled, had been one of the founders of the People's Republican Party.

Once in power, he led his party through politically difficult times and effected a union with the Populist Party, the centre-left party that the military leaders had encouraged to come into being. He then saw a group of deputies and members leave the party to re-establish the People's Republican Party, and he led his party into the current coalition government as a junior partner. At all points in his political career, he indicated that he was interested in leaving politics. The departure of Süleyman Demirel gave him the opportunity to say that the time had come for him to leave, too. He announced his intention in time for the party to be able to consider the election of a new leader at its ordinary convention in October 1993.

Two candidates came to the fore shortly after the leadership race began: Aydın Güven Gürkan and Murat Karayalçın. Gürkan was a university professor who had started his political career in the Populist Party, the centre-left party that the military junta had set up when it embarked on a path towards restoring competitive politics. He did not have wide popular appeal, but appeared to have some support among the deputies and provincial delegates to the convention. Murat Karayalçın, on the other hand, was the charismatic mayor of metropolitan Ankara.

A graduate of the Faculty of Political Science at Ankara University, Karayalçın had done some graduate work in Great Britain. Later, he had worked in the State Planning Organization before moving to head a union of housing cooperatives (organizations that aim to build housing for members who can pay modest monthly instalments). In this job, he demonstrated an unusual ability to get things done, and succeeded in developing a new satellite city outside Ankara. During the municipal elections of 1989, he rode the urban social democratic wave into office as the mayor of the metropolitan municipality of Ankara. He was mayor when he was elected to head his party. A part of his parliamentary party initially resisted his leadership. He was disadvantaged in that he was not a member of parliament. He appears to be slowly assuming full control over the party, however.

The ascension of Yılmaz, Çiller and Karayalçın to the leadership of three major parties in Turkey marks a generational change. The new leaders all have professional backgrounds, and have all received some training abroad. None of them had extensive experience in politics before assuming important political positions, ministerial or mayoral. Their rapid rise to party leadership is in part a consequence of the fact that the military junta of 1980–83 had interrupted the continuity of political organizations and cadres, thus opening the way for the entry of new people into politics. It is also due in part to the change of public attitudes in Turkey, as traditional political cadres came increasingly to be viewed as not being properly equipped for modern times.

LOOKING TO THE FUTURE

Are the newly elected leaders likely to survive for as long as the previous leaders? Or are we perhaps entering a new era in which more frequent

change of party leader will become commonplace? Remembering the forces
that have made it possible for party leaders to retain their positions for long
periods, we may conclude that there are forces at work that will, in all
probability, reduce the tenure of the newly elected leaders while bringing to
an end the tenure of those who have been serving in leadership capacities
for a long time.

First, the tradition of the centralized state is slowly being eroded. There
is intensifying pressure on the government to devolve some of its powers to
local governments. Some analysts have put forward cogent arguments for a
major decentralization of political and administrative authority as well.
Society has become more assertive *vis-à-vis* the state. These developments
may undermine the power of the national party leader, reduce the importance of his/her position, and render it more easy to change him/her.

Second, fragmentation within parties is likely to be reduced as a result
of a process of realignment of both party members and voters. From 1973
on, there has been much mobility between parties involving both party
cadres and constituents. This process is likely to produce less fragmented
parties in which members may be more capable of changing leaders. The
same process may also render leaders less capable of manipulating factions
to serve their own political ends.

Third, the new leaders do not have the weight of history behind them.
Furthermore, a competitive political system appears to be sufficiently established and the possibility of a military intervention sufficiently remote
nowadays for new opportunities for historical achievements by party leaders
to be considerably reduced. From the perspective of party members, it may
no longer be psychologically painful to change leaders, as has been the case
in the past. The new leaders are ordinary leaders. They are more likely to
be judged only on their performance. In operational terms, performance
usually means ability to lead the party to electoral victory.

Fourth, it does appear as if the concerned citizen is finally emerging on
the Turkish political scene. Since 1980 there has been a proliferation of
voluntary associations ranging from greens and feminists to foundations
espousing ultra-conservative ideologies, all providing inputs into the political
process. Sections of the population which were previously not interested in
becoming active in politics (e.g. the business community) are showing a new
interest. Political activity at the local government level is intensifying. In
the future the leaders of political parties may find it less easy to constrain
political activism. In the past, it was precisely the lack of such activism that
made it possible for leaders to retain their positions with relative ease.

Finally, the recent changes of leadership in the major political parties
have shown that changing leaders is not something that is any more prob-
lematical than re-electing the same leader time and again. Having the same
leader stay on for extended periods of time may be just as disturbing or

destabilizing for a political party as the changing of its leader more frequently. The recent change of leaders in major parties may, in fact, generate pressures for change in those parties such as the Welfare Party of Mr Erbakan and the Nationalist Action Party of Mr Türkeş, which have not changed their leaders for a long time.

REFERENCES

Bektaş, Arsev (1993), *Demokratikleşme sürecinde liderler oligarşisi*, Istanbul: Bağlam Yayınları.

Frey, Frederick W. (1967), *The Turkish Political Elite*, Cambridge, Massachusetts: MIT Press.

Kabasakal, Mehmet (1991), *Türkiye'de siyasal parti örgütlenmesi 1908–1960*, Istanbul: Tekin Yayınevi.

Lewis, Bernard (1961), *The Emergence of Modern Turkey*, London: Oxford University Press.

Sayarı, Sabri (1975), 'Some notes on the beginnings of mass political participation', in *Political Participation in Turkey*, Engin Akarli and Gabriel Ben-Dor (eds.), Istanbul: Boğaziçi University.

Shaw, Stanford and Ezel Kural Shaw (1976 and 1977), *History of the Ottoman Empire and Modern Turkey*, 2 vols, New York: Cambridge University Press.

Turan, İlter (1988), 'Political parties and the party system in post-1983 Turkey', in *State, Democracy and the Military in Turkey in the 1980s*, Metin Heper and Ahmet Evin (eds.), Berlin: deGruyter.

Chronology of Events, 1993

JANUARY

1   *Israel/Lebanon*: Prime Minister Rabin announces that he is prepared
    to reduce the sentences of the 450 expelled guerrillas (17 December
    1992) on condition that the Intifada is suspended.
    Spain/UN: Spain becomes a non-permanent member of the Security
    Council.

7   *Algeria/France*: French Foreign Minister Ronald Dumas visits Algeria
    and promises financial support. This is the first visit by a senior French
    politician since Mohamed Boudiaf's assassination.

8   *Bosnia*: Deputy Prime Minister Hakija Turajlic is killed by Serbian
    troops while travelling in a UN convoy.
    Tunisia/Algeria/Egypt: Interior ministers from the three countries meet
    in Tunis to coordinate action against fundamentalist terrorism.
    Libya: The authorities announce the closure of Libya's land borders in
    reaction to the UN embargo imposed over Tripoli's refusal to hand
    over the two men accused of the Lockerbie Pan Am bombing.

9   *FYROM/UN*: The Former Yugoslav Republic of Macedonia
    (FYROM) applies for UN membership.

11 *Islamic Conference Organisation/Turkey/Bosnia*: In a special meeting of
    the organisation in Senegal, Turkey proclaims its support for Bosnian
    Muslims.

12 *UN/Bosnia/Serbia*: Bosnian Serb leader Radovan Karadzic provision-
    ally agrees to the Geneva peace plan.

19 *Syria/Turkey*: President Hafez al-Asad meets Premier Süleyman Dem-
    irel to discuss the Euphrates waters issue and Turkish concerns over
    Syrian backing of the separatist Kurdish Workers Party (PKK).

22 *Spain/Middle East*: During a visit to Jordan, the Spanish Foreign
    Minister Javier Solana condemns the 'illegal deportation' of 450 Pales-
    tinians from Israel.

25 *Tunisia*: Hedi Nouira, 82, prime minister from 1970 until 1980, dies.
    FYROM/UN/France/Spain/UK: The three EC countries propose the
    admission of the republic under the provisional name of 'Former Yugo-
    slav Republic of Macedonia'.

30 *UN/Bosnia*: Mediators Vance and Owen ask the Security Council to
    adopt a 'final decision' on the Balkan conflict, following the refusal of
    Serbs and Muslims to sign the Geneva plan.

FEBRUARY

2   *Tunisia*: eighteen lawyers and students announce the formation of the National Committee for the Defence of Prisoners of Conscience.

4   *Turkey/Iran*: Turkish Interior Minister İsmet Sezgin alleges that Iranian-trained Muslim militants, members of the 'Islamic Movement', have been responsible for at least three political killings.
     Tunisia: Salah Hamzoui, leader of the National Committee for the Defence of Prisoners of Conscience, is arrested.

7   *Cyprus*: President Yorgos Vassiliou, 61, wins the first round of presidential elections, but fails to achieve the 50 per cent needed for outright victory.

11   *EC/Spain*: European Commission President Jacques Delors expresses doubts about Spain's ability to meet the Maastricht terms for economic convergence by 1997.

14   *Cyprus*: Conservative Glafkos Clerides, 73, is the surprise victor of the second round of presidential elections with 50.3 per cent of the vote.
     France/Spain: French police discover an ETA arms factory in the south; some ten members of the organization are arrested.

15   *Algeria*: France offers FFr 6bn worth of tied credits for 1993.

17   *US/Libya*: American government officials claim that Libya is building an underground chemical weapons plant.

26   *Spain*: The government announces a $3bn public works plan to revitalize the economy.

28   *Bosnia/USA*: The US air force begins a relief air-drop to Cerska and other isolated communities.

MARCH

1   *Spain/Gibraltar/UK*: The Spanish government reacts with caution to British proposals for a new constitution for Gibraltar.
     Algeria/Amnesty International: Algeria is accused of widespread torture and an increase in human rights violations since it was placed under a state of emergency in February 1992.

2   *Morocco/Western Sahara/UN*: The UN Security Council unanimously approves a resolution setting a new deadline at the end of 1993 for a referendum in Western Sahara allowing self-determination.
     Bosnia: Cerska falls to Bosnian Serbs.

5   *Egypt*: Gama'a al-Islamiya, which claims to be behind recent attacks on tourists, warns foreigners to leave the country and says that foreign investments 'could soon become a target'.
     Bosnia/UN: UN commander Gen. Philippe Morillon launches a per-

sonal mission to relieve the besieged Srebrenica as Bosnian Serbs in-
tensify their stronghold.

9   *Turkey/Azerbaijan*: The two countries sign an agreement to build a
    pipeline from the Baku oilfields to the Mediterranean coast of Turkey.

12 *Spain*: The government decides to reduce the annual intake of im-
    migrants allowed to work in Spain to below the current 20,600 level.

16 *Algeria*: Djilali Liabes, former minister, head of the 'Group of Experts
    2015' and member of the National Consultative Council (CCN), is
    shot dead.

17 *Turkey*: Abdullah Ocalan, leader of the PKK, announces that it no
    longer seeks complete independence from Turkey; he declares a uni-
    lateral ceasefire from 20 March to 15 April.
    Algeria: Laadi Flici and Hafid Senhadri, members of the CCN, are
    shot dead.

21 *France*: Major defeat for the governing Socialist Party in the first round
    of elections for the National Assembly.

22 *Algeria*: A Muslim extremist operation in Boughezoul (100 km. south
    of the capital) leaves forty-one dead, including eighteen soldiers.
    Algeria: Some 80,000 people demonstrate in Algiers against terrorism.
    Similar marches are held nationwide.
    Bosnia/Serbia: The government of Bosnia-Herzegovina accuses Serbia
    and Montenegro of war crimes.
    Egypt/Amnesty International: the organization accuses the security
    forces of operating a 'shoot to kill' policy against militant Muslims.

25 *Spain*: Prime Minister Felipe González announces that he is prepared
    to accept his share of political responsibility in the Filesa scandal
    (illegal financing of the PSOE).
    Bosnia: President Alia Izetbegovic signs the Vance–Owen peace plan.

27 *Algeria/Iran/Sudan*: Algeria breaks off diplomatic relations with Iran
    and recalls its ambassador from Sudan.

28 *France*: The coalition of Jacques Chirac's Gaullist RPR and Valéry
    Giscard d' Estaing's UDF win 458 out of the 577 seats in the National
    Assembly, in the second round of the legislative elections.

29 *Italy*: Mario Segni, leader of the 'Referendum Movement' that de-
    mands the reform of the electoral system, resigns from the Christian
    Democrat party (DC).

30 *France*: The Gaullist Edouard Balladur is appointed prime minister by
    President Mitterrand.
    Italy: Finance Minister Franco Reviglio resigns after being caught up
    in the corruption investigations.

31 *UN/Bosnia*: A UN Security Council resolution decrees the enforce-
    ment of a no-fly zone over Bosnia.

APRIL

1   *Spain*: Don Juan de Borbón, father of King Juan Carlos, dies.

3   *Egypt/Iran/Sudan*: During a visit to London, President Mubarak accuses Iran and Sudan of encouraging violence in Egypt.

5   *Italy*: Former Christian Democrat prime minister Giulio Andreotti is investigated in connection with the illegal financing of political parties and alleged connections with the Mafia.

7   *Spain*: Four people, three of them terrorists, are killed in an attempted bombing in Zaragoza.

7–8 *FYROM/UN*: Following the unanimous decision of the Security Council, and its approval by the General Assembly, the FYROM becomes the 181st member of the UN.

9–10 *Spain*: The executive commission of the PSOE assumes 'collective political responsibility' for the Filesa scandal.

12 *Greece/FYROM*: Negotiations on the name of the FYROM and confidence-building measures start in New York.
Spain: Prime Minister González calls elections for 6 June.

14 *Israel/UN*: Premier Rabin announces that Israel accepts resolution 242 – which demands its withdrawal from Gaza – as a basis for negotiations with the Palestinians.
Morocco/Amnesty International: A report claims that more than 500 'disappeared' people are still held by the Moroccan authorities.

15 *UN/ CSCE/FYROM*: The two organizations sign a cooperation agreement to prevent the Balkan conflict from spreading to the FYROM.

16 *Turkey/NATO*: Turkey responds to NATO calls to join the force policing the no-fly zone over Bosnia by sending eighteen F-16 fighters to bases in Italy.
Bosnia: Bosnian Serbs capture Srebrenica.

17 *Turkey*: President Turgut Özal, 66, dies in Ankara.

18 *UN/Serbia/Montenegro*: The Security Council, with the abstention of Russia and China, decides to 'totally isolate' the so-called 'New Yugoslavia'.
Bosnia/UN: UN forces enter Srebrenica to disarm the Muslims after a peace agreement is signed between the Bosnian Serb commander, the Bosnian army chief and the UN commander.

19 *Italy*: 82 per cent vote in favour of reform of the electoral system.
Morocco: Some 200 exiled Moroccans form the 'Opposition Movement' (MDOM).

21 *Bosnia*: Muslim fighters in Srebrenica surrender weapons to the UN.
Palestine/Israel: Arafat announces that the Palestinian delegation will return to the Washington talks.

22   *Italy*: Socialist Prime Minister Giuliano Amato resigns.
      Egypt: Seven Muslim militants are sentenced to death.
25   *Albania*: Papal visit.
27   *Italy*: Ex-governor of the Bank of Italy, Carlo Azeglio Ciampi, forms
      a new, 'historic' government.
29   *Italy*: Ciampi's government collapses following the resignation of three
      PDS (Democratic Party of the Left) ministers.

MAY

1   *Bosnia/UN*: After peace talks hosted by the Greek government, the
      Bosnian Serb leader Karadzic signs the Vance–Owen plan, pending
      final approval by the self-proclaimed 'parliament'.
      France: Former Socialist prime minister Pierre Bérégovoy commits
      suicide.
5–6   *Bosnia/UN*: the Bosnian Serb 'parliament' rejects the UN peace plan.
7   *Italy*: Ciampi's government secures a confidence vote with 309 in
      favour, 60 against, and 185 abstentions.
10   *EC/Bosnia/Serbia*: The EC foreign ministers propose the closure of
      the frontier between Serbia and Bosnia.
11   *UN/Cyprus/Russia/UK*: Russia uses its veto in the Security Council
      to block a British-sponsored resolution to share the costs of the 1,500-
      member UN force in Cyprus among all members.
13   *Italy*: The Senate authorizes the inquiry into Andreotti's affairs.
      Spain: The peseta is devalued by 8 per cent.
14   *Council of Europe/FYROM*: The republic fails to obtain full member-
      ship status.
16   *Turkey*: Süleyman Demirel, 68, is elected Turkey's ninth president.
17   *Egypt/Pakistan/Afghanistan/Iraq/Sudan/Iran*: The Egyptian presi-
      dent announces that direct-dial telephone links with these countries
      will be cut, in a move to disrupt contact between Muslim leaders in
      exile and militants at home.
20   *Egypt*: Police Major-General Ahmed al-Adli announces that 822 mem-
      bers of militant Muslim 'Vanguards of the New Holy Struggle' have
      been arrested and charged with forming an illegal organization.
22–23 *Bosnia/USA/UN/Russia*: An agreement is reached between the
      USA, its European allies, and Russia on a plan aiming at the pro-
      tection of Bosnian Muslim communities in UN 'safe areas'.
27   *Italy*: A bomb kills five peple and leaves twenty-nine injured in
      Florence.
28   *Greece/FYROM*: Greece rejects the proposed name of 'New Mace-
      donia' for the FYROM.

JUNE

1   *Serbia*: President Dobrica Cosic, the 'father' of Serbian nationalism, is dismissed by hardliners for 'violating the constitution'.

3   *Western Sahara/Morocco*: Polisario claims that Morocco has managed to secure a promise from the Spanish government that the issue of Western Saharan self-determination will not enter the agenda of the Security Council during the Spanish presidency.

6   *Spain*: The Spanish Socialist Workers Party (PSOE) of Felipe González wins general elections for the fourth consecutive time, but fails to secure an absolute majority with only 159 out of 350 seats in the Congress of Deputies.

8   *Turkey*: The PKK leader Ocalan announces that the unilateral cease-fire has collapsed because Ankara has failed to respond to it.

13   *Turkey*: Tansu Çiller, 47, becomes Turkey's first woman prime minister after being elected leader of the True Path party.
    Egypt: Sherif Hassan Ahmed Mohamed Hassan, a Muslim militant convicted of plotting to overthrow the government, is hanged. He is the first person to be executed for a politically-motivated crime since 1982.

15   *Cyprus/Canada/UK*: Canadian troops start withdrawing from the buffer zone dividing the Greek and Turkish sectors in Nicosia; they are to be replaced by the British Royal Artillery.

16   *Syria/Israel*: Peace talks in Washington appear to progress as the two sides focus discussion on the 'security regime' for the Golan Heights.

17–18   *Algeria/France*: Foreign Minister Redha Malek visits Paris and obtains aid to combat terrorism.

21   *Algeria*: After talks with opposition parties, the presidency unveils a draft blueprint for the 'return of the electoral process'.
    Spain: Seven people are killed and twenty-five injured in a Madrid bombing; responsibility claimed by ETA.

22   *Algeria*: Professor Mohamed Boukhobza, head of Algeria's National Institute for Global Strategy, is assassinated.
    Bosnia: Seven members of the presidency revolt against the decision of Alia Izetbegovic to boycott the Geneva negotiations.

24   *Bosnia/Serbia/Croatia*: Bosnian Serb leader Radovan Karadzic and his Croatian counterpart Mate Boban announce a plan for a confederation combining three ethnic mini-states in Bosnia.

25   *Morocco*: The first round of the general election takes place. A governmental coalition of centre-right parties is eventually formed, despite the strong showing of the left in the first round.

25–27   *Albania/Greece*: Following the deportation of a Greek archimandrite in Northern Epirus, Greece expels thousands of Albanian illegal economic immigrants.

27   *Turkey*: Kurdish separatists bomb a hotel in Antalya, injuring twenty-
      six people, including twelve tourists.

30   *EC/Cyprus*: The European Commission announces that Cyprus may
      be admitted to the Community, even if part of its territory is still
      under Turkish occupation.

JULY

2   *Turkey*: An attack by Muslim fundamentalists against a conference of
      liberal intellectuals in Sivas leaves forty people dead and sixty injured.

4   *Egypt/USA*: The Egyptian government requests the extradition from
      the USA of Sheikh Omar Abdel-Rahman, the spiritual leader of an
      extremist Islamic movement.

5   *Turkey*: Prime Minister Tansu Çiller wins a parliamentary vote of
      confidence.

6   *Egypt/IMF*: Minister of State Youssef Boutros-Ghali announces that
      more than $3bn of western debt will be remitted thanks to an agree-
      ment with the IMF and the World Bank on a programme of economic
      reforms.

8   *Egypt*: Seven Muslim militants are executed for attacks on tourists.

9   *Bosnia*: The collective presidency proposes the transformation of the
      republic into a multi-ethnic federation.

12   *Israel/Palestine*: Arafat confirms rumours about secret high-level con-
      tacts between Israel and the PLO.

16   *Krajina*: Serb and Croat leaders agree to withdraw from the strategic
      area of Maslenica in order to avoid a large-scale confrontation.

17   *Morocco/Western Sahara*: The two sides begin talks in Layoun on the
      future of Western Sahara.

19   *Morocco/Western Sahara*: The two delegations abandon the above
      negotiations in Layoun, but leave open the possibility of future meet-
      ings to be held under the auspices of the UN.

20   *Italy*: Gabriele Cagliari, ex-president of state petroleum company
      Enimont, commits suicide in prison.

23   *Bosnia/NATO*: Official sources suggest that NATO is ready for aerial
      intervention, to enforce compliance with UN resolution 836.
      Italy: Raúl Gardini, a millionaire suspected of being connected to the
      Enimont scandal, commits suicide.

25   *Israel/Lebanon*: Israel commences attacks on Hezbollah positions in
      southern Lebanon.
      Turkey/France: Kurdish separatists belonging to the PKK admit kid-
      napping four French tourists in eastern Turkey.

26–31 *Turkey/Middle East*: Foreign Minister Hikmet Cetin visits the coun-
      tries of the region; he becomes the first Turkish foreign minister to
      visit Israel.

27   *Lebanon/Israel*: 250,000 southern Lebanese civilians flee their homes north of Israel's self-declared 'security zone' inside Lebanon, as Israel continues its strikes against guerrilla positions.
      Italy: Three car-bombs in Milan and Rome kill five people and injure thirty-eight.

31   *Israel/Lebanon*: Israel and Hezbollah agree on a ceasefire in southern Lebanon.

AUGUST

1   *Algeria/Maghreb/Europe*: Bechtel of the USA concludes a contract worth $305m with Sonatrach, the Algerian state hydrocarbons company, for the construction of part of the gas line linking the Maghreb with Europe.

4   *Italy*: The Chamber of Deputies approves a new electoral system based on majority voting.

5   *USA/Israel/Jordan/Syria*: During his visit to the region, Secretary of State Warren Christopher says that the peace process is safe.
      Bosnia: Serbs capture Mount Igman overseeing Sarajevo.

6   *Bosnia*: The Serbs offer to withdraw their forces from the Igman and Bjelasnica mountains.

12   *Palestine*: Representatives from the occupied territories enter the PLO Executive Committee.

13   *Israel/Palestine*: The government expresses its willingness to enter into direct negotiations with Palestinian representatives from the occupied territories.

14   *Bosnia/NATO/UN*: General Jean Cot, head of the UN forces in former Yugoslavia, and Admiral Mike Boorda, commander of NATO for southern Europe, meet to discuss plans for an aerial attack on Serbian positions.

16   *Lebanon/Israel/Syria*: The Lebanese begin top-level talks in Damascus after Syria voices concern over Beirut's plans to deploy troops in the south.

19   *Egypt*: The al-Jihad (Holy Struggle) group claims responsibility for an assassination attempt on Interior Minister Hassan al-Alfi.
      Lebanon/Israel/Hezbollah: Guerillas kill eight Israeli soldiers to avenge the 132 victims of bombardments in southern Lebanon.

21   *Algeria*: Prime Minister Belaïd Abdessalam is replaced by Redha Malek.
      Algeria: Former prime minister Kasdi Merbah is assassinated.
      Palestine/Lebanon: Shafiq al-Hout, the PLO's representative in Lebanon, announces that he is suspending his membership of the executive in protest at a possible agreement for limited Israeli withdrawal from the occupied territories.

23   *Greece/FYROM/UN*: The two governments and the UN mediator
      Cyrus Vance announce the commencement of direct negotiations on
      28 September.
30   *Israel/Palestine*: The possibility of a peace deal between Israel and the
      PLO is made public.
31   *Algeria*: Seven Muslim fundamentalists, found guilty of the Algiers
      bombing in August 1992, are executed.

SEPTEMBER

1   *Libya*: Colonel Qadhafi threatens that Libya will set fire to oil wells if
      it loses its confrontation with the West.
4   *Algeria*: Mourad Benachenou, a technocrat, is appointed finance minis-
      ter in Malek's government.
9   *Israel/Palestine*: Israel and the PLO decide to recognize each other
      and to sign a peace agreement aimed at securing a comprehensive
      settlement of the Arab–Israeli conflict. The accord gives interim and
      partial self-rule to the Palestinians in the occupied territories. The
      PLO agrees to abandon its thirty-year commitment to armed struggle,
      and to unequivocally recognize the Jewish state's right to exist.
      Greece: After the defection of one of its MPs, the conservative New
      Democracy government loses its parliamentary majority, resigns and
      calls early elections for 10 October.
10   *Palestine/Israel*: In Tunis, the executive committee of the PLO votes
      in favour of the agreement with Israel.
      Palestine/USA: President Clinton announces the assumption of official
      US contacts with the PLO.
13   *Israel/Palestine*: The two sides agree on a plan of gradual Israeli with-
      drawal from Gaza and Jericho due to start on 15 December.
14   *Israel/Morocco*: Israeli Prime Minister Yitzhak Rabin, accompanied by
      Foreign Minister Simon Peres, makes a surprise visit to Morocco.
16   *Bosnia*: President Izetbegovic and Bosnian Serb leader Karadjic sign a
      declaration envisaging an immediate ceasefire; fighting continues.
17   *Morocco*: Pro-government parties are the victors of the second round
      of the Moroccan elections, winning ninety seats out of a possible 111.
21   *Algeria*: Two French surveyors are the victims of the first attack on
      foreigners since the violence began in 1992; the Armed Islamic Group
      (GIA) claims responsibility.
23   *Croatia/UN*: Croatia sends an ultimatum to the UN, setting a deadline
      for the disarmament of ethnic Serbs in Krajina.
      Israel/Palestine: The Knesset approves the peace agreement by sixty-
      one votes to fifty.

OCTOBER

3   *Egypt*: Hosni Mubarak is re-elected president unopposed, for a further six years. He retains Atef Sidki as prime minister.

7   *Spain/France/Maghreb*: King Juan Carlos addresses the French National Assembly and speaks of the need to reinforce relations between Europe and the Maghreb.

10   *Greece*: Andreas Papandreou's Panhellenic Socialist Movement (PASOK) is the clear victor in the general elections, winning 46.88 per cent of the vote and 170 out of the 300 seats in parliament.

11   *UN/Egypt*: The UN and Egypt, which holds the presidency of the Organisation for African Unity, call for a summit of African leaders to find a solution to the Somali crisis.

14   *Egypt*: Atef Sidki completes a cabinet reshuffle; the powerful defence, interior, and central economic portfolios are unchanged.

      Turkey/USA: PM Çiller arrives in the USA to request President Clinton's support for an exceptional lifting of UN sanctions against Iraq in order to allow the re-opening of the oil pipeline that runs through Turkey.

15   *Libya*: The Arabic-language daily *al-Haya'* reports that the leaders of three Libyan opposition groups have met in Algeria to discuss a common platform aimed at the overthrow of Colonel Qadhafi.

18–19 *Cyprus/UK*: Cypriots demonstrate against Queen Elizabeth's visit, planned as part of the Commonwealth Conference.

20   *Serbia*: President Milosevic decrees the dissolution of parliament and calls elections for 19 December.

21   *Palestine*: Assad Saftawi, a leading Palestinian peace activist and associate of Yasser Arafat, is shot dead in Gaza.

22   *Palestine/Israel*: Many of the restrictions on Palestinians crossing from the West Bank and the Gaza strip into Israel are lifted.

24   *Algeria*: A police officer is killed and three French diplomatic employees are kidnapped in an attack by the GIA.

      Libya: ABC news reports that an anti-Qadhafi coup led by the commander of Libya's forces in Chad has been thwarted by the air force; 250 soldiers are reported killed and hundreds captured.

25   *Commonwealth/Cyprus/Turkey*: The forty-seven countries participating in the Commonwealth Conference in Limassol call for the immediate withdrawal of Turkish troops and settlers from northern Cyprus, invaded in 1974.

      Egypt/USA: President Mubarak meets President Clinton in Washington to press for the continuation of the $2bn-a-year aid programme.

27   *UN/Western Sahara*: Polisario refuses to re-enter talks with Morocco in New York.

Algeria: Several EC countries warn their nationals to avoid visiting Algeria unless it is absolutely necessary.

29   *Algeria*: Foreign companies, including many of the twenty oil groups exploring new concessions, begin repatriating dependants and non-essential staff.

31   *Algeria/France*: French hostages are released with a warning that all foreign citizens should leave the country before 30 November.

      Israel/Gulf states: Negotiations on sharing the region's waters end in Beijing with an offer by Oman to stage the sixth round. The gesture is rewarded by Israel's backing of Oman's bid to become a member of the UN Security Council.

NOVEMBER

1   *Turkey*: The police announce the arrest of more than 200 Africans, following a crackdown on economic immigrants.

2   *Algeria*: Security forces announce the killing of twenty-eight Muslim militants after two-day operations.

     Lebanon: A £1.8bn company, Solidere, is launched as part of Prime Minister Rafik Hariri's plan to rebuild Beirut's city centre.

     Spain/Palestine/Morocco: The Spanish bank Banesto announces the formation of a $60m joint venture with Israeli, Palestinian and Moroccan groups to fund development in Jericho and Gaza.

3   *Israel*: Ehud Olmert, the right-wing Likud candidate, defeats Labour mayor Teddy Kollek in the Jerusalem municipal elections.

4   *France/Algeria*: Alain Juppé announces that French diplomatic, consular and cultural services in Algeria will be reduced.

     Turkey: Kurd activists launch coordinated attacks against Turkish targets in a dozen European cities.

     Egypt/Libya: President Mubarak and Colonel Qadhafi meet in an effort to find a solution to the crisis in relations over the Lockerbie bombing.

5   *UN/Western Sahara/Morocco*: The UN announces that it has begun the work of identification and registration of voters for the referendum on self-determination.

7   *Palestine/Israel*: Following the attempted assassination of a right-wing rabbi, Jewish settlers go on the rampage; two Palestinians are wounded and two Israelis are killed in clashes.

8   *EU/Turkey*: Meeting of the Association Council to discuss a timetable for an eventual customs union.

9   *Spain/Israel*: In an address to the Knesset, King Juan Carlos defends the right of Palestinians to self-determination.

9–10 *Mediterranean*: Ministers from some forty countries participate in a Mediterranean conference on transport in Trieste.

EU/Middle East/Former Yugoslavia: Assistance to the occupied territories and ways to resolve the Balkan conflict form part of the agenda of the European Union summit in Brussels.

France/Algeria: French police arrest eighty-eight Algerian exiles, of whom eighty-five are released the following day; three are kept for questioning, including two leaders of the 'Algerian Fraternity', believed to be a front organization of the FIS.

11 *UN/Libya*: The Security Council threatens Libya with tighter sanctions unless it hands over the two people suspected of the Lockerbie bombing.

Amnesty International/Egypt: Cairo is accused of the systematic torture of political prisoners.

Israel/Jordan: Israel announces plans for air and road links to Jordan.

12 *Palestine/Israel*: The Israeli army claims that the 29 October killing of a Jewish settler was committed by Fatah. Under pressure from right-wingers opposed to the peace accord, Rabin urges Arafat to unequivocally condemn violence.

13 *Algeria*: Security forces arrest some 200 suspect Muslim militants in Algiers.

15 *Lebanon/Palestine*: Muin Shabaytah, Arafat's representative in Lebanon, dies in Sidon.

Algeria: The FIS 'Provisional Executive Bureau' issues a communiqué rejecting all dialogue with the government.

16 *Lebanon*: Israeli bombardment of Hezbollah positions in southern Lebanon in response to rocket attacks on Israeli troops.

19–20 *Spain/France/EU*: In a meeting in Toledo, Prime Minister González tells President Mitterrand that Spain will contribute 3,500 troops and fifty armoured vehicles to the European Army Corps.

21 *Italy*: The Christian Democrat and Socialist parties suffer a major defeat in municipal elections; former Communists, neo-fascists and separatists make gains.

22 *Turkey*: Eighty-two illegal African immigrants are sent to a camp near the Iraqi frontier and left to make the trip home across a potential war zone.

Egypt/Israel: The Egyptian oil ministry denies that it has agreed to build a pipeline supplying gas to Israel.

23 *Algeria*: The government suspends the execution of 300 Muslim militants in an effort to promote dialogue.

25 *Palestine/Israel*: Thirty-four Palestinians protesting at the killing of a fundamentalist military commander are wounded in an attack by Israeli troops.

Egypt: Prime Minister Atef Sidki escapes an assassination attempt by militant Muslims belonging to Jihad; a schoolgirl is killed and eleven people are injured.

28   *Egypt*: The government forbids newspapers from publishing interviews with Muslim militants.

DECEMBER

1   *Sudan*: Some 500 Islamic radicals from around the world meet in Khartoum to discuss a strategy in response to conflicts involving Muslims; the conference is organized by the Popular Arab and Islamic Congress.

3   *Spain/Morocco/EU*: In a bilateral summit in Madrid, Spain presents itself as the main defender of Moroccan interests in the EU.

5   *Italy*: The PDS-led left alliance defeats the Italian Social Movement (MSI) and the Lega Nord in the second round of municipal elections.

6   *EU/Morocco*: The EU approves the initiation of commercial negotiations with Morocco.

8   *USA/Israel/Palestine*: Secretary of State Warren Christopher says the US would accept a delay in the implementation of the peace plan if both sides agreed.

12   *Israel/Palestine*: Prime Minister Rabin and PLO chairman Arafat agree to postpone the implementation of the plan of gradual Israeli withdrawal from Gaza and Jericho.

13   *Italy*: The Congress of the Lega Nord decides that its deputies will withdraw from parliament, after the approval of the budget, to apply pressure for early elections.

14   *FYROM/EU*: Germany, France, Italy, Holland, Denmark and the UK give full diplomatic recognition to the Former Yugoslav Republic of Macedonia.
     Algeria: Twelve Croatian and Bosnian citizens are killed by fundamentalists.

15   *Israel/Lebanon*: Israel allows the return of 197 Palestinians exiled in southern Lebanon.

17–18 *Spain/Portugal/FYROM*: Following a summit in Palma de Mallorca, Prime Ministers González and Cavaco e Silva announce that their countries will delay recognition of the FYROM in order to give it more time to resolve its dispute with Greece.

19   *Serbia*: The Socialist Party of President Slobodan Milosevic wins its third consecutive electoral victory.
     Algeria: The mandate of the five-man presidency is extended until 31 January 1994.

20   *Lebanon*: One person is killed and ninety injured after an attack on the right-wing Christian Phalange party in Beirut.
     Israel/Palestine: Negotiations resume in Paris, amid signs that the Palestinians are hardening their line on border control.

22   *USA/Egypt/Libya*: President Clinton issues an appeal to President Mubarak on behalf of Mansour Kikhia, an opponent of Colonel Qadhafi and former Libyan foreign minister who disappeared in Cairo in 1983.

30   *Israel/Vatican*: Israel and the Vatican establish diplomatic relations.

31   *Croatia/Bosnia*: In a new year message, President Tudjman hints at possible Croatian involvement in the Bosnian conflict if Muslims continue their attacks against Bosnian Croats.

Compiled by George Doukas

Mediterranean Statistics

Table 1 Key statistics (1992)

	Area (sq. km.)	Population	GDP (US$ billion)	GDP per capita (US$)
Europe				
Albania	28,748	3,363,000	2.0	595
Cyprus	9,251*	716,000*	6.7	9,358
France	543,965	57,372,000	1,322.1	23,044
Greece	131,957	10,300,000	77.9	7,563
Italy	301,302	57,782,000	1,223.0	21,166
Malta	316	359,000	2.7	7,521
Portugal	91,985	9,846,000	84.2	8,552
Spain	504,750	39,085,000	573.1	14,663
Yugoslavia (former)	255,804*	23,930,000*	–	–
Eastern Mediterranean				
Israel	21,946*	4,946,000*	65.6	13,263
Lebanon	10,452	2,838,000	1.8	634
Syria	185,180	12,958,000	34.4	2,655
Turkey	779,452	58,775,000	156.0	2,654
North Africa				
Algeria	2,381,741	26,346,000	45.2	1,716
Egypt	1,002,000	55,163,000	41.8	758
Libya	1,759,540	4,875,000	29.2	5,990
Morocco	458,730*	26,318,000	27.5	1,045
Tunisia	164,150	8,401,000	15.7	1,869

Note: Numbers in parenthesis refer to sources

Area: (3)
*Cyprus: Turkish-occupied area 3,335 sq. km.
*Israel: area within the boundary defined by the 1949 armistice agreement with Egypt, Jordan, the Lebanon and Syria. Area within Israeli jurisdiction following the Six Day War and the withdrawal from the Sinai peninsula 28,188 sq. km. (includes the West Bank of the River Jordan 5,879 sq. km. and the Gaza Strip 363 sq. km.).
*Morocco: excludes the Western Sahara (252,120 sq. km.).
*Yugoslavia: refers to the former Socialist Federal Republic of Yugoslavia (before break-up of the country).

Population: 1992 mid year estimates (6)
*Cyprus: Greek orthodox population 568,600, Turkish Muslim 132,400, other 9,200 in 1992 (1).
*Israel: in 1992 the West Bank contained 973,500 and the Gaza Strip 658,000 people.
*Yugoslavia: refers to the former Socialist Federal Republic of Yugoslavia (before break-up of the country).

GDP and GDP per capita: at current market prices (2 and 5)
Calculated from GDP in national currencies then converted to dollars using average exchange rates for the year in which the GDP was estimated.

Table 2 Population and economic structure

	CBR	CDR	IMR	GR	% Labour force in agriculture
Europe					
Albania	25.2	5.6	28.3	1.96	48.4[a]
Cyprus	19.0	9.0	11.0	1.00	–
France	12.9	9.1	7.2	0.38	5.1
Greece	10.1	9.5	8.2	0.06	22.3
Italy	9.9	9.6	8.3	0.03	7.5
Malta	15.2	7.8	9.1	0.74	2.5
Portugal	11.4	10.0	10.8	0.14	11.2
Spain	9.9	8.7	7.7	0.12	9.5
Yugoslavia	–	–	–	–	–
Eastern Mediterranean					
Israel	21.4	6.3	9.2	1.51	3.3
Lebanon	27.9	7.8	40.0	2.01	–
Syria	44	7	48	3.70	24.0[a]
Turkey	26.1	7.5	63.2	1.86	43.7
North Africa					
Algeria	31	8	74	2.30	24.4[a]
Egypt	30	8	40	2.20	39.5
Libya	46	9	82	3.30	13.4[a]
Morocco	36	10	82	2.60	3.3
Tunisia	26	7	49	1.90	21.6

Note: Numbers in parenthesis refer to sources

Population figures are the latest available estimates (6)
CBR: Crude birth rate, number of births per thousand of the population;
CDR: Crude death rate, number of deaths per thousand of the population;
IMR: Infant mortality rate, deaths of infants aged less than one year per thousand infants aged less than one year;
GR: Natural growth rate in per cent a year.

Labour force data from (4) except 'a' (1)

SOURCES

1. Europa (1993) *The Europa World Yearbook, 1993*, London: Europa Publications Limited.
2. Economist Intelligence Unit, *World Economic Outlook 1994*.
3. Hunter, B. (ed.) (1993) *The Statesman's Yearbook 1993/4*, London: Macmillan.
4. International Labour Office (1993) *Yearbook of labour statistics, 1993*, Geneva.
5. International Monetary Fund (1993) *International financial statistics, 1993*, Washington.
6. United Nations (1993) Statistical papers, Series A, *Population and vital statistics report*, Vol. XLV, No. 3 (July) New York.

Statistics compiled by Keith Salmon

Index